The Quest for Meaning and Wholeness

THE QUEST FOR MEANING AND WHOLENESS

Spiritual and Religious Connections in the Lives of College Faculty

Jennifer A. Lindholm

Foreword by
Alexander and Helen Astin

JB JOSSEY-BASS™
A Wiley Brand

Published by Jossey-Bass
A Wiley Brand
One Montgomery Street, Suite 1200, San Francisco, CA 94104-4594—www.josseybass.com/
highereducation

Jossey-Bass books and products are available through most bookstores. To contact Jossey-Bass directly
call our Customer Care Department within the U.S. at 800-956-7739, outside the U.S. at 317-572-
3986, or fax 317-572-4002.

Wiley publishes in a variety of print and electronic formats and by print-on-demand. Some material
included with standard print versions of this book may not be included in e-books or in print-on-
demand. If this book refers to media such as a CD or DVD that is not included in the version you
purchased, you may download this material at http://booksupport.wiley.com. For more information
about Wiley products, visit www.wiley.com.

Library of Congress Cataloging-in-Publication Data is on file.
ISBN 978-1-118-27147-6 (cloth)
ISBN 978-1-118-41968-7 (ebk.)
ISBN 978-1-118-42127-7 (ebk.)

Printed in the United States of America
FIRST EDITION
HB Printing 10 9 8 7 6 5 4 3 2 1

CONTENTS

ABOUT THE AUTHOR

Jennifer A. Lindholm, PhD, is assistant vice provost in the division of undergraduate education at UCLA. In that capacity, she is responsible for coordinating campus initiatives that focus on enhancing undergraduate teaching and learning, addressing accreditation-related considerations, and facilitating student success. From 2001 to 2006, she served as associate director of the Cooperative Institutional Research Program at UCLA's Higher Education Research Program and as director of the institute's Triennial National Faculty Survey. Lindholm also served as visiting professor of higher education and organizational change in UCLA's Graduate School of Education and Information Studies. She was director and co-investigator for the decade-long Spirituality in Higher Education project and coauthor of *Cultivating the Spirit: How College Can Enhance Students' Inner Lives* (Jossey-Bass, 2011). Her other publications focus on the structural and cultural dimensions of academic work; the career development, work experiences, and professional behavior of college and university faculty; issues related to institutional change; and undergraduate students' personal development. Lindholm also works as a consultant to colleges and universities on topics related to her areas of research and practical expertise.

FOREWORD

Jennifer Lindholm's *The Quest for Meaning and Wholeness* constitutes an invaluable resource in support of efforts to achieve a fuller integration of our "inner" and "outer" selves in higher education. This is the third in a series of related empirical studies with which Jennifer has been involved. The first, *Meaning and Spirituality in the Lives of College Faculty: A Study of Values, Authenticity, and Stress* (Higher Education Research Institute, 1999), was a pilot study that involved in-depth personal interviews with faculty in four diverse institutions. The second, *Cultivating the Spirit: How College Can Enhance Students' Inner Lives* (Jossey-Bass, 2011), which Jennifer coauthored with us, was a longitudinal study of students attending 136 colleges and universities, which also included a detailed survey of faculty in these same institutions. The current study is a natural outgrowth of the first two, in that it provides, for the first time, a comprehensive picture of faculty members' spiritual lives as revealed in a large national sample. Given that many of Jennifer's findings parallel and complement what we found in *Cultivating the Spirit,* her book will be of considerable value to those of us who seek more effective ways to enhance the spiritual growth and development of college students. We believe that her findings should be considered not only for incorporation in graduate courses on college and university faculty but also as a basis for discussions at institutional meetings and retreats.

The findings reported in *Cultivating the Spirit* showed clearly that students benefit in a number of important ways when the college experience enhances their spiritual development. Spiritual growth is positively associated with such outcomes as academic performance, satisfaction with the college experience, psychological well-being, and interest in further education beyond the baccalaureate. Although that study showed that college faculty can play an important role in promoting their students' spiritual development, it also found that faculty seldom encourage their students to engage in spiritual self-exploration. We believe that Jennifer's new study can be of great significance in helping faculty understand the potential value of spiritual self-exploration, not only for themselves but also for their students.

This comprehensive study of faculty spirituality and religiousness comes at an especially opportune time in American higher education. Although most college and university faculty members have traditionally kept their religious and spiritual inclinations pretty much to themselves, in recent years we have seen the emergence of a number of prominent academics—Steven Pinker, Richard Dawkins, and Daniel Dennett, to name just a few—who have become public spokespersons on behalf of atheism. The widespread media attention that these advocates have received has no doubt helped to reinforce the notion, held by many critics of the academy, that most college professors are godless intellectuals devoid of any spiritual or religious values or beliefs. Jennifer's pioneering study clearly puts that myth to rest.

Large numbers of higher education faculty report that they are either religious, spiritual, or both, but what is especially intriguing about Jennifer's data is the extraordinary *diversity* of religious and spiritual perspectives embraced by her respondents. Thus, when it comes to spirituality and religiousness, American college professors turn out not to be a monolithic lot. The same goes for institutions and academic disciplines: faculty in public universities are least likely to see themselves as either religious or spiritual, and those in fields such as education, agriculture, and the health sciences are most likely to view themselves in this way.

Although more than half of Jennifer's respondents consider themselves to be both spiritual and religious at least to some extent, one in five report that they consider themselves to be spiritual but not religious. A slightly smaller number say that they are neither spiritual nor religious. (These figures are remarkably similar to what we found with undergraduates in our earlier study.) Interestingly enough, Jennifer's qualitative data suggest that highly religious faculty view "spiritual but not religious" colleagues even less favorably than they do colleagues who are *neither* spiritual nor religious.

Jennifer's rich qualitative data alone make fascinating reading. Many of her faculty respondents were openly willing to share very personal perspectives about what many of us in academe have long considered to be private and personal matters. A number of faculty obviously put considerable thought and effort into their comments. Taken together, these open-ended data provide us with a rich resource for understanding different perspectives on the interconnections among faculty members' professional, personal, and spiritual lives.

A finding of special interest is that those faculty members who see their profession as a calling or a vocation are most likely to view their work with students (teaching and mentoring) and their scholarly work as an expression of who they are and why they chose to become college professors in the first place. Further, Jennifer's data reveal that some of the same spiritual qualities that we identified in *Cultivating the Spirit*—equanimity, ethic of caring, ecumenical worldview, and charitable involvement—are positively associated with faculty members' teaching practices, how they conduct their research, and their manner of relating to colleagues. To take one striking example, Jennifer found that faculty who demonstrate a high level of equanimity are much more likely to value their students, to have a positive view of their institution, to be supportive of their colleagues, to experience a greater balance between work and personal life, and to experience a high level of satisfaction in their lives. In the same vein, faculty who are able to express their spiritual inclinations openly and who acknowledge that they are "spiritual beings" are more likely to view themselves as being authentic in their work and personal lives. In short, the data provide us with convincing evidence that the work activities, self-concept, and personal values of college and university faculty are closely related to their spiritual inclinations.

Although Jennifer's findings are both powerful and persuasive, questions still remain: How do we create a culture within the academy that celebrates, validates, and cultivates spirituality among our faculty and students? How do we help more faculty members appreciate the importance and practical value of focusing more attention on matters of meaning, purpose, and similar aspects of the "inner self," not only in their students but in themselves? The task of finding practical answers to such questions is being made all the more challenging by at least two current trends in higher education. First is the growing influence of technological innovation, which includes not only the extensive use of such instruments as personal computers, cell phones, and tablets but also the rapid expansion of distance learning and MOOCs (massive open online courses). Although widespread use of such technologies can serve to expand and enhance instruction in certain positive ways, the fact is that focusing on the inner self can be very difficult when teaching and learning are delivered in this manner. Not only does there tend to be a more impersonal connection between the professor and the student, but both teacher and learner are also encouraged to focus almost exclusively on "exteriors" such as course content, screens, and keyboards.

The other limiting trend has to do with academic content. In the past two decades, we have witnessed a remarkable surge of interest in two related subfields of science: evolution and neuroscience. Both of these ascendant fields of inquiry tend to take a materialistic, deterministic view of the human condition: people and societies are the way they are because of genetic factors and brain activity. Of most concern to us, however, is the effect that immersion in these fields tends to have on the way people regard consciousness and the inner self. Human consciousness is seen merely as an epiphenomenon of brain activity, and fundamental psychological qualities such as the sense of self, intuition, and free will are regarded as illusions. From the point of view of those of us who strive to put more emphasis on the "inner life," the unfortunate consequence of these emerging new perspectives is that they tend to trivialize interior realities such as feelings, desires, beliefs, and aspirations and instead focus attention on concrete physical phenomena. Making Jennifer's empirical findings generally available to college and university faculty may be a useful first step in promoting a greater understanding of the importance of spirituality in the academy.

In closing, we quote an excerpt from the white paper that was developed at a retreat that we convened to assess the implications of the findings from *Cultivating the Spirit*:

> One of the single most important steps in advancing students' [and faculty's] interior development on a college campus may be to acknowledge the importance of . . . [the spiritual] dimension of human development. There is a power in naming; it is a liberating experience that can create space for members of the campus community to openly debate the ways in which spiritual development broadly construed might fit into the curriculum and how it aligns with the purposes of liberal learning. We thus believe that the time has come to refocus the discourse on spirituality in higher education away from the question of "whether" to the question of "how."

Alexander W. Astin
Helen S. Astin
December 2013

PREFACE

In 2002, when my colleagues Alexander Astin, Helen Astin, and I began our efforts to examine undergraduate students' spiritual development, colleagues and friends asked—in tones at times genuinely inquisitive and others unmistakably disapproving—whether spirituality (let alone religion) has any rightful place within the modern academy, especially within secular institutions. Not unexpectedly, over the course of the Spirituality in Higher Education project, as well as during administration of the 2012 Faculty Beliefs and Values Survey, queries regarding the "appropriateness" of inquiring about students' or faculty members' spiritual and religious inclinations and perspectives have continued. So too have speculations about the motivations for pursuing this line of inquiry.

Especially given higher education's philosophical foundations, the often strongly expressed resistance to acknowledge as relevant the spiritual and religious dimensions of life and the resistance to exploring how people characterize and navigate their inner lives are somewhat surprising. Beyond personal inclinations to retain as resolutely private our most deeply held beliefs and values, a prominent focal point of contention—particularly within nonsectarian college and university contexts—centers around "separation of church and state" issues, many of which are propelled largely by misunderstandings of the treatment of religion and spirituality under provisions of the U.S. Constitution (see, for example, Clark, 2001). The positivistic culture of academe that conditions faculty and students to separate personal values from disciplinary content, coupled with associated notions that the spiritual dimension of experience is an illegitimate focus for serious scholarly inquiry, represents another, often powerful, source of tension (see, for example, Waggoner, 2011). Also irreparably problematic for some is that, throughout human history, spiritual and religious convictions at times have been used to proclaim the purported superiority of selected belief systems, individuals, races, cultures, and nations. Indeed, so-called dominator conceptualizations of spiritual and religious beliefs, structures, and relationships have also been used to rationalize behavioral atrocities and to justify chronic injustice and misery (Eisler and Montuori, 2003). Associated fears lead some to presume that those who would choose to focus on spiritual or religious dimensions of student and faculty life are motivated by a desire to "convert" others to their own beliefs and practices or to eradicate from the academy those who they feel don't have the "correct" orientations and values.

From the outset of the Spirituality in Higher Education project, our research team has been cognizant of the "dark side" of religion as well as the somewhat ambiguous or negative connotations the term "spirituality" can evoke. Common focal points for critique and contention when referencing the term "spirituality" range from perceptions of its integral association with organized religion to its reflection of meaningless "new age fluff." For those of us on the Spirituality in Higher Education research team, personal judgments about how students or faculty define their spirituality, the role (or lack thereof) of spirituality and religion in their lives, or the particular meaning they make of their lives are not at issue. Rather, we've been motivated to learn how these dimensions of students' and faculty members' lives contribute to shaping how they view their work and their lives and the associated choices made. We have also been compelled by a shared sense that the relative amount of attention that colleges and universities devote to the "inner" and "outer" aspects of students' and faculty members' lives and well-being is largely out of balance. Another compelling motivation for undertaking this work has been the seemingly inherent disconnect between the dominant values of contemporary American society and the perspectives and practices that will enable us to respond effectively not only to our individual needs but also to local, national, international, and global challenges.

SPIRITUALITY AND ACADEMIC WORK

Linkages between spirituality and work can be traced to Greenleaf's concept of servant leadership (1977), a term used to personify individuals within a workplace or, more broadly, a profession who rely on foresight, inspire trust, emphasize personal development, are good listeners, and are masters of positive feedback (see Lee and Zemke, 1993; Ottaway, 2003).

For those who are spiritually oriented, selected work activities and experiences are often viewed with sacred significance (Hill and Dik, 2012). Spiritual or religious people may also view their work itself as a vocation, or calling. Inherent in that conceptualization is an implied responsibility to fulfill one's duty to society and the common good by working in ways that are useful and helpful to others (Dik and Duffy, 2012). As Leider and Shapiro (2001) explain, "calling" is a concept that "challenges us to see our work in relation to our deepest beliefs" (p. 17).

Historically, the notion of having a calling carried with it strong religious connotations, including the notion that one had been "called" by a higher power to pursue a particular line of work (see, for example, Dik and Duffy, 2012). In modern usage, however, "calling" is commonly conceptualized as both a sacred and a secular construct (Dik, Duffy, and Tix, 2012). In the secular sense, a person's calling reflects work that is pleasurable, that is perceived by the individual as fulfilling his or her purpose in life, and that the individual believes is contributing to making the world a better place (see, for example, Wrzesniewski, 2013). Ultimately, alignment between one's sense of purpose and meaning in work and one's broader sense of purpose and meaning in life as a whole provides people with a sense of life stability and coherence (Baumeister and Vohs, 2002). People who characterize themselves as having a calling have been found to be more intrinsically motivated and engaged, more confident that they can make good career decisions, more committed to their jobs and organizations, and more satisfied with their work lives. They also tend to cope more effectively with challenges and are less likely to suffer from stress and depression (Dik and Duffy, 2012). Finally, Dik and Duffy note that those who view their work as a calling are also more likely to engage in good organizational citizenship behavior, which encompasses altruism, civic virtue, conscientiousness, courtesy, and sportsmanship.

Distinguishing workplace spirituality as separate from any particular expression of religiosity, Duchon and Plowman (2005) define it as "a particular kind of psychological climate in which people view themselves as having an inner life that is nourished by meaningful work and takes place in the context of community" (p. 68). Spirituality at work can be conceptualized as having three core dimensions (Ashford and Pratt, 2003). The first, *transcendence of self*, relates to an individual's capacity for, and willingness to, expand his or her boundaries to encompass other people, causes, nature, or belief in a higher power, leading to a sense of connection. The second, *holism and harmony*, pertains to the synergistic integration of various aspects of oneself and one's life, leading to a sense of coherence. Taken together, these two dimensions reflect an ongoing journey of exploration and discovery that is associated with authenticity, balance, and perspective. The third dimension, *growth*, is oriented around self-development and self-actualization leading to realization of one's aspirations and potential, ultimately resulting in a sense of wholeness or completion. As addressed in Chapter Seven of this book, Ashford and Pratt's dimensions provide a useful way of thinking about spiritual and religious connections in the lives of college faculty.

Much of the current research and writing that focuses on higher education emphasizes what is wrong, what is broken, or how all involved are falling short of expectations. Amidst fiscal constraints and shifts in financial support for higher education, growing enrollments and increasing diversity of students, enrollment uncertainties, ever-intensifying pressures for accountability, financial cutbacks, and rapid expansion of knowledge (see, for example, Gappa, Austin, and Trice, 2007), pressures on faculty to be ever more inclusive, expressive, and responsive are intensifying. In the most recently conducted synthesis of research on faculty work, careers, and professional development, O'Meara, Terosky, and Neumann (2008) challenged academic leaders, faculty development specialists, scholars who study faculty, and faculty themselves to "identify ways to foster, in faculty members, the desire and will to craft themselves as teachers, researchers, and partners in service and community engagement who have actively chosen—and continue actively to choose—the academic career as a way to lead their lives" (p. 19). Rather than continuing to rely so heavily on the predominating "narrative of constraint" that tends to frame much of the research and writing on faculty work life and careers, O'Meara and her colleagues proposed application of a "framework for faculty growth" that emphasizes the "synergistic and self-reinforcing" (p. 32) value of learning, agency, professional relationships, and commitments. Such a framework holds potentially promising applications, especially when the spiritual lives and perceptions of college faculty and the associated intersections with their academic work are taken into consideration.

SCOPE AND STRUCTURE

Envisioning campus communities where the life of the mind and the life of the heart are mutually celebrated, supported, and sustained necessitates that we reconsider our habitual perspectives and practices along with our long-standing biases. Toward creating campus environments that provide welcoming and engaging contexts for the personal and professional development of students, faculty, administrators, and staff, all members of campus communities must be willing to look closely not just at what they do (or do not do) on a daily basis, but also why. Those outside the academy must also consider the origins of their presumptions about the nature and purpose of higher education, the roles and responsibilities of faculty, and how their own academic experiences have affected their lives.

One challenge in embarking on such a reconstructive path is the veritable absence of pertinent information and accompanying opportunity for focused dialogue. My aim in writing this book is to offer an evenhanded description of the spiritual and religious inclinations and perspectives of college faculty within the United States. The book's primary purpose is to offer a data-based starting point for such dialogue, featuring faculty perspectives in their own voices. At the outset, it should be recognized that all faculty perspective contained in this book is based on self-reports. Associated measurement problems (corroboration of veracity, response set bias, and social desirability considerations—that is, respondents' potential inclinations to feel they "should" respond in certain ways to selected types of questions) can be magnified when the subject matter encompasses such potentially sensitive topics as spiritual or religious beliefs and experiences (see, for example Hill and Smith, in press). For this reason, I encourage you to consider these findings as suggestive rather than definitive. Regrettably, in-depth analyses on each measure and detailed consideration of the many fascinating demographic, disciplinary, and institutional lenses through which spiritual and religious issues can be framed are beyond the reasonable scope of this book. The findings contained here are presented largely in the aggregate and are focused on traditionally appointed (that is, full-time tenured or tenure-track) faculty at four-year colleges and universities. My hope is that this profile of faculty beliefs and values will help enhance your awareness and understanding of the spiritual and religious lives of college professors as well as your appreciation for the diversity of their values, beliefs, and perspectives.

Chapter One offers contextualizing background on the topic of spirituality in higher education, including introduction to the measures that provide the book's focal points. Chapter Two considers how faculty self-identify with respect to spirituality and religiousness, providing a foundation for addressing in subsequent chapters the salience of the measures described in Chapter One within faculty members' lives and work. Chapter Three highlights faculty members' spiritual quest inclinations. Chapter Four considers the degree to which ethic of caring and ecumenical worldview orientations resonate with college and university faculty, as well as faculty inclinations toward charitable involvement. Chapter Five focuses on faculty members' religious faith and perspectives, looking specifically at religious commitment and engagement as well as skepticism and struggle. Chapter Six addresses the intersections between equanimity and academic work. Chapter Seven revisits key themes and offers faculty perspectives on the connections between spirituality and higher education. A brief Epilogue offers concluding thoughts, along with reference to selected resources for those who are interested in potential institutional and programmatic applications.

ACKNOWLEDGMENTS

The completion of this book would not have been possible without the help and support of many people. I am very grateful to Helen Astin and Alexander Astin for having invited me as a newly minted PhD to embark with them on an extended journey to explore the intersections between spirituality and higher education. Over the course of more than five decades, their visionary leadership on issues related to undergraduate education has been instrumental in shaping the way researchers and practitioners think about many aspects of college and university life. Their founding of the Higher Education Research Institute (HERI), which housed our Spirituality in Higher Education research project, and their creation of the student and faculty surveys that continue to be administered through the institute, provided the foundation that enabled our design of the College Students' Beliefs and Values Surveys and my subsequent development of the Faculty Beliefs and Values Survey. As mentors, colleagues, and friends, you have had an immeasurable impact on my life, and I will always be grateful for the long-term investment you made in my career.

Over the course of the Spirituality in Higher Education project, our creative endeavors were aided tremendously by graduate students from UCLA's Higher Education and Organizational Change program; their contributions remain invaluable with respect to making this new work focused on faculty possible: Shannon Calderone, Christopher Collins, Estella Gutierrez-Zamano, Jennifer Mallen, Kyle McJunkin, Lisa Millora, Nida Denson, Julie Park, Alyssa Rockenbach, Leslie Schwarz, Hanna Song Spinosa, and Katalin Szelényi. Many thanks again to all of you for your terrific work, and continued best wishes in your careers.

Generous funding from the John Templeton Foundation enabled us to conduct the Spirituality in Higher Education project; it included a supplemental grant that was instrumental in supporting survey design, institutional participation, data collection, and analysis in association with the 2004–2005 Triennial National Survey of College Faculty administered by HERI.

My long-term engagement with both the Spirituality in Higher Education project and the extended study of faculty beliefs and values would not have been possible without tremendous support from UCLA's Division of Undergraduate Education. I am especially grateful to Patricia Turner, dean and vice provost for undergraduate education, who, in the midst of her own recent transition to UCLA, has been terrifically supportive of this project. The flexibility, insights, and encouragement you have offered at key points during the writing of this book were invaluable and are greatly appreciated. Many thanks as well to Kathy Oriba, Kathlene Avakian, and Manuela Friedmann, my office mates and terrific colleagues within the Division of Undergraduate Education, whose timely support at key points during this project were especially instrumental in facilitating its completion.

Special thanks as well to Judith Smith, UCLA dean and vice provost for undergraduate education emerita, a phenomenal mentor and wonderful friend and colleague, whose offer to me seven years ago to join the division marked the beginning of a new and transformative chapter in my career. Her creativity in structuring a new role for me that blends administrative work, research, and teaching enabled both my continued involvement in the Spirituality in Higher Education project and the additional data collection on which this book is based. Your dedication to undergraduate education and exemplary contributions as an academic leader are an ongoing source of inspiration. Your kindness, wisdom, patience, generosity, and good humor have made an indelible mark on my heart, and I treasure the insights you continue to offer on academic work and careers as well as life in general.

My work within UCLA's Division of Undergraduate Education offers me the privilege of interacting in various capacities with a wide range of students, faculty, administrators, and staff across campus. On a daily basis, those interactions remind me how fortunate those of us who work on college and university campuses are. Throughout this project—purely in the course of going about their everyday business—many of these individuals (nearly all of whom had no direct knowledge of the project) offered incidental comments, displayed behavior, or shared opinions and experiences that reminded me of the importance of learning more about the intersections between spirituality and life within the academy and of considering the associated applications. Encouragingly, many of those observations and exchanges have exemplified the best of who we can be as members of academic communities. Heartfelt thanks to my fellow Bruins for offering continual inspiration.

Special thanks to Lisa Phan, my undergraduate research assistant and member of the UCLA class of 2013, who worked tirelessly and meticulously on preparations for administering the 2012 Faculty Beliefs and Values Survey and, then again, with selected aspects of the data analysis. My interactions with six other members of the UCLA Class of 2013 who constituted "the red team" within a philanthropy course I team-taught during the 2012–2013 academic year also played an important role in helping me continue to reflect on how the spiritual dimension of life potentially interfaces with undergraduate learning and teaching: Roberto Campos, Elana Gurney, Christine Ristow, Christopher Sirivoranankul, Lauren Van Soye, and Jamecelle Ventura. My heartfelt thanks to all of you, and warmest best wishes as you embark on the next chapter of your lives.

I also express my tremendous appreciation to Sheryl Fullerton, executive editor at Jossey-Bass, for her interest in issues of spirituality and religion in higher education, for the invitation and encouragement to pursue this writing project, and for the terrific insights, support, and general inspiration she so generously provided. My thanks, too, go to Robin Lloyd, Michele Jones, Alison Knowles, and the rest of the fantastic Jossey-Bass team. Working with you has been a true privilege.

Several colleagues—Peter Hill, Jesse Rine, Alyssa Rockenbach, and Michael Waggoner—offered thoughtful and very much appreciated insights and recommendations on the initial draft. Hanna Song Spinosa provided valuable data analysis assistance.

Many thanks to my family and friends for your support in a thousand ways great and small throughout this and every project.

Finally, I offer my deepest gratitude to the faculty who so graciously took time to answer many survey questions about their work lives, values, and beliefs, and to elaborate on their perspectives. Without your thoughtful contributions, this project would not have been possible. Thank you for all that you do and all that you shared.

Jennifer A. Lindholm
University of California, Los Angeles
December 2013

To Judi Smith
With gratitude and admiration

THE QUEST FOR MEANING AND WHOLENESS

CHAPTER ONE

SPIRITUALITY AND HIGHER EDUCATION

The United States is a spiritually engaged nation. Nine in ten adults (91%) believe in God or a Universal Spirit. Fully 80 percent report that religion is "important" in their lives. Just over two-thirds (67%) say they reflect on the meaning of life "often." Only 15 percent report that they are *neither* spiritual *nor* religious (Pew Forum on Religion & Public Life, 2012). Indeed, for most Americans, the meaning-making functions of religion and spirituality play a central role in personal and professional decision making (see, for example, Ammons and Edgell, 2007; Mahoney, 2010; Park, 2012). Nevertheless, within U.S. society, religion and spirituality tend to fall largely outside the realm of socially acceptable public discourse or collective concern. In part, this is attributable to the belief that the spiritual/religious dimension of our lives is intensely personal and should therefore remain completely private.

Like politics, religion and spirituality are potentially inflammatory topics. This is, of course, particularly true in environmental contexts where individuals' associated values, beliefs, and experiences may differ and thus potentially conflict. Within the academy, and especially in secular colleges and universities, resistance to acknowledging the spiritual/religious dimension of life and the often powerful meaning-making influences of people's associated beliefs tends to be especially palpable. Apart from the sources of resistance addressed in the Preface, ambiguities abound regarding what "spirituality" means, whether (and, if so, how) spirituality is distinguishable from religiousness, and how the

1

spiritual dimension of faculty members' lives interfaces (or does not) with their academic work lives. This chapter addresses these considerations and provides an overview of the research on which this book is based.

CONCEPTUALIZING SPIRITUALITY

The English word *spirituality* originated from a merging of the Latin word *spiritus*, meaning "breath," "air," "life," or "courage"— that which gives vitality to a system—with the concept of enthusiasm, from the Greek *enthousiasmos*, meaning "the God within" (Todd, 2004). Although the semantic interpretation of the word spirituality is clear, its meaning in operational terms is more ambiguous. This is attributable, at least in part, to spirituality's highly subjective personal nature (see, for example, Miller and Thoresen, 2003). Before the twentieth century, the term "spiritual" was closely aligned—even synonymous—with religious beliefs and convictions. Current conceptions, however, are much broader. Traditionally, spirituality has been nurtured exclusively within the context of religious faith. For many people, including college and university faculty, it continues to be. However, roughly one in five adults within the United States characterize their spirituality as either loosely, or not at all, associated with an established religious tradition (see, for example, Fuller, 2001). In an era that has been characterized by its spiritual "poverty" (Myers, 2000), we have seen an increased hunger for spiritual growth coupled with a quest by some for nonreligious, nondenominational ways of fostering spirituality.

The terms "spiritual" and "religious" both connote belief in some type of higher power; imply a personal desire to relate with that higher power; and support "rituals, practices, and daily moral behaviors" that nurture that relationship (Fuller, 2001, p. 5). Over time, though, a convergence of intellectual and culture forces have highlighted distinctions between "public" and "private" dimensions of life. For those who differentiate between the two, religion tends to be connected with the so-called public realm. Spirituality, in contrast, is more commonly associated with "private" thought and experience. More specifically, whereas religion is characterized by "group activity that involves specific behavioral, social, doctrinal, and denominational characteristics," spirituality is commonly conceived as "personal, transcendent, and characterized by qualities of relatedness" (Fetzer Institute/ National Institute on Aging Working Group, 2003, p. 1). Paloutzian and Lowe (2012) maintain that in terms of psychological function, "spiritual" (rather than "religious") is the broader category because "it includes the values, priorities, overall purposes, and principles that a person may use to live by, whether or not these are stated in identifiably religious terms or are conceptualized as religious by the individual" (p. 181). They go on to explain that, in keeping with the existential views of Frankl (1963), "any superordinate value or principle by which one lives or that a person uses to guide his or her life" can be regarded as "functionally spiritual for her or him" (p. 182).

Spirituality is often characterized within both academic and popular literature as involving the internal process of seeking personal authenticity, genuineness, and wholeness; transcending one's locus of centricity; developing a greater sense of connectedness to self and others through relationship and community; deriving meaning, purpose, and direction in life; being open to exploring a relationship with a higher power that transcends human existence and human knowing; and valuing the sacred (Hill et al., 2000; Love and Talbot, 1999; Zinnbauer, Pargament, and Scott, 1999). Spirituality has also been described as an animating, creative, energizing, meaning-seeking and meaning-making force; a source of inner strength; an inner moral orientation; a way of knowing and of being in the world; a source of connection that brings faith, hope, peace, and empowerment; and a "dynamic expression" of ourselves that gives shape to, and is shaped by, who we really are (Baker, 2003; Dawson, 1997; Dyson, Cobb, and Forman, 1997; Geroy, 2005; Goddard, 2000; Hindman, 2002; King, 1996; Tanyi, 2002). Kazanjian (1998) maintains that "spirituality in education is that which animates the mind and body, giving meaning, purpose, and context to thought, word, and action" (p. 38).

Some contend that although it may be expressed through highly variable personal mechanisms, spirituality is a biologically integral component of being human; we are genetically predisposed to be spiritual (see, for example, Aldridge, 1998; Hamer,

2004; Narayanasamy, 1999; Stoll, 1989; Wright, 2000). Within the spiritual domain, human development has been characterized both by one's increased capacity to integrate the many other aspects of development—cognitive, social, emotional, moral— and by one's enhanced capacity for integrity or wholeness, openness, self-responsibility, and authentic self-transcendence (Helminiak, 1987). Developing people's abilities to access, nurture, and give expression to the spiritual dimension of life has been found to impact how people engage with the world and fosters within them a heightened sense of connectedness that promotes empathy, ethical behavior, civic responsibility, passion, and action for social justice (Allport and Ross, 1967; Batson, 1976; De Souza, 2003; Klaassen and McDonald, 2002). Spiritual well-being tends also to be positively associated with self-confidence, general assertiveness, and inclinations toward offering praise, and to be negatively associated with depression, aggressiveness (including passive aggressiveness), dependency, conflict avoidance, and negatively experienced effects of potentially stressful situations (see, for example, Ellison and Smith, 1991).

Irrespective of the presence or absence of clearly defined linkages between religion and spirituality, or the personally presumed "goodness," "badness," or "irrelevance" of the manifestations of such connections, to ignore the role of spirituality in personal development and professional behavior is to overlook a potentially powerful avenue through which people construct meaning and knowledge (see, for example, Tisdell, 2001). Indeed, it is the spiritual component of human beings that gives rise to questions about why we do what we do, pushes us to seek fundamentally better ways of doing it, and propels us to make a difference in the world (Zohar and Marshall, 2004). Steger (2012) contends that spirituality relates to the "ability for people to extend who they are into a broader and more significant sphere of activity" (p. 236). Within the context of higher education, spirituality can be viewed as "rooted and sustained through the social and psychological connections of communal life on campus" (Dalton, 2006, p. 165).

From the outset of the Spirituality in Higher Education project, and still resonant with my own orientation in writing this book, our research team conceptualized spirituality as pointing to the individual's inner, subjective life, as contrasted with the objective domain of observable behavior and material objects that can be readily pointed to and measured. In other words, the spiritual domain has to do with what one experiences privately in one's subjective consciousness. As explained in *Cultivating the Spirit*, spirituality has more to do with individuals' qualitative or affective experiences than it does with reasoning or logic. It is reflected in the values and ideals people hold most dear, their sense of who they are and where they come from, their beliefs about why they are here—the meaning and purpose they see in their lives—and their connectedness to one another and the world around them. Spirituality also captures those aspects of human experience that are not easy to define or talk about, such as intuition, the mysterious, and the mystical (Astin, Astin, and Lindholm, 2011b). Although thematic overlaps are identifiable, we would expect that each individual will view his or her spirituality in a unique way. For some, traditional religious beliefs compose the core of their spirituality; for others, such beliefs or traditions may play little or no part (see, for example, Fuller, 2001). This holds true for college and university faculty as well.

HIGHER EDUCATION AND THE LIFE OF THE SPIRIT

Historically, spiritual and religious considerations were foundational in U.S. higher education. Scholars have written extensively about the founding of U.S. colleges and universities—their strong early ties to religious orders, close connections with local communities, and traditional missions not only to enhance the breadth and depth of students' knowledge but also to foster "a sense of purpose that included an awareness of the soul's relationship to God" (Cohen, 1998; Marsden, 1994; Murphy, 2005; Reuben, 1996). In the late nineteenth century, however, Enlightenment ideals, positivistic modes of thinking, and scientific worldviews began to exert rapid, markedly different, and powerful influences on American thought, social values, and individual goal orientations (see, for example, Marsden, 1994).

One manifestation of the transformed worldview that persists today is that people tend to diminish the value of institutional and developmental contexts that are characterized by self-reflection, open dialogue, and thoughtful analysis of alternative perspectives. Instead, many of today's colleges and universities mirror the strong societal emphasis on individual achievement, competitiveness, materialism, and objective knowing (Astin, Astin, and Lindholm, 2011b). These orientations, coupled with the post–World War II emphasis on business-oriented approaches to education that emphasize productivity and cost effectiveness, have resulted in a shift away from holistic, integrative approaches to teaching and learning along with a devaluing of the liberal arts (Murphy, 2005). The development of self-understanding, in particular, receives very little attention in our schools and colleges today, even though most of the great literary and philosophical traditions that constitute the core of a liberal education are grounded in the maxim "know thyself." This is a pertinent disconnect, because self-understanding is a necessary prerequisite to our ability to understand others and resolve conflicts. It is difficult to imagine, for example, how most of our contemporary domestic and world problems can ever be resolved without a substantial increase in individual and collective self-awareness. Yet, as a society, we continue to give very high priority to outcomes that are unrelated—even antithetical—to the enhancement of self-awareness and understanding.

Over the past decade, higher education has come under increasing criticism for its too often fragmented approach to undergraduate education. Today, society is also voicing more loudly the claim that faculty have a social responsibility to contribute more fully to the well-being of their students and their institutions, as well as the broader community. In response, growing numbers of educators today are calling for a more holistic education, one that underscores the importance of attending to both mind and spirit and that returns to the core values of liberal education—an education that examines teaching, learning, and knowledge in relation to an exploration of self (see, for example, Braskamp, Trautvetter, and Ward, 2006; Chickering, Dalton, and Stamm, 2006; Tisdell, 2003; Trautvetter, 2007). Such a reinvigorated liberal arts curriculum would necessarily pay closer attention to existential questions. At the same time, and in parallel with a broader societal movement that reflects a growing concern with establishing or recovering a sense of meaning in our lives and work, we have seen a movement gradually emerging in higher education in which many academics find themselves actively searching for meaning and trying to discover ways to make their lives and their institutions more whole (Astin, 2004). The particular "spiritual questions" that give rise to these concerns encompass a broad set of issues:

- How do we achieve a greater sense of community and shared purpose in higher education?
- How can we provide more opportunities for individual and institutional renewal?
- What are the causes of the division and fragmentation that some academics experience in their institutional and personal lives?
- What does it mean to be authentic, both in our interactions with students and in our relationships with colleagues?
- What are some of the practices and traditions that can make it difficult for us to be authentic in academic settings?
- What are some of the disconnections that higher education is experiencing in relation to the larger society? How might we better serve the public good?
- How can we help our students and ourselves achieve a greater sense of meaning within the academic and personal realms of life?

THE SPIRITUALITY IN HIGHER EDUCATION PROJECT

In 2002, my colleagues Alexander Astin, Helen Astin, and I launched a decade-long program of research to examine undergraduate students' spiritual development.[1] Specifically, we were interested in learning how college students conceive of spirituality, understanding the roles that spirituality and religion play in their lives, examining how their spiritual qualities change during the course of their undergraduate careers, and considering how colleges and universities could potentially enhance their effectiveness in facilitating students' spiritual development. To raise awareness among faculty, academic administrators, and the public at large of the vital role that spirituality plays in promoting student learning and development, the Astins and I wrote *Cultivating the Spirit* (2011), which documented empirically how students change spiritually and religiously during their undergraduate years. We also identified how college experiences, including interactions with faculty, can contribute to students' spiritual growth and development.

The primary focus of this book shifts to faculty. Building on a research report titled *Spirituality and the Professoriate* (Lindholm, Astin, and Astin, 2005) and associated quantitative and qualitative faculty-focused analyses we conducted over the course of the Spirituality in Higher Education project, the chapters that follow examine in greater depth how professors conceptualize and experience the spiritual and religious dimensions of their own lives. The book also addresses how faculty members perceive the intersections between spirituality and higher education and considers the implications that their spiritual inclinations and interests may have for undergraduate education and for the nature of faculty life within academic workplaces.

WHY FOCUS ON FACULTY?

With few exceptions (see, for example, Astin and Astin, 1999; Braskamp, 2003; Shahjahan, 2010; Tisdell, 2003), research on spiritual and religious dimensions of life that has been conducted within higher education institutions has focused primarily on students, largely ignoring the experiences, attitudes, expectations, and influences of faculty. There is thus a substantive gap both in our general awareness and knowledge of this realm of faculty members' lives and in our understanding of how to create educational environments that maximize the personal and professional potential of students and faculty. Indeed, faculty, who play a central role in determining both the culture and the climate of their institution, are at the heart of higher education's capacity to change.

The norms, values, beliefs, assumptions, and behaviors of faculty shape—and are shaped by—the individual inclinations and orientations of those who pursue professorial careers as well as by the structural and cultural characteristics of their disciplinary and institutional affiliations. Within academic contexts, the normative values and beliefs of faculty represent the fundamental standards by which institutional decisions are made and priorities are set (see, for example, Astin and Twede, 1989). Astin (2004) has noted that, like many others, academics who consider themselves spiritual have for far too long been living fragmented and sometimes inauthentic lives, where they act either as if they are not spiritual beings or as if their spiritual side is irrelevant to their vocation. Under these conditions, academic work can become divorced from faculty members' most deeply felt values, and they hesitate to discuss issues of meaning, purpose, authenticity, wholeness, and fragmentation with their colleagues. Inadvertently or intentionally, faculty likewise discourage their students from engaging these issues among themselves or with their professors.

Within higher education, there has been increased interest recently in issues of meaning, purpose, and spirituality. However, there has been very little empirical research on how faculty view spirituality or how they experience its expression in their professional lives. Faculty have rarely been asked questions related to how they view themselves, how they conceive of their life missions and purposes, what personal meaning they make out of their work, or how the spiritual dimension of their lives interfaces (or does not) with their institutional roles and responsibilities as well as their additional professional pursuits. Apart from the two dozen or so specifically related items that our Spirituality in Higher Education research team included on the Higher Education Research Institute (HERI) 2004–2005 Triennial National Survey of College Faculty, such questions have never been asked of large numbers of faculty from many different backgrounds, disciplines, geographical regions, or types of institutions, and never has there been such an opportune time to do so. Previously, through interviews conducted with seventy professors from a wide array of disciplinary backgrounds and professional fields who were employed in diverse types of institutions, Astin and Astin (1999) found that interviewees *wanted* to talk about issues of meaning, purpose, and spirituality. However, their employing institutions provided few, if any, opportunities for such conversations. At this critical juncture for the professoriate, questions of meaning, purpose, connection, and authenticity are arguably more important than ever before.

The myriad ways in which higher education institutions are evolving compel us to reconsider long-standing expectations and deeply held assumptions about many aspects of undergraduate education. As part of that process, we must reflect on our work as educators, especially with respect to the effects that our values, beliefs, and behaviors have on our own and others' lives, both within and beyond the academy. To enhance the capacity of colleges and universities to support the personal and professional growth of faculty themselves and, by extension, to facilitate students' growth and development, it is essential that we understand what faculty think, what they believe, what they do, and why. It is also important that we go beyond those pursuits to listen to the heart of who faculty are and what they feel. In turn, these efforts can contribute to enhancing higher education's capacity to effect positive change beyond institutional borders. Nationally normative data collected by our Spirituality in Higher Education research team coupled with additional national data collected in summer and fall 2012 provide a unique opportunity to explore faculty-focused issues of spirituality within higher education.

STUDYING FACULTY BELIEFS AND VALUES

Broadly speaking, values can be conceptualized in two main ways. One way to think about values is as a set of guidelines and core beliefs that we rely on when we are confronted with situations in which a choice must be made (Gibson, Ivancevich, and Donnelly, 1994). Viewed this way, values represent "general modes of conduct" or notions of what we "ought" to do in various contexts and under certain circumstances (Rokeach, 1973). Values can also be conceptualized as preferences (see, for example, Locke, 1976). Viewed from this perspective, values provide the standards by which we determine whether particular objects (or personal and professional pursuits, ideologies, institutional missions, processes, outcomes, and so on) have "value" or are to be preferred. In this way, values represent a primary "organizing structure" for much of the rest of our belief system. Inherently judgmental, values "carry" our ideas as to what is good, right, or desirable (Robbins, 1998). As Robbins explains, values are important to the study of organizational behavior not only because they lay the foundation for understanding the attitudes, motivations, and goal orientations of individuals but also because they influence people's perceptions of their work environment. Ultimately, the "collective, mutually shaping patterns of norms, values, practices, beliefs, and assumptions that guide the behavior of individuals and groups" characterize the cultural contexts within which we experience our lives and our work (Kuh and Whitt, 1988, pp. 12–13).

The overarching meaning systems we possess as individuals provide us both with an orientation to the world and directions for living in that world (Pargament, 1997). As conceptualized by Park (2012), global meaning systems comprise individuals' sweeping assumptions about the world and themselves (that is, beliefs) and the high-level ideas, states, or objects toward which people work (that is, goals, as defined by Karoly, 1999). Park describes the final component of global meaning as an emotional one, involving the degree to which an individual experiences a sense of meaning and purpose in life or feels connected to causes greater than himself or herself (Klinger, 1977; Reker and Wong, 1988). Global meaning systems are important because they provide the "general framework through which individuals structure their lives" (Park, 2012, p. 26). Essentially, meaning is "the sense made of, and significance felt regarding, the nature of one's being and existence" (Steger, Frazier, Oishi, and Kaler, 2006, p. 81). Seeing one's behaviors as oriented toward desired future goals leads to a sense of meaningfulness (Emmons, 1999).

Meaning-making is the process of resolving discrepancies between one's appraised meaning of a particular situation and one's global meaning system (Park 2010). The process involves "reappraising a situation and thinking through its implications for one's life," which helps people "restore a sense of the world as coherent and their own lives as meaningful" (Park, 2012, p. 29). Positive shifts in one's spiritual or religious life as a result of meaning-making have been identified as an important component of stress-related growth (Park, 2009).

Silberman (2005) contends that, in many people's meaning systems, religiousness and spirituality play a major role. Drawing on the work of Emmons (1999) and Lewis and Cruise (2006), Park (2012) explains that religious and spiritual aspects of global meaning "can influence individuals' lives through their interpretation of occurrences in their daily lives, the ways they structure their daily pursuits, and their general sense of well-being and life satisfaction" (p. 27). Park posits that religious and spiritual meaning systems potentially influence many aspects of work life through four pathways: (1) career choice and development, (2) on-the-job conduct, (3) work-related stress and coping, and (4) work-related well-being. As reaffirmed in some of the faculty comments that are incorporated throughout this book, our human need to be connected to something larger than ourselves translates into a "need to do good and be good—to make a difference in the world" (Wigglesworth, 2013, p. 694). Work can be especially meaningful when individuals seek "paths of integration" between their personal and professional lives (Dik and Duffy, 2012), focus on the broader purpose(s) of their work, are able to use their personal talents to promote others' well-being, and perceive their work as contributing to the greater good of society (see, for example, Schlegel, Hicks, King, and Arndt, 2011; Steger, Dik, and Duffy, 2012; Steger, Hicks, Kashdan, Krueger, and Bouchard, 2007). Comprehension (that is, making sense of one's experiences) and purpose (that is, identifying and intending to pursue highly valued overarching goals) play central roles in people's perceptions that their work is meaningful (Steger, 2010). Comprehension and purpose are also important in that they provide potential pathways for helping people align and integrate the personal and professional aspects of their lives (Dik, Duffy, and Tix, 2012). Dik and his colleagues maintain that, by extension, those who approach their work holistically tend to be highly motivated and productive, which in turn reinforces their work organization's commitment to maintaining their well-being.

As mentioned earlier, the Spirituality in Higher Education project focused primarily on the beliefs and values of college students. However, to understand the role that college faculty play in affecting undergraduate students' spiritual development, we also included a secondary focus on faculty beliefs and values. Supported by supplementary grant funding from the John Templeton Foundation, we collected extensive survey data during the 2004–2005 academic year from 65,124 faculty members at 511 U.S. colleges and universities through the HERI Triennial National Survey of College Faculty (Lindholm, Szelényi, Hurtado, and Korn, 2005). In keeping with traditional versions of the survey dating back to 1989, the survey questionnaire focused on goals for undergraduate education, preferred teaching styles, and institutional perspectives. The 2004–2005 survey also included roughly two dozen items that queried faculty members' own spiritual inclinations as well as their attitudes about the potential role that colleges and universities might play in facilitating students' spiritual development.

Aggregated normative findings for two- and four-year college and university faculty related to those spirituality oriented items were featured in *Spirituality and the Professoriate* (Lindholm, Astin, and Astin, 2005). Respondents to the 2004–2005 HERI faculty survey included professors at the 236 four-year colleges and universities that also participated in the 2004–2007 longitudinal College Students' Beliefs and Values (CSBV) Survey. As elaborated in *Cultivating the Spirit* (Astin, Astin, and Lindholm, 2011b), this overlap enabled our Spirituality in Higher Education research team to address as part of our 2004–2007 longitudinal analyses how faculty beliefs and behaviors contribute to shaping undergraduate students' spiritual development. To enhance our understanding of faculty survey respondents' perspectives—especially as they related to spirituality and undergraduate teaching and learning—we also conducted individual interviews with twenty-three faculty members at four-year colleges and universities nationally.

THE FACULTY BELIEFS AND VALUES SURVEY

Space constraints on the 2004 HERI faculty survey prevented us from exploring at that time the degree to which the spirituality and religiousness measures that our Spirituality in Higher Education research team had developed through our student-focused analyses were germane to faculty members' lives. Building on the 2004 Triennial National Survey of College Faculty and the 2004 and 2007 CSBV Surveys, the 2012 Faculty Beliefs and Values Survey was designed to facilitate learning more about the values and beliefs of college faculty and to begin to develop greater understanding of how faculty construct a sense of meaning and purpose in their lives, including through their professional pursuits. The survey also enabled both broader and more in-depth analysis of spiritual and religious dimensions of faculty members' lives as reflected by many of the spirituality and religiousness measures that our research team had developed earlier. (Those measures are addressed in more detail later in this chapter.) In addition to the 148 items that focused directly on the spiritual/religious dimensions of life, the 2012 Faculty Beliefs and Values survey also included approximately 135 items that addressed various aspects of faculty members' daily work and lives. Including these questions enabled further exploration of how the values and beliefs of faculty, including their spiritual/religious inclinations (or lack thereof), correlate with their personal and professional priorities and practices. The survey was completed electronically as a web-based survey in summer and fall 2012 by 9,291 faculty at a diverse sample of 264 baccalaureate colleges and universities.[2] Additional methodological details are provided in the Appendix.

MEASURING SPIRITUALITY AND RELIGIOUSNESS

As addressed earlier in this chapter, a number of researchers have attempted to distinguish between "spirituality" and "religiousness" (see, for example, Strohl, 2001; Tanyi, 2002; Testerman, 1997; Zinnbauer et al., 1997; Zinnbauer, Pargament, and Scott, 1999). However, there is no generally agreed-on set of definitions for these two terms. In 2001, when we began our work to develop scales to measure the spirituality and religiousness of American college students, our Spirituality in Higher Education research team was guided by two basic principles: (1) that spirituality is a multidimensional concept and that no single measure can adequately capture all that individuals mean when they use the term (Elkins, Hedstrom, Hughes, Leaf, and Saunders, 1988; Hill et al., 2000; MacDonald, 2000); and (2) that although many individuals no doubt express their spirituality in terms of some form of organized religion, the fact that others do not necessitates that we view religiousness and spirituality as separate qualities and that we attempt to develop separate measures of each.

Our research team's process of developing the CSBV Survey began with an exploration of various definitions of spirituality proposed by scholars in business, education, health, psychology, sociology, and other fields (see, for example, Ashmos and Duchon, 2000; Baker, 2003; Burack, 1999; Cannister, 1998; Cook, Borman, Moore, and Kunkel, 2000; Dehler and Welsh, 1997; Dyson, Cobb, and Forman, 1997; Gibbons, 2000; Hayes, 1984; Hill and Pargament, 2003; Hodge, 2003; Krahnke and Hoffman, 2002; Pargament, 1999; Rose, 2001). The team also reviewed previously developed measures of spirituality and religiousness. One key resource on which our team relied heavily in developing the CSBV survey was a comprehensive analysis of 125 different scales compiled by Hill and Hood (1999). In consultation with our Technical Advisory Panel,[3] which comprised expert researchers in the fields of religion, psychology, sociology, and education, we determined that although the existing scales contained a number of interesting and potentially useful items, no single instrument appeared to be uniformly well suited to the purposes of the Spirituality in Higher Education project.[4]

Our preliminary work resulted in the identification of content areas or "domains" to be considered in designing items and scales to measure spirituality and religiousness. As incorporated in the 2012 Faculty Beliefs and Values Survey, these include

- Spiritual or religious outlook (orientation/worldview)
- Spiritual well-being
- Spiritual/religious behavior/practice
- Self-assessments
- Caring/compassionate behavior
- Sense of connectedness to others and the world
- Spiritual quest
- Theological/metaphysical beliefs
- Attitudes toward religion/spirituality
- Religious affiliation/identity

Using these domains as a framework, our research team developed a large number of potential survey items. In addition to modifying many of the items developed by earlier investigators, we also created a number of new items.[5] Ultimately, over the course of three student survey administrations that were conducted in 2003, 2004, and 2007, we developed and refined scales of spirituality and religiousness.[6,7] Students' responses to the individual items in both of the latter surveys formed patterns that were nearly identical to those identified in the 2003 pilot survey, giving us confidence that we were dealing with measures that carried potentially wide application. Nine of those measures (five spirituality measures and four religiousness measures) served as focal points for learning more about faculty members' spiritual and religious lives.

SPIRITUALITY MEASURES

The first group of spirituality measures focuses on two "internally" directed aspects of spirituality:

Spiritual Quest is a nine-item measure that assesses interest in the search for meaning and purpose in life, finding answers to the mysteries of life, attaining inner harmony, and developing a meaningful philosophy of life. The process orientation of this measure is reflected in the prevalence of such words as "finding," "attaining," "seeking" "developing," "searching," and "becoming."

Equanimity includes five items reflecting the extent to which an individual feels at peace or is centered, is able to find meaning in times of hardship, sees each day as a gift, and feels good about the direction of his or her life. Equanimity plays an important role in the quality of people's lives because it shapes how they respond to their experiences, particularly those that are potentially stressful.

The second set of spirituality measures are "externally" directed aspects, focusing on individuals' connectedness to those around them and reflecting "caring about" and "caring for" one another:

Ethic of Caring is an eight-item measure that assesses one's degree of commitment to such values as helping others in difficulty, reducing pain and suffering in the world, promoting racial understanding, trying to change things that are unfair in the world, and making the world a better place.

Charitable Involvement is a four-item behavioral measure that includes such activities as participating in community service, donating money to charity, and helping friends with personal problems.[8]

Ecumenical Worldview is a twelve-item measure that indicates the extent to which the individual is interested in different religious traditions, seeks to understand other countries and cultures, feels a strong connection to all humanity, believes in the goodness of all people, accepts others as they are, and believes that all life is interconnected and that love is at the root of all the great religions.

Working within the framework of these measures, our Spirituality in Higher Education research team developed the following definition:

> Spirituality is a multifaceted quality that involves an active quest for answers to life's "big questions" (Spiritual Quest), a global worldview that transcends ethnocentrism and egocentrism (Ecumenical Worldview), a sense of caring and compassion for others (Ethic of Caring) coupled with a lifestyle that includes service to others (Charitable Involvement), and a capacity to maintain one's sense of calm and centeredness, especially in times of stress (Equanimity).

RELIGIOUSNESS MEASURES

The religiousness measures address four aspects of individuals' religious lives:

Religious Commitment is an "internal" measure comprising twelve items. It reflects the individual's self-rating on "religiousness" as well as the degree to which she or he seeks to follow religious teachings in everyday life, finds religion to be personally helpful, and gains personal strength by trusting in a higher power. In particular it measures the extent to which the individual's spiritual/religious beliefs play a central role in his or her life.

Religious Engagement, an "external" measure that represents the behavioral counterpart to Religious Commitment, includes seven items reflecting such behaviors as attending religious services, praying, engaging in religious singing/chanting, and reading sacred texts.[9]

Religious Skepticism includes nine items reflecting such beliefs as "the universe arose by chance" and "in the future, science will be able to explain everything," and disbelief in the notion of life after death.

Religious Struggle includes nine items reflecting the extent to which the individual feels unsettled about religious matters, disagrees about religious matters, feels distant from God, or has questioned her or his religious beliefs.

To determine whether someone possesses a high (or low) degree of the trait in question, we considered what pattern of responses to the entire set of items that make up that scale a person would need to show.[10] Not surprisingly, and in keeping with our team's previous findings related to undergraduate students, faculty members' scores on some of these measures are related to each other. (See the Appendix for a table of correlations among the measures.) For example, individuals who obtain high scores on Religious Commitment are also likely to obtain high scores on Religious Engagement and low scores on Religious Skepticism. In other words, if an individual is strongly committed to his or her religious faith, that individual is also likely to engage frequently in prayer and attend religious services regularly. At the same time, that individual is unlikely to express much religious skepticism.

Although the correlations are not as strong as in the case of the religiousness measures, some spirituality measures are also associated with one another. For example, those who have high Spiritual Quest scores also tend to obtain high scores on Ethic of Caring and Ecumenical Worldview. Those who demonstrate high levels of Charitable Involvement also tend to score high on Ethic of Caring.

Finally, as was the case with the college student analyses we conducted previously, the faculty Religious Struggle measure does not show any substantial relationship with other religious or spiritual measures. This means that individuals who are highly engaged in a religious struggle are not especially likely to score either high or low on any of the other measures.

MEASURES IN CONTEXT

As we also described in *Cultivating the Spirit*, taken together these measures constitute a framework for assessing individuals' spiritual and religious qualities. Because of substantial differences in survey design, it is difficult to make direct comparisons between measures we created as part of the Spirituality in Higher Education project and those developed by earlier investigators. Some of our scales, however, do share enough item content with earlier efforts to warrant mention here. In particular, our Religious Commitment scale appears to share a good deal of content with Allport and Ross's Intrinsic Religious Orientation scale (1967), which has been identified as perhaps the most widely used measure of religiousness in social science research. Religious Commitment also appears to share common elements with Williams's Commitment scale (1999), Seidlitz and colleagues' Spiritual Transcendence index (2002), Hall and Edwards's Awareness scale (2002), MacDonald's Religiousness factor (2000), and Underwood and Terisi's Daily Spiritual Experience scale (2002).

Our Religious Engagement scale shares some item content with Levin's Private Religious Practices scale (1999), MacDonald's Religiousness factor (2000), and especially with Idler's Organizational Religiousness scale (1999). The positive pole of Genia's Spiritual Experience index (1991) in some respects resembles our Ecumenical Worldview scale. Finally, at least two earlier measures appear to contain elements of our Equanimity scale: Underwood and Terisi's Daily Spiritual Experience scale (2002) and MacDonald's Existential Well-Being scale (2000).

Our Ethic of Caring and Charitable Involvement measures appear to tap spiritual qualities that may be especially relevant to the goals of education. For example, in arguing that spiritual development "should be a focus in the schools," Beck (1986) includes "love" and a "caring approach to other people" as essential qualities of a spiritual person. Similarly, Noddings (1984, 1989) argues that the cultivation of caring ought to be a basic goal of education. She also distinguishes two forms of caring: "caring-about," which resembles our Ethic of Caring measure, and "caring-for," which resembles our Charitable Involvement measure.

Finally, our spirituality measures appear to incorporate the two dimensions of spirituality proposed by Elkins and colleagues (1988): Mission in Life (our Spiritual Quest) and Altruism (our Charitable Involvement and Ethic of Caring). In discussing altruism, Elkins and colleagues also refer to "a sense of . . . belonging to a common humanity" (p. 11), which seems to relate directly to our Ecumenical Worldview.

Conclusion

As a foundation for the material presented in subsequent chapters, this chapter has highlighted common conceptualizations of the often nebulously perceived construct of "spirituality." It also addressed intersections between higher education and the life of the spirit and described the foundational work that has enabled the writing of this book. Using as an organizing structure the spirituality and religiousness measures that have been outlined in this chapter, the chapters that follow explore how college faculty view and experience the spiritual and religious dimensions of their lives. As noted in the Preface, the approach taken in presenting the findings, based primarily on two large, multifaceted national surveys of college faculty, is primarily descriptive. Speculation about cause-and-effect relationships is not appropriately a central feature of this work. Chapter Two provides a profile of how faculty characterize their spiritual and religious self-identities and offers insight on the meaning they perceive spirituality as having within their lives. The focus of Chapters Three through Six shifts to considering the salience of selected spirituality and religiousness measures in faculty members' lives, including connections between those measures and aspects of faculty members' work lives. The final chapter considers the findings as a whole with respect to faculty work and undergraduate teaching and learning. Considered there too are faculty attitudes about selected spirituality issues as related to higher education.

NOTES

1. All student-focused aspects of the Spirituality in Higher Education project were generously funded by the John Templeton Foundation. The foundation also provided additional, supplemental funding to support our Spirituality in Higher Education research team's sampling and data collection interests relative to the 2004–2005 HERI Triennial National Survey of College Faculty. The Templeton Foundation, however, has played no role in the analysis or interpretation of the student or faculty data we have collected.

2. The institutional sample was designed to ensure diversity with respect to type (colleges and universities), control (public, private nonsectarian, Roman Catholic, Protestant, Evangelical), and selectivity level. In creating the sample, geographical location along with prior institutional participation in the 2004–2005 HERI Triennial National Survey of College Faculty and the 2004–2007 longitudinal CSBV Survey were also taken in to consideration. For more detail on the 2012 Faculty Beliefs and Values Survey methodology, see the Appendix.

3. John A. Astin (California Pacific Medical Center), Arthur W. Chickering (Goddard College), Peter C. Hill (Biola University), Ellen L. Idler (Emory University), Cynthia S. Johnson (American College Personnel Association), Michael McCullough (University of Miami), William L. (Scotty) McClennan Jr. (Stanford University), Kenneth I. Pargament (Bowling Green State University), and Christian Smith (University of Notre Dame).

4. The limitations inherent in many of these instruments were expressed in different ways. For example, "spirituality" is typically equated with traditional religious practices and beliefs. Questions tend to assume, either explicitly or implicitly, that the respondent embraces a monotheistic, Judeo-Christian belief system (Moberg, 2002). Further, no distinction is made between one's spirituality and one's theological perspective, nor is a distinction made between spiritual attitudes, beliefs, or perspectives and spiritual action or behavior—that is, "inner" versus "outer" manifestations of spirituality. In developing the CSBV Survey, our team sought to design a set of questions that would meet the following criteria: (1) No assumptions would be made about the student's spiritual-religious perspective or lack thereof; regardless of their theological or metaphysical perspective or belief system, all individuals should be able to respond to items in a meaningful way; (2) References to "God," "supreme being," or a similar entity would be held to a

minimum; instead, respondents would be given an opportunity to specify what such a concept means to them, including an option to reject the concepts. (3) Both religious beliefs and perspectives and religious practices and behaviors would be covered, although the use of specific denominational or sectarian terminology would be avoided; for example, "sacred texts" would be used instead of "Bible" or "Koran." (4) The items would accommodate those who define their spirituality primarily in terms of conventional religious beliefs and practices as well as those who define their spirituality in other ways.

5. Throughout this process, Technical Advisory Panel members and the research team served as "judges" in finalizing the relevant domains and selecting the most appropriate items for each domain. Ultimately, this preliminary work led to the development of a pilot survey that included approximately 175 items having to do with spirituality and religion and 50 to 60 additional items addressing students' activities and achievements since entering college, as well as posttests on selected items from the freshman survey question- naire that these same students had completed three years earlier (Fall 2000) when they entered college. Readers who are interested in more information about the pilot 2003 CSBV Survey are advised to consult www.spirituality.ucla.edu.

6. Once students had completed and returned their CSBV Surveys and the resulting data were prepared for analysis, our next major task was to develop "scales" by searching for clusters of survey items that formed consistent patterns in terms of how students responded. In other words, if a given student endorsed one item within a particular scale, that student also tended to endorse other items in the scale and, ultimately, would obtain a high score on that scale. Conversely, if the student did not consistently endorse the items comprised by a particular scale, he or she would obtain a low score on that scale. Our principal means of identifying such patterns was a statistical method known as factor analysis, a procedure that examines the correlations among a set of variables (in this case, individual ques- tionnaire items) with the aim of reducing the variables to a smaller set of more general "factors," or scales. Compared to individual items, scales have at least two other advantages. Primarily, they are more reliable than individual items, but they also facilitate the task of interpreting results. Because there is likely to be a good deal of redundancy in individuals' responses to 175 spirituality and reli- giousness items, it becomes much easier to make sense out of the results if these items can be reduced to a much smaller number of

multi-item scales (Moberg, 2002). Final versions of each spirituality and religiousness scale were developed using factor analysis and item analysis. Possible scales (that is, groups of similar items) were identified using principal components analysis with Varimax rotation, following which each potential scale was subjected to an item analysis (Cronbach's alpha) to eliminate items that were not contributing to scale reliability. Considerations of appropriateness of item content were also applied in each stage of scale development. Those who are interested in additional information about scale development are advised to refer to *Cultivating the Spirit* (Astin, Astin, and Lindholm, 2011b) and to an associated article, "Assessing Students' Spiritual and Religious Qualities" (Astin, Astin, and Lindholm, 2011a).

7. In 2004, we created a slightly modified version of the CSBV pilot survey that incorporated these measures as part of a two-page addendum to the four-page freshman survey administered annually by the Cooperative Institutional Research Program (CIRP) at HERI (Sax, Hurtado, Lindholm, Astin, Korn, and Mahoney, 2005). A total of 112,232 entering freshmen at 236 four-year colleges and universities completed that special six-page 2004 CSBV Survey. Resulting data were weighted to approximate the responses we would have expected had all first-time, full-time students attending baccalaureate colleges and universities across the country participated in the survey. In late spring 2007, the final CSBV Survey was administered at 136 institutions to randomly selected samples of students who had participated in the 2004 CIRP/CSBV Freshman Survey. Data from 14,527 respondents were weighted to approximate the results that would have been obtained if all 2007 "juniors" (2004 freshmen who were still enrolled in 2007) at baccalaureate-granting institutions in the United States had responded to follow-up. Findings from the subsequently conducted analyses were addressed in *Cultivating the Spirit* (Astin, Astin, and Lindholm, 2011b).

8. The faculty version of the Charitable Involvement measure includes three fewer items than were included in the student version. (See the Appendix for specific items included in the measure along with alpha reliability and score ranges.)

9. The faculty version of the Religious Engagement measure includes two fewer items than were included in the student version. (See the Appendix for specific items included in the measure along with alpha reliability and score ranges.)

10. Raw scores on scales have no absolute meaning. Therefore, interpretive difficulties arise when attempting to compare group differences

in average scores. A potentially useful way to contend with such challenges is to define high and low scores. In doing so, it becomes possible to compare groups by determining what proportions of each group obtain high (or low) scores. For example, how do the proportions of men and women who score high on Equanimity compare? Because an individual's score on any particular spirituality or religiousness measure reflects the degree to which he or she possesses the quality being measured, defining high or low scores is, to a certain extent, arbitrary. Nevertheless, in making those determinations, our Spirituality in Higher Education research team tried to take a rational approach to such definitions by posing the following question: In order to defend the proposition that someone possesses a high (or low) degree of the trait in question, what *pattern* of response to the entire set of items that make up that scale would the person have to show? Our final definitions of high and low scores on each spirituality and religiousness measure were quite stringent. For example, on the five-item Equanimity scale, the respondent would have to give the strongest possible response on at least four of the five items to qualify as a high scorer. A more detailed description of the process we followed in defining high and low scores is provided in the Appendix.

CHAPTER TWO

THE MEANINGFULNESS OF SPIRITUALITY AND RELIGION IN FACULTY MEMBERS' LIVES

Today's four-year college and university faculty report relatively high levels of spiritual interest and involvement. Nearly nine in ten (87%) say that they believe in the sacredness of life. Roughly three in four indicate having an interest in spirituality (77%) and say that they believe we are all spiritual beings (73%). Fully three-fourths say that they are searching for meaning and purpose in life, and 70 percent report having discussions about the meaning of life with friends. Nearly two-thirds (65%) say that to at least "some" extent, they seek out opportunities to grow spiritually, and 54 percent believe that "we cannot really understand the world that lies outside of us without understanding the deeper spiritual aspects of ourselves." Overall, 47 percent give high priority to integrating spirituality in their lives.

Just over three-fourths (78%) of faculty consider themselves a "spiritual" person at least "some" extent. Four in ten embrace a spiritual self-identity "to a great extent," and just 22 percent say they are "not at all" spiritual. Data collected as part of the 2012 Faculty Beliefs and Values Survey reaffirm our earlier normative findings and show that, when asked to rate their own spirituality inclinations relative to others their age, 30 percent of faculty characterize themselves as "above average," and 12 percent designate themselves in the "highest 10%." As illustrated in Table 2.1,

TABLE 2.1 "CONSIDER MYSELF SPIRITUAL" BY DEMOGRAPHIC CHARACTERISTICS (PERCENTAGES)

	Consider Myself a Spiritual Person	
	To a Great Extent	Not at All
Sex		
Female	50.5	16.3
Male	40.2	24.5
Race		
African American/Black	64.5	8.9
Mexican American/Chicano	45.5	17.7
Puerto Rican	58.1	5.1
American Indian	56.7	13.7
Native Hawaiian/Pacific Islander	54.8	23.6
White/Caucasian	43.6	21.8
Other Latino	36.2	26.8
Asian American/Asian	30.9	28.7
Other Race	46.7	20.0
Lesbian, Gay, Bisexual, Transgender Identity		
Yes	35.1	21.9
No	39.2	20.9
Age		
Under 35	37.3	26.8
35–44	41.8	21.9
45–54	46.6	20.2
55–64	43.7	21.4
65+	42.9	24.0
Marital Status		
Married	43.4	22.2
Living with Partner	35.6	26.1
Single	46.6	18.6

Table 2.1 (continued)

| | Consider Myself a Spiritual Person | |
	To a Great Extent	Not at All
Children		
Yes	38.2	21.1
No	44.1	25.4
Political Views		
Far Right	64.6	16.3
Conservative	67.0	9.8
Middle-of-the-Road	46.3	16.6
Liberal	36.4	26.2
Far Left	35.8	30.3

Source: 2004–2005 HERI Triennial National Survey of College Faculty (except for LGBT identity: 2012 Faculty Beliefs and Values Survey)

across different disciplines and institutional types, and in parallel with broader adult spirituality data, women faculty are generally are more likely than men to characterize themselves as spiritual. African American faculty members are most inclined to characterize themselves as spiritual "to a great extent." On the whole, middle-aged faculty are also comparatively more inclined than their younger or older colleagues to characterize themselves as highly spiritual, as are those who have self-described "conservative" political beliefs. Reflective of the close associations many faculty perceive between spirituality and religion, nearly two-thirds of those who describe themselves as spiritual also describe themselves as highly religious. Another 19 percent consider themselves "somewhat" religious; 16 percent say they are "not at all" religious.

Across different types of four-year colleges and universities, faculty also show a moderate degree of religious involvement. Nearly two-thirds (63%) say they pray; 51 percent pray at least weekly, and 29 percent pray daily. About six in ten (61%) report that they attended religious services in the past year. More than half (56%) believe in God, 37 percent say they read sacred texts at least weekly, and roughly the same proportion (36%) consider it "essential" or "very important" to follow religious teachings in their everyday lives.

Nearly two-thirds of faculty (64%) also say that they feel a "sense of connection" with God or another higher power that "transcends my personal self." More than half (54%) say that they gain spiritual strength by trusting in God or another higher power. Four in ten say that, in the past year, they frequently "felt loved by God." Whatever their particular spiritual/religious beliefs may be, fully three-fourths of faculty indicate that those beliefs "have been formed through much personal reflection and searching." For more than half (57%), those beliefs "lie behind my whole approach to life."

Overall, faculty tend to demonstrate a high level of religious tolerance and acceptance. For example, the majority agree at least "somewhat" that "non-religious people can lead lives that are just as moral as those of religious believers" (94%) and that "most people can grow spiritually without being religious" (78%). More than eight in ten faculty (85%) also disagree with the proposition that "people who don't believe in God will be punished." When it comes to their spiritual existence, more than six in ten (62%) concur that "questions are far more central than answers."

Across different types of four-year colleges and universities and disciplinary contexts, 60 percent of four-year college and university faculty consider themselves a "religious" person to at least "some" extent. Just under one-third (32%) self-identify as religious "to a great extent." Fully four in ten, however, say they are "not at all" religious. When asked to rate their "religiousness" relative to others their age, just 22 percent characterize themselves as "above average"; 9 percent designate themselves as in the "highest 10%."

Table 2.2 highlights demographic differences in faculty members' "religious" self-identity. Across different disciplines and institutional types, women faculty generally are more likely than men to characterize themselves as religious. African American and Mexican American/Chicano faculty members are most inclined to characterize themselves as religious to at least "some" extent. Overall, younger faculty are considerably more inclined than their older colleagues to say that they are "not at

TABLE 2.2 "CONSIDER MYSELF RELIGIOUS" BY DEMOGRAPHIC CHARACTERISTICS (PERCENTAGES)

	Consider Myself a Religious Person	
	To a Great Extent	Not at All
Sex		
Female	31.4	39.9
Male	32.4	40.7
Race		
African American/Black	46.0	22.8
Mexican American/Chicano	36.5	28.2
Puerto Rican	32.5	37.0
American Indian	36.3	36.3
Native Hawaiian/Pacific Islander	34.9	41.6
White/Caucasian	32.1	40.5
Other Latino	21.9	53.0
Asian American/Asian	21.8	48.6
Other Race	31.8	40.0
Lesbian, Gay, Bisexual, Transgender Identity		
Yes	14.9	51.3
No	32.4	35.6
Age		
Under 35	26.4	48.8
35–44	30.2	43.4
45–54	33.1	39.5
55–64	31.8	38.9
65+	37.4	34.0
Marital Status		
Married	33.8	38.5
Living with Partner	11.9	63.4
Single	28.6	43.2

(continued)

Table 2.2 *(continued)*

	Consider Myself a Religious Person	
	To a Great Extent	Not at All
Children		
Yes	33.8	37.2
No	22.1	51.9
Political Views		
Far Right	70.1	10.6
Conservative	66.8	12.3
Middle-of-the-Road	38.0	28.2
Liberal	19.7	51.7
Far Left	12.1	71.0

Source: 2004–2005 HERI Triennial National Survey of College Faculty (except for LGBT identity: 2012 Faculty Beliefs and Values Survey)

all" religious. Politically liberal faculty—especially those who characterize their views as "far left"—and those who identify as lesbian, gay, bisexual, or transgender (LGBT) are less likely than any other demographic subgroup of faculty to self-identify as religious.

Despite their relatively strong spiritual/religious interests, many faculty also express doubts and reservations with respect to spirituality and religion. More than half of faculty indicate that they have at least occasionally disagreed with their families about spiritual/religious matters (57%) and questioned their own spiritual/religious beliefs (54%). Fully four in ten report feeling "disillusioned" with their religious upbringing, and roughly the same proportion (39%) agree that "most religious people are hypocrites who don't practice what they believe." Additional spiritual/religious reservations among faculty are reflected by the roughly one-third or more who report that "whether there is a Supreme Being is not a matter of concern to me" (38%), indicate that "believing in supernatural phenomena is foolish" (35%), and feel that it is "futile to try and discover the purpose of existence" (31%). Nearly one-quarter (24%) do not believe in God; 20 percent are "not sure" they believe in God. Figure 2.1 illustrates faculty responses to the question, "How would you describe your

FIGURE 2.1 CURRENT VIEWS ABOUT SPIRITUAL/RELIGIOUS MATTERS

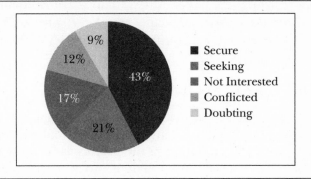

Note: These figures add up to more than 100 percent because faculty were permitted to choose more than one response option.

Source: 2012 Faculty Beliefs and Values Survey

current views about spiritual/religious matters?" Fewer than half of faculty indicate that they feel "secure" in their views. Considered within the context of the broader U.S. population, the religious faiths and perspectives of faculty are addressed in greater depth in Chapter Five.

THE SPIRITUAL AND RELIGIOUS SELF-IDENTITIES OF COLLEGE PROFESSORS

Researchers have attempted to distinguish between "spirituality" and "religiousness" (see, for example, Strohl, 2001; Tanyi, 2002; Testerman, 1997; Zinnbauer et al., 1997; Zinnbauer, Pargament, and Scott, 1999). However, there is no generally agreed-on set of definitions. Conceptions of the term "spirituality" tend to be especially slippery. Paralleling the approach our Spirituality in Higher Education research team used with each administration of the CSBV Survey, neither the 2004–2005 HERI faculty survey nor the 2012 Faculty Beliefs and Values Survey defined for survey respondents how the researcher(s) preferred them to conceptualize spirituality. Rather, in keeping with the majority of previous surveys that query individuals' spiritual/religious beliefs and values, that conceptualization was left to respondents to determine. The 2012 Faculty Beliefs and Values Survey did include an open-ended item that asked respondents to explain what meaning the term "spirituality" has to them. Those conceptualizations, framed within the context of faculty members' spiritual/religious self-identities, are the focal point of the remainder of this chapter.

"Spiritual and Religious"

Overall, 57 percent of four-year college and university faculty self-identify, at least to "some" extent, as both spiritual and religious. Of these, 28 percent characterize themselves as being both spiritual "to a great extent" and religious "to a great extent"; 17 percent indicate that "to some extent" they self-identify with both characterizations. The remainder within the "spiritual and religious" group view themselves either as more spiritual than religious (8%) or as more religious than spiritual (3%).

Demographically, African American faculty are the most inclined to describe themselves as spiritual and religious. Asian American/Asian faculty and those who identify as "other" Latino (that is, not Mexican American/Chicano) are the *least* likely to resonate with a "spiritual and religious" personal identity. On the whole, women faculty are also marginally more inclined than their male counterparts—both overall and within different racial/ethnic groups—to embrace a "spiritual and religious" self-identification. Relative to their younger counterparts, older faculty are also more inclined to embrace "spiritual and religious" personal identities. Married faculty and those who have children are more likely to characterize themselves as spiritual and religious as well. Pronounced differences in "spiritual and religious" self-identification based on political inclinations are also apparent. For example, whereas more than 80 percent of politically conservative faculty at four-year colleges and universities within the United States and roughly 70 percent who characterize their political beliefs as middle-of-the-road self-identify as spiritual and religious, just 46 percent of politically liberal (and 28% of far left) faculty describe themselves similarly (Table 2.3).

Many "spiritual and religious" faculty say that despite attempts within popular culture to define the spiritual and religious

Table 2.3 "Spiritual and Religious" Self-Identity by Demographic Characteristics (Percentages)

	"Spiritual and Religious"
Sex	
Female	58.7
Male	56.3
Race	
African American/Black	75.1
Mexican American/Chicano	61.8
Puerto Rican	66.9
American Indian	63.5
Native Hawaiian/Pacific Islander	62.1
White/Caucasian	57.1
Other Latino	44.6
Asian American/Asian	46.9
Other Race	57.2
Lesbian, Gay, Bisexual, Transgender Identity	
Yes	47.7
No	62.5
Age	
Under 35	49.3
35–44	54.4
45–54	58.4
55–64	58.3
65+	62.4
Marital Status	
Married	58.8
Living with Partner	35.9
Single	55.2
Children	
Yes	60.1
No	46.2

(continued)

TABLE 2.3 (continued)

	"Spiritual and Religious"
Political Views	
Far Right	81.9
Conservative	85.5
Middle-of-the-Road	68.6
Liberal	45.9
Far Left	28.1

Source: 2004–2005 HERI Triennial National Survey of College Faculty (except for LGBT identity: 2012 Faculty Beliefs and Values Survey)

dimensions of one's life as separate entities, they view the two constructs as highly complementary and essentially intertwined. For these individuals, spirituality is most often described as pertaining to one's "personal journey enabled by reflection and prayer." The religious aspect of their inner lives is often viewed as akin to the "corporate element of faith," which "connects me to others and gives me identity in the community and society." As one professor elaborated:

> I tend to think of "spiritual" as almost synonymous with religious, although spiritual is somewhat broader and more vague, incorporating less specific ideas about unexplained forces that seem to be present in the universe and in people's lives . . . religious without naming names.

As illustrated by the remarks that follow, many "spiritual and religious" faculty view the term spiritual as necessarily "referring to faith and religious values" and as "essentially meaningless taken outside a particular epistemology":

> Religion is the structure and process, while spirituality is the lived experience of those ideas and practices. Spirituality without some kind of religious framework is akin to metaphysical pornography: all kicks, no commitment! But without spirituality, religion is dry and dead. Both are needed. We all share a common bond at some level . . . a capacity for spiritual involvement . . . but that capacity must be directed in proper ways.

Although most "spiritual and religious" faculty tend to see the two constructs as necessarily part of the same whole, some view them as clearly distinct. The elaborated response of one professor illustrates key elements of that contrast especially well:

> I tend to separate "spiritual" from "religious." For me, being spiritual means being cognizant of forces greater than oneself and of outcomes of our behavior that can have ripple effects that go far beyond our immediate purview. "Spiritual" is an adjective, which means it can only modify what something is; by the nature of the word, it cannot completely define you. Thus, one can be partly spiritual and partly not. I don't mind the conflict resulting in that conceptualization. I don't mind being somewhat spiritual and somewhat in doubt. I think I live my life in a spiritual way and that I am guided by lessons I learned as a child growing up in the Roman Catholic church, but I don't want to be a follower of any single organized religion because their use of religion has poisoned many parts of society and led to counterproductive behaviors, that is, war, intolerance, even abuse. I think anything done fanatically is done at great risk. I really get tired of other people using religiosity to mean spirituality and using both to press political views of intolerance. So, I'm conscious of how spiritual I claim to be and what kind of spirituality I work to hold. Ultimately, being spiritual means being in touch with my best self and trying to connect that self to everyone else out there who is hopefully working at the same thing.

Another professor, who characterizes herself as more spiritual than religious, noted these distinctions:

> "Spiritual" means something different from "religious" for me. "Spiritual" refers to reflections on my experience of existence, my place in the universe, the meaning of life, the conduct of a moral life, and similar ideas. "Religious" refers to practices of a particular religion—rituals, scriptures, doctrines, etc. The practice of a particular religion is secondary for me to the authenticity of a spiritual practice that prioritizes love and nurturing.

A subset of religiously inclined faculty (roughly 20%) who also consider themselves at least somewhat spiritual express offense at what they view to be the "co-opting" of spirituality as "quasi-religious experience" or "religion without responsibility." Those within this group tend to view "spirituality" as a "far too vague," "weak" word for "New Age people who don't want to use the more accurate term, religion" or who have "given up their natal religion but can't let go of their religious mindset." One faculty member elaborated further on this view:

> Spirituality, to me, is an aspect of my religious life—the lens through which I see the beauty of creation and try to align myself with the spirit of all life. The word has been taken over by non-religious people who say they are "spiritual but not religious," which makes no sense to me at all. Why care about a "spirit" if you don't believe we have a source and a reason for being? When I hear the word spiritual from non-religious people, I usually think it's a cop-out and that they don't want to yoke themselves to any religion that requires them to change their attitude. I have many academic friends who call themselves "spiritual but not religious" and we drift apart over time, because I have a simple word ("God") to describe this source, and they don't. I don't understand why they can't cross the line and just say the word, you know?

As illustrated by many of the accompanying sentiments they shared, faculty who characterize themselves as spiritual and religious tend to view the two as playing different, but often collaborative and mutually reinforcing, roles in their lives. For some of these "religious" faculty, there is reluctance to characterize themselves as spiritual "to a great extent" given the wide-ranging ways in which people tend to use the term, including ways that they feel diminish the value of "traditional" religiosity.

"RELIGIOUS BUT NOT SPIRITUAL"

As reflected in Table 2.4, a very small proportion (roughly 2%) of faculty at four-year colleges and universities embrace the personal characterization "religious but not spiritual." Demographically, this self-identification is most prevalent among Asian American/Asian faculty along with those whose political beliefs are "far right." Some self-proclaimed religious faculty, especially those who have very strong faith-based worldviews, dismiss "spirituality" as a personally meaningless term in their own lives given their perception that it is "overused" and "annoyingly vague," ultimately reflecting little more than a "safe," "amorphous,"

TABLE 2.4 "RELIGIOUS BUT NOT SPIRITUAL" SELF-IDENTITY BY DEMOGRAPHIC CHARACTERISTICS (PERCENTAGES)

	"Religious but Not Spiritual"
Sex	
Female	1.3
Male	3.0
Race	
African American/Black	2.1
Mexican American/Chicano	1.7
Puerto Rican	1.0
American Indian	0.4
Native Hawaiian/Pacific Islander	2.9
White/Caucasian	2.4
Other Latino	2.4
Asian American/Asian	4.3
Other Race	2.9
Lesbian, Gay, Bisexual, Transgender Identity	
Yes	1.0
No	2.1
Age	
Under 35	1.8
35–44	2.2
45–54	2.1
55–64	2.9
65+	3.5
Marital Status	
Married	2.7
Living with Partner	0.7
Single	1.7

(continued)

TABLE 2.4 *(continued)*

	"Religious but Not Spiritual"
Children	
Yes	2.7
No	1.9
Political Views	
Far Right	7.4
Conservative	2.2
Middle-of-the-Road	3.1
Liberal	2.4
Far Left	1.0

Source: 2004–2005 HERI Triennial National Survey of College Faculty (except for LGBT identity: 2012 Faculty Beliefs and Values Survey)

"watered down" form of religiosity that "has no teeth." At its essence, spirituality is what some dubbed "religious light," "disorganized religion," or "religion without the effort" for those who "lack the discipline to practice a religion" or who are inclined to "pick and choose what feels good to them across religious traditions and cultures." As one professor remarked,

> When people say they are spiritual (as opposed to religious), I usually assume that means they want the personal benefits of faith (peace, centeredness, etc.) without the responsibilities or rules demanded by organized religions. I consider that a rather self-centered attitude.

As further illustrated by the following remark, the "self-centered" conceptualization of spirituality is particularly off-putting for many who characterize themselves as religious but not spiritual:

> "Spirituality" is self-created and self-focused and, consequently, can turn one away from God and others. I hope to be a religious person . . . love God, love neighbor . . . not a spiritual one . . . find MY peace, etc.

Other "religious but not spiritual" faculty offered similarly negative sentiments in association with the term spirituality:

> I tend to think that "spiritual" has become a kind of place holder that may not mean much, despite it obviously having some meaning to the person who uses it. For example, "I'm a spiritual person, but I don't believe in anything." I've heard that before. Well, without faith, what is spirituality? I can't say that I understand that formulation. So I think it's a word that's used as a place holder for the person who doesn't want to admit that they, in fact, do have faith. In certain places in our culture—particularly in some sub-sets of academic culture, faith is somewhat looked down upon.

> I don't really like the word "spiritual." It sounds like the people we called "God botherers" at school. I know who I am and what I believe and I believe in God. I don't go to church regularly but I consider myself religious and I feel a deep connection to the earth—the ocean, sky, birds, animals. Perhaps that is spiritual, but I would never describe myself that way.

Overall, the small proportion of college and university faculty who consider themselves religious but not spiritual share many of the same negative reactions to the term spirituality that some "religious and spiritual" colleagues do. However, the comparatively greater intensity of their negative sentiments leads them to reject the term entirely.

"SPIRITUAL BUT NOT RELIGIOUS"

In recent years, self-identification as "spiritual but not religious" has been referenced more prevalently within the American spiritual/religious landscape, sparking, as described earlier in this chapter, sometimes strong critique from those who hold more traditional views regarding the "inseparability" of the two constructs. Those who characterize themselves as spiritual but not religious account for the largest proportion of "unchurched Americans" and are inclined to "reject traditional organized religion as the sole—or even the most valuable—means for furthering their spiritual growth" (Fuller, 2001, p. 6). Fuller goes on to explain that those who identify as spiritual but not religious account for the largest proportion of those who have no substantive connection with organized religion but who nevertheless consider themselves as spiritual, sometimes highly so. Within the United States, 18 percent of adults self-identify as spiritual but not religious (Pew Forum on Religion & Public Life, 2012).

Individuals who characterize themselves as spiritual but not religious tend to value curiosity and religious freedom. They may have had negative experiences with organized religion or find traditional expressions of religiosity "stifling." On the whole, they tend to embrace a more "individualized" spiritual life, preferring a focus on "private reflection" and "private experience" that facilitates a journey of personal growth and development. That journey may be supported (although not necessarily so) by various religious traditions and other philosophies, but that incorporation does not translate into self-identification as a "religious" person (Fuller, 2001). Many who describe themselves as spiritual but not religious can be considered "spiritual seekers" rather than "spiritual dwellers." As Wuthnow (1998) explains, whereas spiritual dwellers embrace an "orderly, systematic understanding of life" (p. 8) that is rooted in a single faith tradition or community, spiritual seekers are inclined to "create a sense of personal identity through an active sequence of searching and selecting" (p. 10). Within the U.S. population, those who self-identify as spiritual but not religious are more likely to be college educated and to be employed in white-collar professions. They are also more inclined to be liberal in their political views and to be more self-reliant as well as more likely to have been raised in families where religious service attendance was relatively infrequent (see, for example, Roof, 1993).

Turning to the professoriate, 21 percent of four-year college and university faculty characterize themselves as spiritual but not religious. This includes 7 percent who describe themselves as "highly" spiritual. As reflected in Table 2.5, women faculty are more likely than men to identify as spiritual but not religious. In terms of racial/ethnic groups, faculty who identify as "other" Latino and Puerto Rican are the most likely to resonate with the spiritual but not religious self-characterization, whereas African American and Native Hawaiian/Pacific Islander faculty are the least inclined. Younger faculty are also more likely than their most senior colleagues to identify with being spiritual but not religious. Faculty

TABLE 2.5 "Spiritual but Not Religious" Self-Identity by Demographic Characteristics (Percentages)

	"Spiritual but Not Religious"
Sex	
Female	24.9
Male	19.3
Race	
African American/Black	15.9
Mexican American/Chicano	20.5
Puerto Rican	27.9
American Indian	22.7
Native Hawaiian/Pacific Islander	14.3
White/Caucasian	21.0
Other Latino	28.5
Asian American/Asian	24.2
Other Race	22.8
Lesbian, Gay, Bisexual, Transgender Identity	
Yes	30.5
No	16.6
Age	
Under 35	23.9
35–44	23.7
45–54	21.3
55–64	20.3
65+	13.6
Marital Status	
Married	19.0
Living with Partner	38.0
Single	26.1

(continued)

TABLE 2.5 *(continued)*

	"Spiritual but Not Religious"
Children	
Yes	18.8
No	28.4
Political Views	
Far Right	1.8
Conservative	4.7
Middle-of-the-Road	14.8
Liberal	27.9
Far Left	36.1

Source: 2004–2005 HERI Triennial National Survey of College Faculty (except for LGBT identity: 2012 Faculty Beliefs and Values Survey)

who identify as LGBT, those who do not have children, and those who characterize their political beliefs as far left or liberal are also generally more likely than their colleagues to resonate with being spiritual but not religious.

For those who self-identify as spiritual but not religious, clearly articulated distinctions between the two terms—including notation that, at least for them personally, being spiritual does *not* necessarily imply a belief in God or another deity—tend to be especially critical. For these faculty, spirituality is viewed as an essentially "secular construct" that reflects "a concern with life's meaning and value" and a recognition that there is a "force greater than all of us that connects us in unseen ways and influences our lives in mysterious ways." Such orientations are viewed as distinct and otherwise independent from belief in the doctrines, dogmas, and "fantastic narratives" of institutionalized religions. The elaborated comments of two faculty members who resonate with this identity capture well a frequently expressed view:

> To me "spiritual," or more specifically "spirituality," is that aspect of the human mind or human senses that reflects the recognition

there is more to our experience than what we can readily perceive or describe. It is the sense of awe in the magnitude of the Universe and its apparent systematic organization that begs speculation about "supreme beings" and the like. My experience, limited as it is in space and time, has convinced me that none of the organized religions have a legitimate claim on an accurate description of the metaphysical realities of the Universe, if there are any. I learned long ago that they all share in common some valuable insights into human behavior and relationships, and on that basis may offer valuable guidance to people. But they get so many other things wrong about reality that it nearly or, in some cases, completely overwhelms their value to society. So, when I think or talk about "spirituality" it has nothing to do with religious beliefs, almost all of which I think are bereft of any validity.

Being spiritual for me means believing that human beings . . . animals . . . nature . . . are more than simply biological entities, without having to believe in a sacredness that has to be tied to a god or a specific religion. I think all religions communicate some sense of the spiritual, but so do some philosophies as well as works of literature. If I were to pin down my sense of the spiritual, I would invoke the works of Thoreau and transcendentalists, who saw in all life forms an energy or force that binds us together. We don't need a god or a religion to support such a system, which demands that we respect all life regardless of religious, political, or even species affiliations.

These conceptions also mesh well with others' definitions of spirituality as the search for one's ultimate significance (Potts, 1996) or as related to a personal belief system that provides a sense of meaning and purpose to existence and that offers an ethical path to personal fulfillment (Waite, Hawks, and Gast, 1999).

Many "spiritual but not religious" faculty members perceive spirituality as going "beyond religion" into "engaging with ultimate questions and values" and "thinking about the philosophy of being human . . . what we are here on earth to do, how we need to treat others, and how we need to treat ourselves." What some view as the "foundational" or "core" aspects of spirituality in their lives is reflected in these remarks:

Spirituality refers to matters of the soul, the part that is not cognitive. It is not a religious concept and has nothing to do with believing in god. It means understanding that the mind, body, and soul are different aspects of self. The soul is that part that is intuitive, reads the unwritten/unspoken part of others. It is the part that is connected to the earth, other living things, and the energy of the universe.

Another professor's comments captured other commonly expressed conceptions well:

[Spirituality refers to] what satisfies the human spirit beyond religion. Spiritualism is the ground where people of different belief systems can meet because spiritualism belongs to no human institution, so it is above politics. It is not concrete, but an inner satisfaction in the sense that it leads to inner peace. And inner peace leads to feeling at one with nature. Spiritualism is the search for harmony between what is within oneself and what is outside oneself.

For many who characterize themselves as spiritual but not religious, spirituality is often linked with considerations regarding one's "inner self" or "inner life." This new kind of faith—driven, at least in part, by what Wuthnow (1998) terms "the quest to overcome estrangement" (p. 166)—requires "inner knowledge that must be renewed and renegotiated with experience" (p. 167). As Wuthnow has detailed, the late 1980s and 1990s marked a period of renewed interest among Americans in relating to the sacred by focusing on the inner self. Researchers have categorized this inner orientation in terms of relationship with oneself (Chiu, Emblen, Van Hofwegen, Sawatzky, and Meyerhoff, 2004), which involves ambition for better self-understanding and inner balance (Astedt-Kurki, 1995), authenticity and openness (Hall, 1998), striving for self-actualization (Fryback, 1993), ability to draw on inner strength and resources (Burkhardt, 1993), and affirmation and satisfaction with life (Mickley, Socken, and Belcher, 1992).

In contrast to what some of their colleagues denounce as the highly "self-absorbed" or "selfish" orientations of self-proclaimed spiritual people, many faculty who consider themselves spiritual but not religious describe the meaning of spirituality in terms of "interconnectedness," "respect," "care," and "compassion." As delineated by Chiu and colleagues (2004), relationships with others and relationships with nature (both addressed in more detail in Chapter Four) involve a sense of community, compassion, and altruism as well as awareness of human-environmental integrality (Sherman, 1996). Such views are illustrated well in the following remarks:

> For me, spiritual has nothing to do with religion and everything to do with my inner self, my desire to be a good and kind person, to treat others as I would have them treat me, to connect with the natural, physical world, and to love.

> To me, "spiritual" means that I feel a sense of respect, appreciation, wonder and awe for the natural world around me, and the way in which the processes that govern what happens can . . . and do . . . influence our lives in positive and negative ways. Spirituality to me is a non-religious phenomena that has been, unfortunately, in large part co-opted by the religions of the world.

> [Spirituality] indicates a sense of interconnectedness, that there is more to this world than our material existence. It is a faith in the shared experience of humans and animals and nature. It is religious feeling without religious orthodoxy.

> If "spirituality" is used to refer to a secular, humanist ideology that encompasses a commitment to general values that are not couched in terms of religious doctrine, then I'm happy to include myself among the "spiritual." I don't need to practice [a particular] faith or subscribe to [specific] doctrine or believe in a higher power in order to live a life that is committed to the expression of compassion, tolerance, forgiveness, concern for others, empathy, etc.

> I do not see "spiritual" as overtly religious, nor necessitating the belief in supernatural entities or phenomena. It can come from within and is derived from the unique social structures that define our evolutionary history and resulted in the human brain. The ability to empathize, to think abstractly, to appreciate aesthetic beauty, and to see value in things that goes beyond our immediate well-being are uniquely human and this is what I believe is spiritual.

Indeed, "spiritual but not religious" faculty tend to conceptualize spirituality in the broadest and most consistently positive ways. For many who value cultivating their inner lives but who do not believe in a higher power or who are generally resistant to institutionalized religion, spirituality is an "integrating and empowering" force that is often viewed as enhancing one's own and others' lives. Especially for those who have struggled with what they describe as "discompassionate" and "discriminatory" treatment within religious contexts, or for those who experienced an "eclectic" religious upbringing, embracing an entirely separate "spiritual" identity that supports a life journey of service, compassion, and acceptance of self and others can provide fulfillment and promote healing. As Wuthnow (1998) detailed based on the life stories of some of those he interviewed, "being exposed to trauma that could not be understood in terms of traditional beliefs" or "being exposed to many different beliefs" can make it difficult for people to use religious teachings and doctrines to make sense of their spirituality (p.147).

ON TRANSCENDENCE, SACREDNESS, AND CONNECTION WITH A HIGHER POWER

Irrespective of whether they conceptualize their own or others' spirituality as independent from religion or as integrally linked with religion, many faculty reference aspects of transcendence, sacredness, and connection with a higher power. As reflected in the following remark, spirituality (as compared to religion) exemplifies more directly a "concern for the spirit"; an appreciation of "the sacred elements of the world"; and "openness to sacred influence, experience and perception":

> To be spiritual is to have a sense of transcendence and sacredness in this world; that people are sacred, that the natural earth is sacred, and that there is a loving sacredness that enfolds all of humanity and all of the cosmos. Religion, or religiousness, has to do with the cyclical nature of practices and rituals that express our beliefs, our prayers, our thanks, and our petitions.

For some, spirituality refers to the "life giving aspect" or "essence" of who we are. As one faculty member explained, spirituality is "that which makes me, me . . . the most real thing about me." Thus, being spiritual relates to "the importance one places on nourishing his/her spirit" and to "knowing and understanding yourself and having a sense of who you are in that inner place." From a spiritual standpoint, "cultivating the mind and heart" requires one to "reflect on what it is to be human, and how one would like to be—and be with others (human and non-human)—in the world." It implies a personal commitment to "exploring the greater purpose, meaning, mystery, and sacredness of life," "being aware of and seeking for meaning in life that goes beyond the scientific, factual world," and showing "concern for the intangible aspects of life, whether universal qualities and values or personal feelings and beliefs."

Necessarily, such commitment involves recognizing that "individuals are part of a larger life that can be intimated but never fully grasped," accepting that there are "forces of vitality that are more than merely the energy of our physical bodies," and "being aware of things about the world and about myself that are beyond the realm of understanding." As one professor noted, spirituality is "the greater reality on which the material world is contingent." In keeping with this perspective, another faculty member remarked:

> Spirituality, to me, means recognizing the energy and life force, acknowledging things outside of yourself and valuing relationships over material things. Although I believe strongly in science, spirituality adds the sense of wonder and beauty to what seems to happen accidentally.

For faculty who embrace this conceptualization of spirituality, there is a broadly shared acknowledgment that there are "forces more powerful than myself that tie all things together in some way" and that the spiritual dimension of our lives pertains to experience that is "not empirically verifiable" but that nevertheless "provides meaning and purpose in our lives." Elaborations on these perspectives include conceptions that spirituality

> refers to aspects of existence and reality which cannot be measured by physical means. In referring to my spiritual life, there is a part of my brain function which cannot be reduced to chemical and electromagnetic interactions like some computer circuitry. Subparts of spirituality are altruism, self-awareness, self-sacrifice, jealousy, kindness, love, self-control. The spiritual interacts with the physical and provides mystery and beauty beyond the stimulation of nerve endings, synapses and neurons. Spiritual gives awareness and appreciation of physical beauty.

reflects a recognition that there exists and inanimate, non-physical aspect to consciousness that cannot be fully understood by reference to the physical universe—that is simply beyond the capacity of the "human computer" system to understand.

refers to what is transcendental about our existence, beyond just each of us—but present in the collective, present in nature, present in all forms of love, beauty and aesthetics—what defies easy comprehension, easy definition. A place where the personal and the universal come together and produce in us awe and appreciation—the spiritual is eternal and infinite and therefore infinitely and eternally mysterious, not meant to be explained. Only appreciated and basked in. To explain it all in terms of a god diminishes it.

is the essence of the mind-heart connection that truly makes us human. All people are spiritual beings, whether they see it in that context or not. Our values are formed in many ways that go beyond the biochemical. The cosmos of spirituality transcends the material into un-measurable realities.

"My spirituality," one faculty member explained, "connects to the non-physical part of me but is not disconnected from my brain or body either . . . My physical, mental, and spiritual body all connect, and what influences one will influence the another."

In contrast to many of the conceptions included earlier in this chapter, some faculty members' spirituality relates very specifically to (or is the direct expression of) "belief in," "connection to," or "authentic relationship with" with one's Creator, the Divine, God, or other higher power that "cares about us . . . loves us . . . and wants to be with us, or us to be part of it," and who "communicates to us through the events that occur in our daily lives." For this group, which primarily comprises faculty who characterize them-selves as spiritual and religious but also includes some who do not resonate at all with a "religious" self-identity, spirituality is rooted in "feeling called and known" by that higher power and believing that "one is somehow responsible to this force for other aspects of creation." "Trying to see the world and other people the way God sees them" and "listening for how you can be used to bring about redemption and hope" also tend to be prominently fea-tured elements. For some, "feeling confirmation that my life is acceptable in God's eyes" and "living a moral lifestyle that acknowledges the dignity of human life" are also central considerations. Still others refer to spirituality as a relatively individualized "pathway" through which "unmediated" personal connections with a higher power serve to "connect the dots in our lives." The following elaborations further illustrate this aspect of spiritual meaningfulness:

> Being spiritual means having a sense of one's place in the universe, a sense of purpose in one's life, an appreciation of the interdependence of all life, and a connection to the creator and sustainer of life.

> For me personally, "spiritual" means that I believe in a Power greater than myself and that I work daily to improve my conscious contact with that Power. [This process] takes place through prayer and meditation, but self-examination, making amends, and helping others are also central. In order to live a spiritual life, I believe I must live by spiritual principles (such as honesty, faith, integrity, love, compassion, and tolerance). If I am not acting on those principles, then I am not living a spiritual life. For me, spirituality and religion are not the same thing. One can be religious without being spiritual, and vice versa. I also believe that each person (myself included) may have his/her own understanding of the spiritual—your understanding of "spiritual" does not need to match mine. My own spiritual growth is best supported through a particular structure and with the help of a mentor, but I am not religious, nor do I participate in any organized religion. Spiritual growth and living a spiritual life are hugely important to me.

> Spiritual is an adjective that I use to describe a range of situations or feelings. Most relate directly to the knowledge that there is a loving God that seeks to guide us. I love my family, I love my friends, but I love God most. This realization that I have a spiritual connection . . . that is, a feeling of love and guidance in situations that is from God . . . allows me patience and understanding despite differences and trials. My actions should speak louder than my words, and therefore my lifestyle on a daily basis (certainly not only on Sunday!) should match my beliefs. Spiritual is how I feel when I know I have followed a loving path or made a decision out of love and concern for others, not myself or my judgmental tendencies. Spiritual is how I feel when I am at a Native American Pow Wow dancing with the heartbeat of the

drum and the wind blowing, knowing that God (the Great Spirit) is in control. (I don't feel a dissonance between my heritage and my Christ-following beliefs, as some texts might suggest.)

Whether experienced within the context of a specific faith tradition or not, connection with a higher power is a "compelling positive force" for those whose spiritual lives are defined in whole or part through that relationship .

Thematically, faculty members' references to transcendence closely parallel others' conceptions (see, for example, Chiu et al., 2004; Klaas, 1998). For example, on the basis of their review of spirituality conceptualizations, Chiu and her colleagues highlighted the significance of transcendence in terms of one's capacity for expanding conceptual boundaries of the self beyond constricted views of life and human potential (see also Reed, 1991). Through such heightened awareness, people may ultimately achieve new perspectives and experiences that exceed ordinary physical boundaries (Kaye and Robinson, 1994).

"NOT SPIRITUAL AND NOT RELIGIOUS"

In the United States, roughly 15 percent of the adult population can be considered completely disengaged both spiritually and religiously (Pew Forum on Religion & Public Life, 2012). Among four-year college and university faculty, that proportion is somewhat higher. Normative faculty data show that 19 percent of four-year college and university faculty reject both "spiritual" and "religious" as even minimally relevant self-identifications. As illustrated in Table 2.6, politically "far left" faculty are the most likely to denounce spiritual and religious self-identities. More than one-third characterize themselves as "not at all" spiritual and "not at all" religious. Roughly one-quarter of "liberal" faculty are similarly inclined, compared to just 13 percent of their politically "middle-of-the-road" colleagues and less than one in ten of those who are politically "conservative" or "far right." Irrespective of political orientation, the "not spiritual and not religious" faculty population comprises more men than women. It also includes comparatively higher proportions of those who characterize themselves as "other" Latino, Asian American/Asian, Native Hawaiian/Pacific Islander, and white/Caucasian. Age variations are also evident.

TABLE 2.6 "Not Spiritual and Not Religious" Self-Identity by Demographic Characteristics (Percentages)

	"Not Spiritual and Not Religious"
Sex	
Female	14.9
Male	21.5
Race	
African American/Black	6.8
Mexican American/Chicano	16.0
Puerto Rican	4.5
American Indian	13.3
Native Hawaiian/Pacific Islander	20.5
White/Caucasian	19.4
Other Latino	24.6
Asian American/Asian	24.4
Other Race	17.0
Lesbian, Gay, Bisexual, Transgender Identity	
Yes	21.1
No	18.8
Age	
Under 35	24.9
35–44	19.8
45–54	18.2
55–64	18.5
65+	20.6
Marital Status	
Married	19.5
Living with Partner	25.5
Single	17.0
Children	
Yes	18.4
No	23.6

(continued)

TABLE 2.6 *(continued)*

	"Not Spiritual and Not Religious"
Political Views	
Far Right	8.9
Conservative	7.6
Middle-of-the-Road	13.4
Liberal	23.9
Far Left	34.9

Source: 2004–2005 HERI Triennial National Survey of College Faculty (except for LGBT identity: 2012 Faculty Beliefs and Values Survey)

Younger faculty are comparatively more inclined than their older colleagues to identify as neither spiritual nor religious.

❧   ❧

Some who offered elaboration as to why they do not characterize themselves as either spiritual or religious noted that although these concepts are "irrelevant" in their own lives, they "recognize" and "appreciate" that "religion and spirituality are very important to most people," including, in some cases, "people I care about." These faculty acknowledge that spirituality is "clearly important sociologically," and they "respect" others' use of the term to describe selected aspects of their lives. One faculty member's remarks illustrate this perspective especially well:

> When making choices in my life, there is nothing that I consider spiritual that plays any part. I value the beauty of the world, and I work to be good rather than bad, and I know that many people would be hard put to see a difference between those parts of life and spirituality. For me, they are in no way enhanced or assisted by being taken as an expression of spirituality. If a person's spirituality includes the connectedness of all things, and all of them being expressions of a larger, pervasive force, then spirituality is everywhere and everything. That does not happen to be the world I live in. That said, I am fascinated by the different ways people get on with their lives. I have known wonderful

people whose lives are deeply informed by religion, or something spiritual, or both. I do not believe that my way of experiencing the world is the correct way, and anyone on a different path is a fool or in need of correction. I believe that for some people spirituality makes them more creative, kinder, and understanding. I want to learn from such people. I also know some people whose beliefs seem organically connected to being able to justify doing bad things, or being the excuse for avoiding aspects of life that would be better served if confronted. Some people who define themselves in terms of their spirituality can only be approached in terms that they recognize, and, sometimes, in order to have useful interactions with them, the only way to do it is on their terms. In such cases, suspension of disbelief is very useful.

Asked what meaning the term spirituality has for them, others explained that they do not identify themselves as spiritual primarily because they elect not to spend their time pondering "unanswerable questions about the meaning of life" and prefer "leaving the thinking about such matters to others":

> To me, being spiritual is being someone who is concerned about an aspect of life beyond the physical or intellectual and who actively tries to attend to this side of his/her existence. I am not one of these people.

> I do not pretend to understand the mind of God or how He works on earth. I am too busy to spend time on wondering about such questions. If I have any extra time, I sleep.

More prevalent, however, were distinctly varied explanations for why the term spirituality is personally objectionable. Among self-proclaimed "not spiritual and not religious" faculty, three categories of resistance to the term spirituality were primarily evident: (1) concerns related to spirituality being too closely associated with religion; (2) notions of spirituality as "self-indulgent, squishy nonsense"; and (3) relative indifference altogether to spirituality and religion.

"Too Close to Religion"

One notable subset of faculty who self-identify as not spiritual and not religious are repelled by the term spirituality based on their conceptions of its inherent associations with organized religion, which they tend to characterize as "fraud," "empty," or "soulless." For some, the terms spiritual and religious evoke common images of "rigid proselytizers" who "act with cruelty, superiority, and scorn" toward those who disagree with their beliefs. As one professor underscored, "I think the world would be much better off if religion and spirituality vanished tomorrow." As further illustrated through the following comments, some faculty explicitly reject the term spirituality because it "cannot be extricated from religious doctrine at this point in our society" and has been irreparably "tainted by its traditional association with organized religion":

> Since [the term spirituality] is usually associated with religion, I have long avoided its use. While many wonderful things have been accomplished in the name of religion, I feel that, over the centuries, religions have done more harm than good in the ways they have constricted personal and intellectual freedom, encouraged intolerance and persecution, and been the ostensible cause of wars and miseries of many kinds. In particular, in today's world, I consider any form of fundamentalism, and the bigotry and intolerance that it fosters, a form of evil.

> The term "spirituality" creates a lot of conflicting responses in me. When I reflect on it in the historical sense, I have an enormous amount of respect for "spiritual" persons, because their connection with something that is more important to them than their own self-interest has been enormously beneficial, not necessarily for themselves, but for society. Unfortunately, in modern usage, "spiritual" often refers to a form of narcissistic religiosity—which has often been pillaged from other cultures, and ripped out of its meaningful context—in which the goal of religion is to make persons feel better about themselves, and particularly to feel less empty in their materialism, and often to feel less guilty about their lifestyles.

> [I equate spirituality with] non-rational thinking and beliefs that are double-edged swords. It can help you find peace and understanding of self and others, and it can also lead to hatred/ misunderstanding toward other groups when relying on text-based instruction of the sacred texts (e.g., views against abortion, homosexuality/queer identities, etc.). In other words, spirituality

helps to create tautological reasoning and limit the exploration of certain topics ("narrow mindedness").

"SELF-INDULGENT, SQUISHY NONSENSE"

Irrespective of the term's perceived associations (or lack thereof) with religion, many faculty who self-identify as not spiritual and not religious underscored a variety of other, often colorfully described, reasons for their personal disassociation with the term spiritual. Within this group, spirituality was most commonly denounced as a construct that is "wishy-washy, individualistic, and vacuous"; "superficial, fake, self-delusional, politically correct"; "a hokey, sappy way to dance around the idea of a supreme being or beings"; "blather, balderdash, cant, boloney"; "a meaningless buzzword"; "sanctimonious hypocrisy"; "a waste of time"; "a useful synonym for myopic self-worship"; and "internalized silliness." As one faculty member offered, hearing someone use the term spirituality is a clear signal for him to "ignore the person . . . as he/she is an idiot."

Among those who elaborated on their distaste for the term, one focal point for critique was spirituality's "anti-intellectual" nature. Illustrative characterizations included conceptions of spirituality as "synonymous with mushy thinking," characterized by "fuzzy minded introspection" and indicative of "a reliance on intuition instead of intellectual skills," "irrational thinking and behavior," and "pseudo-psychology for those too lazy to think." Essentially, as one professor noted, "spirituality is a crutch for the weak minded." For others, spirituality is best considered "a quirk of the human mind," "a misunderstanding of neurobiological phenomena," or indicative of self-delusional proclivities for "believing in things you know are not true." As one professor lamented:

> [Embracing the term spirituality] signifies a sense of ignorance of science and intellectual laziness on the part of people who fail to seek mechanistic explanations for their observations. It also indicates a lack of deep questioning and an inability to think critically.

Others—many of whom underscored their preference for "using evidence to understand the universe"—offered additional perspectives that align closely with the following elaborated sentiments:

> I take [the term spirituality] in the narrow sense of finding a connection/relationship with a higher power or entity. In this sense, I consider spirituality to be primarily a defense mechanism that helps people feel special, have a sense of purpose, etc. Of course, the term is also used much more broadly and hazily. One meaning is just a sense of wonder and awe with the world we live in—with the enormity of the universe, the evolutionary inter-connection of all life we know of, the enormous improbability of our existence. I suppose I'm spiritual in this specific sense, but the term is usually too bound up in a bunch of wishful/magical/self-interested thinking that I don't really care for. To my mind, an accurate view of the universe does allow us to achieve purpose, calm, balance, and a consistent moral code. We don't need to fool ourselves with notions of an afterlife, deities, auras, vortexes and the like.
>
> I would like to be able to use this term, but it has been much tarnished by the squee and ick of self-appointed "seekers." It strikes me as ridiculous for any human to suppose they have a handle on how the world really works, whether they are coming from a scientific or religious or spiritual perspective. All that a lifetime of education has taught me is that what we are capable of knowing, even in a single field of study, amounts to very little. How much less so for the enormous universe that we inhabit? There are aspects of existence that I'm willing to term "spiritual," but I don't believe I or any human being has the capacity to achieve much in this area, judging from how ethically compromised most "spiritual leaders" throughout history and contemporary society appear to be, and I'm comfortable with my doubts. There's something pathetic and desperate about the human desire for certainty that becomes the basis for self-righteousness on all sides of the question of spirituality versus science.

Still other self-described "practical" people highlighted their more specific issues related to what they perceive to be the "self-absorbed," "self-indulgent," and "highly individualistic" nature of spirituality. Too often, from their vantage point, so-called spiritual worldviews prioritize "individual knowledge" and "personal fulfill-ment" at the expense of attention toward "broader social needs" and "commitment to community." The following comments fur-ther illustrate this viewpoint:

I understand spirituality as my need to relate to what is outside of me in a respectful, thoughtful, and sometimes helpful way. I know that it may be strange to many, but somehow I feel the expression "being a spiritual person" too egocentric. It seems too much about oneself. I would prefer to be considered an ethical person. It would describe me more in terms of relationship with the rest of the world, which is what matters most to me.

[Spirituality means] nothing that I can relate to as it seems that one is putting too much emphasis on oneself and being busy telling others how to live their lives. Also, this business of seeking the meaning of life takes too much away from living life. We live, we do, we care for, we attach, we love, we procreate, we try to do work that will help others that we love or ourselves, but eventually sooner or later we die.

"DON'T KNOW WHAT SPIRITUALITY MEANS, DON'T REALLY CARE"

Finally, although not necessarily associated with "negative" conceptions, for some faculty who self-identify as neither spiritual nor religious, spirituality is simply an "overly broad," "baffling," "largely ambiguous," "catch all" term that is impossible for them to resonate with or understand. As one faculty member noted, "It's a nebulous word that cannot accurately be defined in the same way for everyone." Another remarked that the term is "undecipherable to me; I simply cannot relate." Others offered similar sentiments:

Spiritual is one of the most vague terms . . . Whenever someone tells me that s/he is spiritual, I ask what that means and almost never get an answer. I think it probably refers to a need to believe in something godlike, if not in God as defined in traditional religions. It is not a personally meaningful term for me.

I don't make a distinction between spirituality and religion. Frankly, spirituality is a dubious term for me. I'm not sure what people mean by it. It seems to be a New Age-ish concept about expanded consciousness and feelings of oneness with the universe. People I know who call themselves spiritual appear to believe in a vague higher power that is not strictly speaking a deity. But this is not my belief. People who are spiritual and those who are religious both believe (not rationally) in some higher guiding force in the universe that is separate from the physical world. I don't see any evidence for that.

I find the word "spiritual" somewhat confusing, since it is so intimately tied to religious myths/stories that I do not see as "truth." I certainly have a sense of awe and wonder when I look at nature and the complexity of the universe, and even more awe and wonder when I think about human capacity to understand that complexity. I read and study and contemplate the universe almost every waking hour of every day of my adult life, and in some sense I have devoted myself to the appreciation of nature. However, I do not think of this as meditation or prayer or spirituality. Instead, it is thoughtfulness, curiosity, analysis, and just plain hard work. To use words like "spiritual" or "faith" conflates curiosity and devotion with specific mythologies.

I don't find it's a term with much relevance to my life. It seems to point to ineffable experiences and higher powers. People speak about "spiritual" experiences while looking at art or tripping on mushrooms or going on religious retreats. All these instances cluster around rarefied moments of existence, held apart from everyday life by some kind of special value-added. I prefer to think in terms of solidarity, fellowship, and kindness with other people and in terms of clarity and beauty with regards to sensory experiences. I live a happy life, full of grassroots activism, teaching, writing, and great friendships. I don't feel that "spirituality" describes my commitments or my experiences in any of those spheres.

Spirituality has very little personal meaning for me. When I think of the kind of "inner life" and questions that I consider on a daily basis, I think of them as ethical, psychological, moral, or of that nature. I have never been religious and have never believed in a higher power, so I don't relate to that term. I do, however, believe in taking responsibility for my conduct, and ethical considerations are extremely important to me, as are questions of the motives for my conduct.

Among college and university faculty, questions related to spiritual/religious identity and, particularly, to the personal meaning that spirituality has (or does not have) in one's life tend to evoke strong reactions. As illustrated in their own voices throughout this chapter, the relevance of spirituality and religion in the lives of college and university faculty ranges from critically important to completely nonexistent. In keeping with the variety of spirituality conceptualizations highlighted in Chapter One, there also tends to be considerable variation with respect to the particular meaning that spirituality has for them. For some, issues of sacredness, transcendence, and connection with a higher power are central. For others, such considerations are not at all applicable. Demographic differences in spiritual/religious self-identification tend to mirror patterns that are consistently evident within the broader U.S. adult population. As addressed in subsequent chapters, these differences are associated, at least to some degree, with the extent to which faculty tend to embrace (or reject) selected spiritual and religious qualities. As with all aspects of professorial work, disciplinary and institutional contexts also figure prominently.

THE IMPORTANCE OF DISCIPLINARY AND INSTITUTIONAL CONTEXTS

College and university faculty live and work within the context of multiple professional affiliations and their associated cultures, most notably those of a discipline and department, a specific college or university, a national system of higher education, and a profession. The overarching and integrative values that characterize the culture of the academic profession have been a focal point for much research and writing (see, for example, Clark, 1986; Rice, 1986). As summarized by Austin (1990, pp. 62–63), core values of the academic profession include:

1. A notion that the fundamental purpose of higher education is to "pursue, discover, produce, and disseminate knowledge, truth, and understanding"
2. A belief that "autonomy and academic freedom in teaching and research are valued as ways to maintain quality and protect creative as well as controversial ideas"
3. A commitment to "intellectual honesty and fairness"

4. A belief that collegiality is the "ideal framework for faculty interactions as well as institutional decision making"
5. A commitment to "service for society"

Faculty share a fundamental responsibility for educating young adults. However, their daily routines, their approaches to academic work, and their professional perspectives and priorities vary considerably depending on contextual considerations, including their disciplinary training, the nature of their academic appointments, their specific departmental roles, and the particular institutions and academic units in which they work.

Organizational values encompass both implicit and explicit views. They also address both (1) external adaptation (that is, how a given unit should relate to external constituencies and competitors) and (2) internal integration (that is, how members of a given unit should relate to and work with one another) (Schein, 2004). One of the central challenges within institutions, educational or otherwise, is to achieve the common good of the unit while simultaneously meeting the needs and safeguarding the rights of its various constituencies. Within organizational contexts that are characterized by diverse needs and expectations, a primary challenge is to find ways of helping people transcend their focus on individual concerns and forge a common path that leads toward the fulfillment of community-based goals. Taken together, the prevailing values, beliefs, and assumptions of an academic unit constitute its culture and are, to a large extent, reflected in its climate.

Academic institutions have long been characterized as "value-rational" organizations (Dill, 1982; Satow, 1975), reflecting the fact that the individuals who are affiliated with them tend to be committed to, and find meaning in, specified ideologies. As Satow explains, value-rational organizations are bound together by members' broadly shared beliefs about primary roles and responsibilities (for example, research, teaching, and service) as well as collectively valued personal traits and behaviors (for example, production and communication of knowledge, sustained curiosity, honesty, and ongoing intellectual growth and development). Thus the power and authority of value-rational institutions ultimately rests on members' allegiance to shared sets of values and ideological norms. From a value-rational perspective, shared values are also important because they serve as an organization's cultural foundation. At the organizational level, values function as important guidelines for human behavior within work environments and affect all aspects of organizational life and culture. Within organizations, the influence that values exert on individual and collective action tends to be subtle yet undeniably powerful, permeating every facet of organizational life and culture. However, it is also important to keep in mind that within various environmental contexts, the "weight" of individual values may be differentially accounted for based on power dynamics, tradition, and the like.

Normative values of the academic profession and employing institution exert strong forces that affect faculty values and activities. Demographic differences also contribute to shaping faculty members' personal and professional perspectives, practices, and experiences. However, the most fundamental distinctions among U.S. academics tend to be based on disciplinary context. As both the "primary units of membership and identification within the academic profession" (Clark, 1987, p. 7) and the basic organizational element of U.S. colleges and universities, academic disciplines are the "value-laden cultures that frame the beliefs and behaviors of faculty members" (Austin, 1990, p. 64), including assumptions about what is to be known and how.

Important to note is that while disciplinary (and institutional) cultures contribute to shaping the values, beliefs, and behaviors of the faculty, so too are disciplinary and institutional cultures shaped by the individuals who are attracted to them. To be sure, the puzzle of faculty–work environment fit comprises a wide range of individual and organizational "pieces" that do not necessarily come together in a universally applicable "solution." However, those pieces—coupled with faculty members' spiritual/religious inclinations and their perceptions of congruence between their own values, needs, and attributes and those of the college or university contexts within which they work—have important implications for individuals and institutions.

With respect to the spiritual and religious dimensions of life, evidence of the distinctive disciplinary and institutional differences in the values, beliefs, perspectives, and priorities of college and university faculty is clearly evident. Overall, 40 percent of four-year college and university faculty describe themselves as being spiritual "to a great extent," and 22 percent say they are "not at all" spiritual. However, with the exception of engineering, half or more of faculty in applied fields (education, health sciences, agriculture/forestry, fine arts, and business) characterize themselves as highly spiritual. Health sciences and education faculty are also the least likely to consider themselves "not at all" spiritual: only about 9 percent in each field describe themselves in that way. The most balanced proportions of those who do (and do not) characterize themselves as spiritual are found in the physical and biological sciences. In these disciplines, roughly 30 percent of faculty consider themselves spiritual "to a great extent," and approximately the same proportion consider themselves "not at all" spiritual. (Figure 2.2 summarizes these results.)

With respect to religious self-identity, 32 percent of faculty characterize themselves as religious "to a great extent"; 40 percent

FIGURE 2.2 "CONSIDER MYSELF SPIRITUAL" BY ACADEMIC DISCIPLINE/FIELD

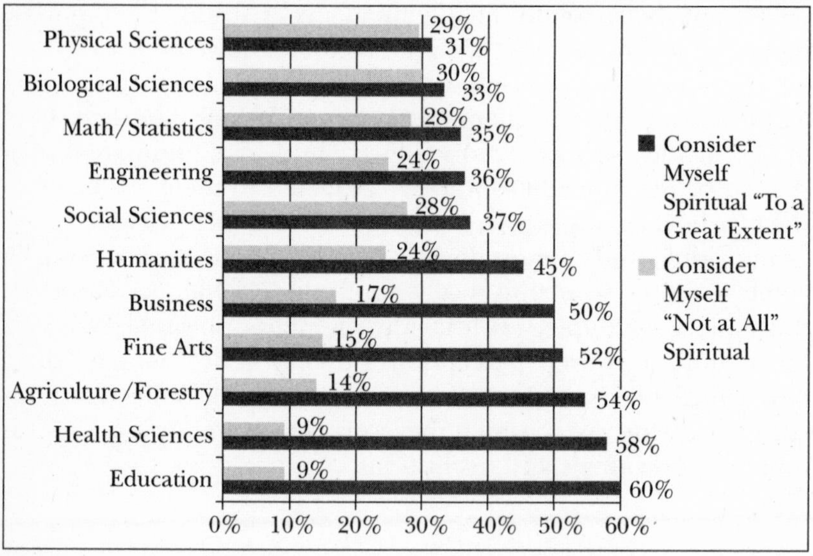

Source: 2004–2005 HERI Triennial National Survey of College Faculty

indicate that they are "not at all" religious. As was the case with spiritual self-descriptions, these proportions vary considerably based on academic field and disciplinary affiliations. Generally speaking, as depicted in Figure 2.3, those in applied fields (with the exception of engineering and fine arts faculty) are considerably more likely than colleagues in the sciences and humanities and in math/statistics to characterize themselves as highly religious. In contrast, half of faculty in the biological sciences, physical sciences, and social sciences are "not at all" religious. Engineering faculty tend to reflect the most balanced proportions of highly religious and completely nonreligious faculty (35% and 32%, respectively).

Table 2.7 shows differences in the prevalence of various spiritual/religious self-identities based on disciplinary/academic field affiliation. As might be expected given the characterizations just described, the highest proportions of "spiritual and

FIGURE 2.3 "CONSIDER MYSELF RELIGIOUS" BY ACADEMIC DISCIPLINE/FIELD

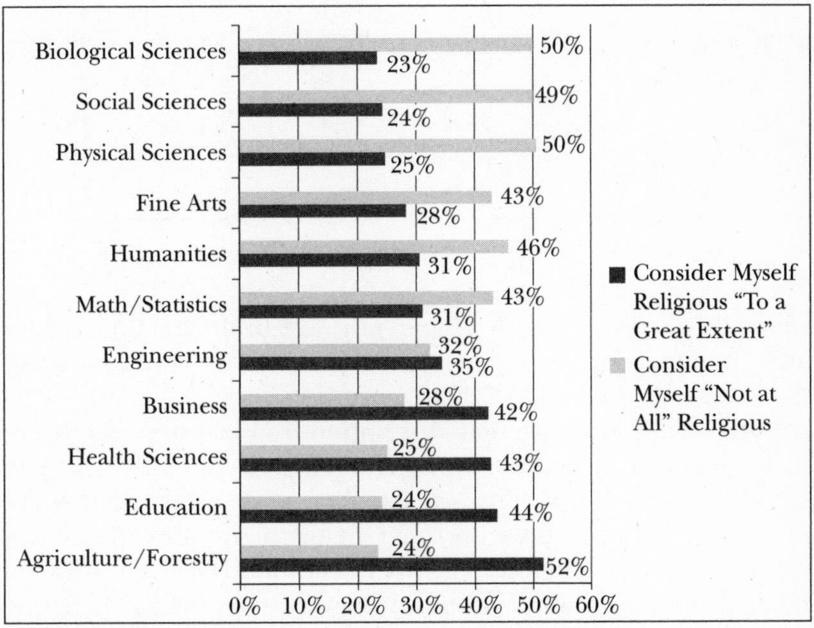

Source: 2004–2005 HERI Triennial National Survey of College Faculty

TABLE 2.7 SPIRITUAL/RELIGIOUS SELF-IDENTITY BY ACADEMIC
DISCIPLINES/FIELDS (PERCENTAGES)

	Spiritual/Religious Self-Identity			
	Spiritual and Religious	Spiritual but Not Religious	Religious but Not Spiritual	Not Spiritual and Not Religious
Academic Discipline/ Field				
Agriculture/Forestry	73.1	13.0	3.4	10.6
Biological Sciences	47.5	22.9	2.4	27.1
Business	68.3	14.9	3.6	13.0
Education	74.2	16.6	1.6	7.6
Engineering	63.5	12.1	4.0	20.3
Health Sciences	74.5	16.0	0.4	22.0
Humanities	51.1	22.9	1.9	21.9
Fine Arts	55.8	29.2	1.0	13.9
Math/Statistics	53.7	18.1	3.1	25.1
Physical Sciences	46.4	24.2	3.1	26.3
Social Sciences	46.3	23.9	3.3	25.3
Other (Technical Field)	59.8	17.4	4.4	18.5
Other	62.9	20.0	2.6	14.6

Source: 2004–2005 HERI Triennial National Survey of College Faculty

religious" faculty (roughly 75 percent) are in the health sciences and in education and agriculture/forestry. In contrast, fewer than half of biological science, physical science, and social science faculty embrace that description. Engineering faculty are most likely to consider themselves religious but not spiritual; those in the fine arts, physical sciences, and social sciences are more inclined than those in other fields to consider themselves spiritual but not religious. Faculty in the biological and physical sciences and in math/statistics are more likely than their colleagues in other disciplines/fields to describe themselves as not spiritual and not religious.

FIGURE 2.4 "CONSIDER MYSELF SPIRITUAL" BY INSTITUTION TYPE

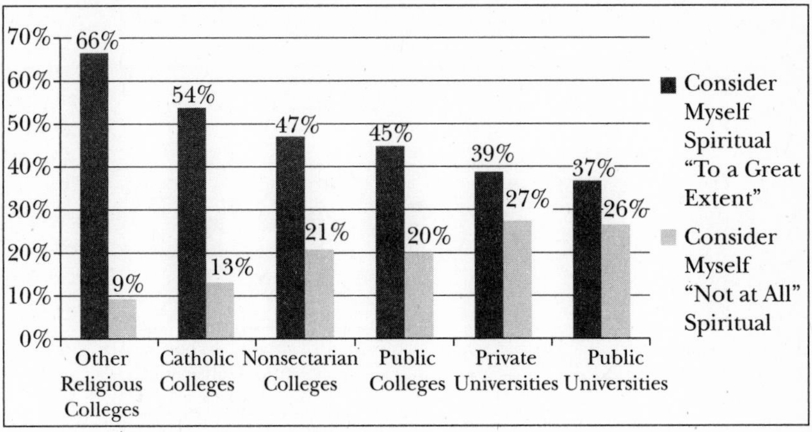

Source: 2004–2005 HERI Triennial National Survey of College Faculty

Not unexpectedly, faculty at faith-based colleges are more likely than their colleagues at public colleges and universities or at private nonsectarian colleges to consider themselves spiritual "to a great extent." More than half of Catholic college faculty and fully two-thirds of those at "other" (mainly Protestant) religiously affiliated institutions identify this way. Overall, private and public university faculty are the most disinclined to identify with being spiritual; roughly one-quarter of faculty indicate that they are "not at all" spiritual (Figure 2.4).

Inclinations toward "religious" self-identification follow a similar pattern, with those at "other" religious colleges considerably more inclined to identify as religious "to a great extent" and least likely to characterize themselves as "not at all" religious. In the aggregate, public university faculty are the least likely to describe themselves as religious "to a great extent" (Figure 2.5). As illustrated in Table 2.8, the "spiritual and religious" self-identity is most prevalent at faith-based institutions; faculty at public and private universities are more likely than their colleagues at other types of institutions to be among the small population who consider themselves religious but not spiritual. On the whole, "spiritual but not religious" faculty are most prevalent at public colleges

FIGURE 2.5 "CONSIDER MYSELF RELIGIOUS" BY INSTITUTIONAL TYPE

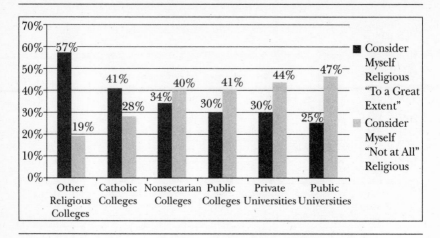

Source: 2004–2005 HERI Triennial National Survey of College Faculty

TABLE 2.8 SPIRITUAL/RELIGIOUS SELF-IDENTITY BY INSTITUTIONAL TYPE (PERCENTAGES)

	Spiritual/Religious Self-Identity			
	Spiritual and Religious	*Spiritual but Not Religious*	*Religious but Not Spiritual*	*Not Spiritual and Not Religious*
Institutional Type				
Public Universities	50.6	23.0	2.8	23.5
Private Universities	52.8	19.9	3.2	24.2
Public Colleges	57.1	23.1	2.4	17.4
Private Nonsectarian Colleges	58.4	21.0	1.6	19.0
Catholic Colleges	70.0	17.2	2.0	10.8
Other Religious Colleges	79.1	11.8	1.5	7.6

Source: 2004–2005 HERI Triennial National Survey of College Faculty

and universities, and public and private university faculty are comparatively more inclined than their colleagues at other types of institutions to identify as not spiritual and not religious.

Conclusion

The spiritual and religious self-identifications of college and university faculty that have been delineated in this chapter, coupled with faculty members' views on the meaning of the term spirituality, paint a portrait of the professoriate that is multifaceted with respect to spirituality and religiousness. On the whole, college faculty are less likely than other U.S. adults to consider themselves religious. However, in parallel with U.S. adults as a whole, and reflecting the considerable conceptual overlap that many people perceive between the constructs of spirituality and religiousness, most faculty consider themselves to be at least somewhat spiritual and religious. Similarly small proportions of college faculty and the U.S. adult population at large consider themselves religious but not spiritual. Finally, relative to other U.S. adults, college faculty are somewhat more inclined to characterize themselves as spiritual but not religious or as neither spiritual nor religious. As previewed here, faculty members' spiritual qualities and religious inclinations vary notably depending on their disciplinary and institutional affiliations.

Taken together, the profiles included here serve as a foundation for considering in the chapters that follow how faculty who self-identify in different ways (spiritual and religious, religious but not spiritual, spiritual but not religious, and not religious and not spiritual) view their work and lives. Building on information contained in this chapter, subsequent chapters also consider how faculty who are "high," "moderate," and "low" scorers on a Spiritual Self-Identification measure that our Spirituality in Higher Education research team initially developed in 2005 are differentiated with respect to their responses to items comprised by the Ethic of Caring, Ecumenical Worldview, Charitable Involvement, and Equanimity measures.

CHAPTER THREE

SPIRITUAL QUEST

Spiritual quest is a form of existential engagement that emphasizes individual purpose and meaning-making in the world (Klaassen and McDonald, 2002). Essentially, it represents the "seeking"
in us that can lead to a better understanding of who we are, why
we are here, and how we can live a meaningful life—the "big
questions" we confront at different stages throughout our lives:
Who am I? What are my most deeply felt values? What is the
meaning of life? What is my mission or purpose in life? What kind
of person do I want to be? What sort of world do I want to help
create? How will I go about building and sustaining the life I
desire? Dalton (2001) contends that "it is possible to speak of
spirituality as a universal human activity because life is filled with
experiences that drive us to question and seek answers on the
meaning and purpose of existence" (p. 18).

Faculty members' quest-oriented conceptions of spirituality
are reflected in references to "feeling one's place in the universe" and descriptions regarding the life of an "inner self" that
"seeks to find meaning in life," "questions, seeks, and wonders
about how to be in the world," that has "faith—and doubt—that
there is purpose and meaning in the universe," and that is
"willing and committed to a quest to understand our existence."
Also prevalent were characterizations of searching for "explana-
tion and meaning that is outside the easily measureable physical
world," "making sustained effort to own and understand belief
in an immaterial reality" and to "deeply question what it means
to be human and to (attempt to) understand what it means to

live a life," as well as a commitment to "interrogate and develop one's inner life." For some, this quest involves a "knowledge of something higher, or other than the self," a "search for something . . . a power of being . . . beyond the self," including a "personal quest for the sacred."

For many who embrace quest-oriented conceptions of spirituality, the journey of self-discovery and understanding primarily requires "intellectual humility" and a "realization that there are sweeping, universal truths about human existence that are almost never clearly understood in detail, but can be experienced." These conceptions parallel others' characterizations of spirituality as a personal journey to discover meaning and purpose in life (Fryback and Reinert, 1999) and to deal with the unknown (Burkhardt, 1993). For those who are quest oriented, the processes of seeking such understanding and establishing "deeper connection with that which unites all beings and the rest of the world" have direct implications for our "moral beliefs and our behavior" and "help us cultivate morality and goodness."

Composed of nine items, the Spiritual Quest scale is the most process-oriented of the measures we developed over the course of the Spirituality in Higher Education project. Primarily, the measure reflects an engagement in the search for meaning and purpose in life as grounded in several key aspirations, including finding answers to the mysteries of life, seeking beauty in one's life, developing a meaningful philosophy of life, becoming a more loving person, attaining inner harmony, and attaining wisdom. Acknowledging that spiritual growth is facilitated through interactions with others, the measure also considers how commonly individuals' close friends are searching for meaning and purpose, along with the frequency with which individuals talk with their friends about life's purpose and meaning. The active or process-oriented aspect of spiritual quest is reflected by such words as "searching," "developing," "finding," "seeking," "becoming," and "attaining," which are contained within each of the items that the measure comprises. The self-discovery inclinations of those for whom a quest orientation resonates are reflected in the relatively strong positive associations between faculty members' scores on the Spiritual Quest scale and the personal value they place on "discovering who I really am" ($r = .65$) and "knowing my purpose in life" (r = .65) as well as the degree to which their "beliefs have been formed through much searching" (r = .42).

How individuals perceive their position in the world, develop a sense of meaning and purpose in life, and seek inner harmony and self-awareness are all critical components of healthy identity development and psychological well-being. Earlier research has shown, for example, that those who view themselves as being on a spiritual quest tend to exhibit an active, open disposition to tackling the perplexing and otherwise challenging issues we face in life (see, for example, Klaassen and McDonald, 2002). At its core, a quest orientation entails "honestly facing existential questions in all their complexity while resisting clear-cut, pat answers" (Batson, Schoenrade, and Ventis, 1993, p. 163). Developing people's abilities to access, nurture, and give expression to the spiritual dimension of life has an impact on how they engage with the world and fosters within them a heightened sense of connectedness that promotes empathy, ethical behavior, civic responsibility, passion, and action for social justice (Allport and Ross, 1967; Batson, 1976; De Souza, 2003; Klaassen and McDonald, 2002). The spiritual growth process has been described as evolving (see, for example, Dobbie, 1991) and integrative (Riley, Perna, Tate, Forcheimer, Anderson, and Luera, 1998).

As we highlighted throughout the course of the Spirituality in Higher Education project, spiritual quest is in many ways at the core of spiritual development. The individual items comprised by the Spiritual Quest measure speak to aspects of many of the other measures that we developed. "Attaining inner harmony," for example, has implications for dealing effectively with stress and maintaining a healthy perspective and capacity for resilience in the midst of inevitable trials and tribulations (equanimity). Similarly, "becoming a more loving person" implies a commitment to caring for others and contributing to the welfare of the community (ethic of caring and charitable involvement) as well as to valuing the interconnectedness of life, embracing common elements of our human journeys, and respecting the differences among us that can provide texture and richness in our lives (ecumenical worldview). "Attaining wisdom" and "developing a meaningful philosophy of life" reflect the aims of many religious faiths (religious commitment, religious engagement), and "working toward finding answers to the mysteries of life" is often at the root of religious struggle.

QUEST PERSPECTIVES

As a starting point for understanding faculty members' spiritual quest inclinations, were used the same criteria for determining high and low scorers that our Spirituality in Higher Education research team had previously established (see Appendix). As illustrated in Figure 3.1, across different types of four-year colleges and universities, 30 percent of traditionally appointed faculty members register as high scorers on the Spiritual Quest measure, 44 percent are moderate scorers, and the remainder (26%) are low scorers. Quest-related interests are not exclusive to "religious" faculty or even more broadly characterized "spiritual" faculty. However, patterned responses to items that constitute the Spiritual Quest measure show that those who self-identify as "religious and spiritual" are the most inclined to be high Spiritual Quest scorers, followed by those who consider themselves "spiritual but not religious." More than half of those who characterize themselves as "religious but not spiritual" or neither religious nor spiritual are low scorers on Spiritual Quest (Figure 3.1).

FIGURE 3.1 SPIRITUAL QUEST HIGH AND LOW SCORERS BASED ON
SPIRITUAL/RELIGIOUS SELF-IDENTITY

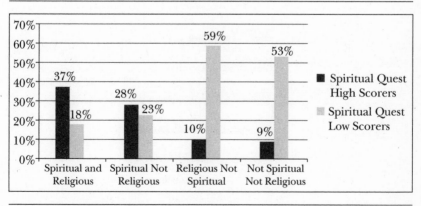

Source: 2012 Faculty Beliefs and Values Survey

Overall, just under two-thirds (64%) of faculty say that, to at least "some" extent, they seek opportunities to grow spiritually. Among high Spiritual Quest scorers, roughly half (48%) indicate that they pursue spiritual growth opportunities "to a great extent." Figure 3.2 displays variations in faculty members' responses to individual items that constitute the Spiritual Quest measure based on their score ("high," "medium," or "low") on a Spiritual Self-Identification measure that our Spirituality in Higher Education research team originally developed in the course of our 2004–2005 HERI faculty survey analyses. The measure, which comprises three items ("consider myself a spiritual person," and the personal priorities placed on "integrating spirituality into my life" and "seeking opportunities to grow spiritually") reflects an individual's propensity to engage actively with the spiritual dimension of life.[1] Faculty responses show that the greatest differentials in quest-related interests between high and low scorers are reflected in the degree to which attaining inner harmony and developing a meaningful philosophy of life are given high priority.

The most current scholarship on spiritual questing emphasizes variations in how individuals grapple with existential issues and the multidimensional ways in which quest is enacted (see, for example, Beck and Jessup, 2004; Burns, Jackson, Tarpley, and

FIGURE 3.2 "ESSENTIAL" OR "VERY IMPORTANT" SPIRITUAL QUEST PURSUITS BY SPIRITUAL SELF-IDENTIFICATION

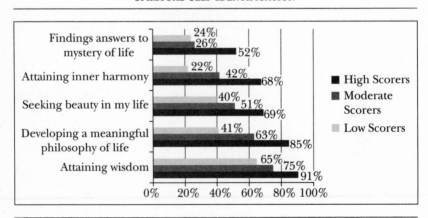

Source: 2012 Faculty Beliefs and Values Survey

Smith, 1996). An important distinction to be made is that spiritual quest is not synonymous with being committed to a particular faith tradition or being otherwise settled in one's religious perspectives. Indeed, actively engaging in a spiritual quest may be a manifestation of several different religious orientations. For example, when asked to characterize their current spiritual/ religious beliefs, college and university faculty who are high scorers on Spiritual Quest are nearly four times more likely than low scorers (46% vs. 12%) to say they are "seeking," which points to the relative fluidity of their belief system. Roughly one-third of high Spiritual Quest scorers (34% vs. 13% of low scorers) say that they "frequently" question their own assumptions and "agree strongly" that "questions are far more central to my spiritual existence than answers" (31% vs. 12% of low scorers). "Daily" self-reflection is also a way of life for 62 percent of high scorers, compared to just 18 percent of low scorers. At the same time, 36 percent of high scorers, compared to only 20 percent of low scorers, say they are "conflicted," which indicates that an element of religious conflict may be an underlying component of seeking for some of those who are more deeply engaged in questing. Similarly, more high scorers (30%) than low scorers (21%) say they are "doubting" their religious beliefs, which suggests that for some faculty, spiritual quest itself may be rooted in a fundamental examination of their religious faith.

In contrast, those who are high scorers on Spiritual Quest are also more likely than their low-scoring colleagues to say they are "secure" in their religious beliefs (32% vs. 23%). Spiritual Quest high scorers are also comparatively more inclined to say that they "frequently" find new meaning in the rituals and practices of their religion (27% vs. 4%), and to report that they pray (45% vs. 14%) or meditate (15% vs. 1%) on a daily basis. These findings illustrate the variable and sometimes complex relationship between spiritual questing and religious conviction. Indeed, although religiosity may play a key role in the process by which individuals formulate responses to core questions of meaning and purpose, resolution of these concerns may result in deepening of religiosity or, for some, perhaps a rejection of it. It is also important to understand that, for some, spiritual quest inclinations are not at all linked with personal religiosity. For example, 62 percent of those who say they are "not at all" religious score at least moderately on the Spiritual Quest scale. Within that group, 18 percent are high Spiritual Quest scorers. In addition, just under half (47%) of those who do not believe in God also register at least moderately on the Spiritual Quest measure, including 8 percent who are high scorers.

DEMOGRAPHIC DIFFERENCES

Women faculty are somewhat more likely than men to register as high scorers on the Spiritual Quest measure (32% vs. 28%) and marginally, although statistically significantly, less likely to be low Spiritual Quest scorers (25% vs. 27%). African American faculty members are considerably more likely than their colleagues of other races or ethnicities to be high scorers (48%). About one-third of Hispanic[2] (35%) and Asian (34%) faculty score similarly compared to just 29 percent of those who are white non-Hispanic. Roughly one-quarter (27%) of non-Hispanic whites are low Spiritual Quest scorers as compared to just 21 percent of Asians, 18 percent of Hispanics, and 11 percent of African Americans. On the whole, older faculty tend be more quest oriented than their younger colleagues: nearly one-third (32%) of those fifty-five years or older register as high Spiritual Quest scorers relative to roughly one-quarter (26%) of those who are forty-four years or younger. Spiritual quest inclinations also resonate strongly with many LGBT faculty, 41 percent of whom register as high Spiritual Quest scorers. Politically conservative faculty are somewhat more likely to score high on Spiritual Quest (34%) than their more moderate (31%) or liberal (28%) colleagues. However, roughly one-quarter of each group also register as low scorers.

QUEST AND ACADEMIC WORK

As elaborated in Chapter One, global meaning systems are "pervasive in determining the course, direction, and tenor of individuals' existence" (Park, 2012, p. 31). For many people, meaningful work is foundational to their sense of well-being. When work is meaningful to them, people tend to be more creative, productive, committed, and collegial (Amabile and Kramer, 2012). When not moving toward fulfilling their full potential, people tend to become bored and uncreative, spend too much time on nonessential activities, and, ultimately, underachieve (Lips-Wiersma and Morris, 2011).

What makes work meaningful? Lips-Wiersma and Morris (2011) identified seven common sources of meaning that are important both for individual performance, satisfaction, and well-being and for organizational performance: unity with others, expressing full potential, service to others, developing the inner self, balancing "being" and doing, balancing "self" and "other," and relating both to inspiration and reality. Important too are notions that the dimensions of meaningful work are in "constant and dynamic movement" (p. 381) and that focusing too much on only one of these dimensions over too long a period of time tends to undermine meaning. Dik and Duffy (2012) offer additional perspective on job characteristics that tend to increase the likelihood that people will find their work meaningful. These include autonomy; possibilities for using a variety of personal skills and talents; a sense of how your work contributes to a tangible, personally identifiable product or service; a sense of how that contribution matters to society; and coworkers who value your work and with whom you get along well. Also important are an institutional mission that aligns well with one's individual values and broader sense of purpose, and supportive organizational leaders who communicate a clear vision that one also values and who express genuine care and concern about one's well-being.

Faculty members' inclinations toward spiritual questing may affect both their motivations for pursuing academic work and how they view their work. For example, compared to their colleagues who score low on Spiritual Quest, those who score high are more inclined to say that it is "essential" for them to have intellectual freedom (68% vs. 49%), freedom to pursue ideas (62% vs. 46%), and opportunities for teaching (46% vs. 28%). High scorers are also more likely to rate as "essential" the availability of strong collegial networks (40% vs. 21%), the potential for mentoring others (28% vs. 11%), and the opportunity to influence social change (25% vs. 7%).

For some faculty, the decision to become a professor was motivated by a "sense of calling" to pursue work that resonates deeply with their own beliefs, values, and passions and that enables them to integrate key aspects of their own life journeys. As discussed in the Preface, callings can be conceptualized as either sacred or secular (see, for example, Dik, Duffy, and Tix, 2012). In either case, they can be characterized by three core elements: a transcendent summons, purpose and meaning in work, and other-oriented motivations (Dik and Duffy, 2012). Overall, 56 percent of faculty report that, "to a great extent," they feel that they are fulfilling a calling through their work. Just 13 percent indicate that this is "not at all" the case. The 2012 Faculty Beliefs and Values Survey did not define for respondents how they should interpret the word "calling" in the context of that particular survey item, nor were respondents asked specifically whether they personally conceive of their calling to academic work in sacred or secular terms. Their comments about selected aspects of their work, however, reflect clearly the components of calling that Dik and Duffy (2012) delineated.

For example, as described by faculty members themselves, core elements of their work as teachers involve "sharing knowledge," "learning along with" and "mentoring" students, including "validating students' efforts at speaking in their own authentic voices." For faculty who view their professorial careers as a "vocation" that is rooted in creative discovery, critical reflection, and the sharing of ideas, some of the most spiritual aspects of professorial work are helping students "seek deeper purpose and engagement in the world," "respect and appreciate diverse people and worldviews," and "think critically about ethical issues and social change." Describing the connections between her spiritual life and her work with students, one faculty member remarked:

> As a teacher I am inspired by the enthusiasm that I feel in my search for knowledge and meaning and my desire to impart it to others. It often seems to me that this zeal comes from a spiritual source that is both within and without. I am part of something larger than myself.

Reaffirming Astin and Astin's earlier findings (1999), for some faculty, research also provides an avenue for facilitating one's own spiritual quest:

Research is all about questions. My career as an academic is guided by Rilke's words: "Live the questions." This is in line with how I define spirituality as a search for meaning, a search which has to be guided by questions.

Illustrating the views of those who view their entire professional lives as tightly integrated with the so-called spiritual dimension of their lives, another professor remarked:

I do what I do because I feel I am supposed to make the world a better place through all I do, from teaching students the things they need to know and showing them the joy of knowledge to guiding students through advising and supporting them in the positive things they do.

DISCIPLINARY DIFFERENCES

Overall, humanities and fine arts faculty tend to be the most quest oriented, with more than four in ten respondents in these fields registering as high scorers. Roughly one-third of education and health science faculty indicate similarly strong quest proclivities, along with about one-quarter of social science and business faculty. By comparison, the largest proportions of low Spiritual Quest scorers are found in engineering, the physical sciences, and the biological sciences (illustrated in Figure 3.3). Across academic disciplines, the intersections some faculty members perceive between their spiritual and professional lives are further reflected in the following comments:

As a teacher educator I am always working with my students to understand that what they teach (content) is only a small part of the act of teaching and learning. Their ability to make the human connection with their students, both on a one-on-one basis and with them as a group, will make the biggest difference in whether their students actually learn. This is in part an expression of the spiritual nature of what it means to be a good teacher.

I am a scientist. Science informs my entire concept of the world and myself. In some ways my scientific quest to understand things is identical to my spiritual quest to understand the mystery of the universe.

As an artist, I derive meaning from the act of creative expression as a divine reflection of the Creator God, and teaching as an

FIGURE 3.3 SPIRITUAL QUEST HIGH AND LOW SCORERS BY ACADEMIC
DISCIPLINE/FIELD

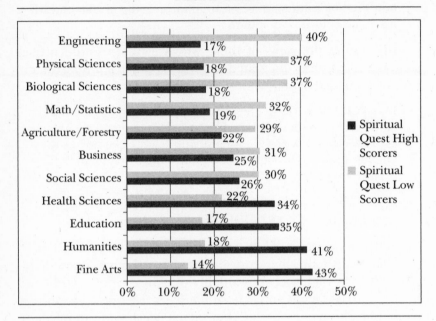

Source: 2012 Faculty Beliefs and Values Survey

equally sacred act of seeking/imparting wisdom in a learning
community.

I teach Biology. Understanding the subtlety and complexity of the
workings of the cell provides about the greatest opportunity for
being awed by existence outside of galactic astronomy.

Being a scientist helps me appreciate the Universe and approach
it both scientifically and worshipfully. It helps confirm the
spirituality I feel as a deeply religious atheist. One of the rewards
of being a teacher of science is to see students gain a deeper
understanding of and appreciation for all of the Universe and its
workings.

I teach and do theatre and theatre has deep spiritual roots and is
a constant investigation into all that is human which encompasses
our spiritual questing. My own quest supports and influences how
I teach and how I interpret the plays I direct, the roles I play, and
the writing that I encourage.

My work as a poet and essayist is what gives my life its meaning and focus. I teach creative writing which means that I am teaching the same subject that drives and moves me beyond the classroom.

Why are there apparent disciplinary differences in faculty members' spiritual quest inclinations? One might reasonably speculate that these differences are attributable simply to faculty demographic differences, such as the relative balance of women versus men, within selected disciplines or fields. Through statistical analyses, we can test the veracity of such speculations by holding constant the potential effects of core demographic variables (gender, race/ethnicity, and age) and then examining whether there remains a significant correlation between faculty affiliation with a particular academic discipline/field and a given measure (in this case, Spiritual Quest). The results of this process reveal that irrespective of their gender, race/ethnicity, or age, faculty in the humanities, fine arts, health sciences, and education are comparatively more likely than their colleagues in other fields to resonate with a quest orientation. Further, above and beyond the potential influence of their particular demographic characteristics, physical science faculty as a whole are negatively inclined toward spiritual questing. Patterned findings of this nature (with some variation depending on the specific measure under consideration) are replicated across many of the measures that are focal points of subsequent chapters. This suggests that, on the whole, faculty in selected academic disciplines and fields are differentially inclined (or *dis*inclined) to resonate with spiritual/religious dimensions of life.

The disciplines/fields where faculty as a whole are more inclined toward a quest orientation tend to attract what Smart, Feldman, and Ethington (2000) determined to be predominately "social" (education, health sciences, humanities) or "artistic" (fine arts) type personalities, based on Holland's personality-based career development framework (1973, 1997). In contrast, per Smart and his colleagues' classification, the predominately "investigative" types who are drawn to the physical sciences may be inherently less inclined to embrace ineffable pursuits. Additional interpretive insight may be gleaned by considering Biglan's classification (1973) of disciplinary groupings based on the nature of knowledge ("hard" vs. "soft") and disciplinary culture ("pure" vs. "applied") as well as the "life" versus "nonlife" orientation of the subject matter. Generally speaking, in the case of Spiritual Quest, it is faculty in "soft" and "applied" disciplines/fields who resonate more with spiritual questing relative to those in "hard" and "pure" disciplines/fields.

INSTITUTIONAL TYPE DIFFERENCES

Looking at differences across institutional types, the largest proportions of high Spiritual Quest scorers are found at Catholic institutions and other religiously affiliated campuses (see Figure 3.4). One-third of private university faculty also score high on Spiritual Quest, although there are comparatively larger proportions of private university faculty who are low scorers than is the case at faith-based institutions. Equivalent proportions of faculty at both private nonsectarian colleges and public colleges register as high and low scorers. On the whole, public university faculty are the least likely to embrace a quest orientation. Not unexpectedly, highly spiritual and/or religious faculty who are employed at faith-based colleges where the spiritually infused institutional missions are highly congruent with their own spiritual beliefs and life priorities tend to experience the most seamless integration between their professorial work and their own quest interests. The importance to some of working in an environment that supports such connection—in many cases independent of a direct parallel between the faculty members' specific religious faith (or lack thereof) and the institutional denomination—is illustrated through the following faculty comments:

> I teach in a Christian university with an emphasis on the integration of faith and learning. I left a state-institution for this place at lower pay and higher teaching in order to be in this environment.

> I teach in a faith-based college that centers principles on social justice. I strongly believe in social justice and therefore feel there is a connection between my social justice beliefs and the beliefs

FIGURE 3.4 SPIRITUAL QUEST HIGH AND LOW SCORERS BY INSTITUTIONAL TYPE

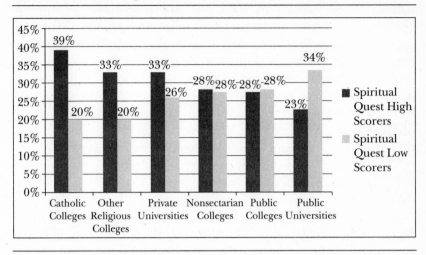

Source: 2012 Faculty Beliefs and Values Survey

upon which the institution was founded, even though I am not of the same religious persuasion.

Because I teach at a religious university that is committed to the intentional spiritual formation of both staff and students, many aspects of my professional life are associated with my spirituality: teaching is integrative, mentoring is focused on disciplining Christian students, relationships with colleagues are predicated on robust spiritual lives, and collaboration with colleagues tends towards the integration of spirituality with both teaching and service.

I teach at a Catholic university. While not a Catholic, the questions we ask here about meaning and belief and service pertain directly to questions I ask about myself and my own life.

Irrespective of disciplinary or institutional affiliation, Spiritual Quest high scorers are generally more likely than their low-scoring colleagues to say that, "to a great extent," they are grateful to be involved in the work they do (87% vs. 67%), feel that work adds meaning to their lives (83% vs. 64%), and feel passionately about their work most of the time (83% vs. 63%). Relative to low scorers, they are also more likely to report that they have intentionally focused their careers in ways that are personally meaningful (82% vs. 49%) and to say that they experience joy in their work (80% vs. 63%). Similarly, high scorers are more inclined ("to a great extent") than low scorers to believe that they are fulfilling a calling through their work (73% vs. 37%) and to reflect on the meaning of their work (70% vs. 13%). Nearly three-quarters (65%) of high scorers, compared to just under one-third (32%) of low scorers, also say that, "to a great extent," they see connections between their work and the betterment of society.

For many college and university faculty who view themselves as being on a spiritual quest and who strive to live "well-integrated" personal and professional lives, "making sure I am the person I aspire to be" can be a perpetual challenge. As illustrated by sentiments expressed by respondents to the 2012 Faculty Beliefs and Values survey, faculty often have "minimal time to reflect" in the midst of "limitless requests that are reasonably worthy of attention" and work demands that otherwise "are based on the expectation that there are more than 24 hours in a day." For some, work often creates "obligations" and "threats to my peace of mind, to my security, and confidence" that are "exhausting." Tensions created between the "push to produce versus to reflect and seek" can make it difficult to "hold service and self-care in balance" and "easy for spiritual aspects of life to get lost." These tensions have been the focal point of previous research and writing (see, for example, Gappa, Austin, and Trice, 2007; O'Meara, Terosky, and Neumann, 2008; Philipsen, Bostic, and Mason, 2010), and their prominence with respect to compromising the spiritual well-being of faculty resurfaces in subsequent chapters.

For some faculty, self-characterized "preoccupation," even "obsession," with "professional achievement, advancement, and recognition" ultimately serves to impair "openness to experience and practice that would likely promote personal and spiritual growth." Illustrative of comments that others shared, one faculty member commented:

> My own pride, vanity, ego—whatever you want to call it—has continually asserted itself into my work and often almost disabled my ability to act with humility and genuine curiosity about [my work]—and, most mysteriously, other persons.

To be sure, as Dalton (2001) has pointed out, a spiritual quest that "focuses primarily on self-definition and self-understanding fails to consider equally serious concerns about relationships with others and the search for transcendence that are central to that quest" (p. 23).

Conclusion

On the whole, and in keeping with our Spirituality in Higher Education research team's earlier findings on college students, faculty who are on a spiritual quest tend to view their place in the world and their relationship to, and with, others as embodying a number of qualities that are found in other measures that are a focal point of this study. For example, those who are high scorers on Spiritual Quest also tend to exemplify an ethic of caring, as illustrated by their commitment to such values as helping others in difficulty, working to reduce pain and suffering in the world, and looking to make the world a better place. They also tend to possess an ecumenical worldview, as indicated by their interest in understanding other countries and cultures as well as different religious traditions, and by their belief that love is at the root of all the great religions. Finally, those who are high scorers on Spiritual Quest also tend to demonstrate equanimity, as reflected in feeling at peace and centered, being able to find meaning in times of hardship, and sensing a strong connection to all of humanity. In the chapters that follow, these dimensions of spirituality and their connections with professorial work and faculty members' lives are addressed in detail.

NOTES

1. The 2012 Faculty Beliefs and Values Survey Spiritual Self-Identification measure has an alpha reliability of .86.
2. Race/ethnicity response options on the 2012 Faculty Beliefs and Values Survey did not exactly parallel categorizations that were used on HERI's 2004–2005 Triennial National Survey of College Faculty.

Racial/ethnic differences discussed in this and subsequent chapters that are based on analyses conducted using 2012 Faculty Beliefs and Values Survey data use the following categorizations: "African American," "American Indian or other Native American," "Asian" (which includes "Asian, Asian American, or Pacific Islander"), "Hispanic" (which includes "Mexican or Mexican American," "Puerto Rican," and "Other Hispanic or Latino"), and "white non-Hispanic."

CHAPTER FOUR

ETHIC OF CARING, ECUMENICAL WORLDVIEW, AND CHARITABLE INVOLVEMENT

The previous two chapters focused primarily on how faculty characterize themselves in terms of their spiritual and religious self-identities. Are they spiritual? Religious? Both? Exclusively one or the other? Neither? The answer to all these questions is yes. As illustrated in Chapter Two, faculty members' spiritual identities are highly varied. Many also have strong feelings (both for and against) the value of spirituality in their own and others' lives. Most (roughly three-fourths) are at least moderately engaged in existential pursuits, including developing a meaningful philosophy of life, attaining wisdom, seeking beauty in their lives, and attaining inner harmony. In this chapter, we turn our attention to three spirituality-related measures: Ethic of Caring, Ecumenical Worldview, and Charitable Involvement. These measures help us explore externally directed aspects of individuals' spirituality.

ETHIC OF CARING

The Ethic of Caring measure comprises eight items that reflect people's sense of caring and concern about the welfare of others and the world around us. More specifically, the measure reflects a desire to assist those who may be troubled ("helping others who are in difficulty") and those who are suffering ("reducing pain and suffering in the world"). Also included are items that convey concern about what today are commonly termed "social justice" issues ("trying to change things that are unfair in the world" and "helping to promote racial understanding") as well as an interest in the welfare of one's community and the environment ("becoming involved in programs to clean up the environment" and "becoming a community leader") and proclivity for activism ("influencing social values" and "influencing the political structure").

Patterned responses to the individual survey items that make up the Ethic of Caring measure show that the majority (60%) of four-year college and university faculty register as moderate scorers on Ethic of Caring. So-called high scorers encompass 21 percent of faculty, and 19 percent can be categorized as low scorers. Faculty who consider themselves spiritual but not religious are marginally (although statistically significantly) more likely than "spiritual and religious" faculty to register as high scorers on Ethic of Caring. Those who are not spiritual and not religious and those who are religious but not spiritual are markedly more likely to be low scorers (see Figure 4.1). Across the individual Ethic of Caring items, the most pronounced differences in the relative value

FIGURE 4.1 ETHIC OF CARING HIGH AND LOW SCORERS BY
SPIRITUAL/RELIGIOUS SELF-IDENTITY

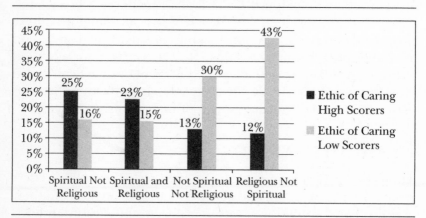

Source: 2012 Faculty Beliefs and Values Survey

ascribed to particular pursuits between those who are high versus low scorers on the Spiritual Self-Identification measure are found with respect to the personal value placed on helping others in difficulty, influencing social values, and reducing pain and suffering in the world (see Figure 4.2).

Variations based on demographic, disciplinary, and institutional affiliations are also evident. For example, nearly identical proportions of men and women faculty are moderate scorers on Ethic of Caring. However, men are comparatively less likely than women to register as high scorers (17% vs. 26%) and more likely to be included among low scorers (23% vs. 14%). African American (36% of who score high on Ethic of Caring) and Hispanic faculty (29% are high scorers) are comparatively more likely than Asian (21%) or white non-Hispanic (20%) faculty to exercise an ethic of caring. On the whole, politically liberal faculty (24% of whom are high scorers) are more likely than their politically middle-of-the-road (18%) or conservative (11%) colleagues to embrace an ethic of caring. So, too, are LGBT faculty, 35 percent of whom register as high scorers. Roughly one-quarter (24%) of faculty who are fifty-five years of age or older also score high on Ethic of Caring relative to just 17 percent of those who are under forty-five years of age.

FIGURE 4.2 "ESSENTIAL" OR "VERY IMPORTANT" ETHIC OF CARING
CONSIDERATIONS BY SPIRITUAL SELF-IDENTIFICATION

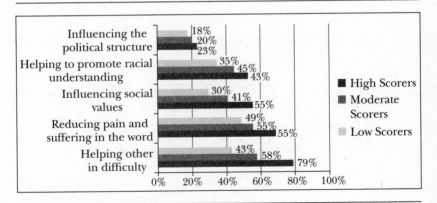

Source: 2012 Faculty Beliefs and Values Survey

High scorers on Ethic of Caring tend to be more prevalent in the health sciences, education, the humanities, and the fine arts. The smallest proportions of high Ethic of Caring scorers tend to be concentrated in math/statistics, engineering, the physical sciences, and business (see Figure 4.3). Across different types of four-year colleges and universities, largely equivalent proportions (roughly 21%) of faculty are high scorers on Ethic of Caring. Somewhat stronger ethic of caring inclinations tend to be evident among faculty at Catholic institutions, where 24 percent are high scorers. The highest proportions of low scorers (23%) within a particular type of college or university are found in public research universities.

Faculty members' ethic of caring inclinations can be further illustrated by their responses to individual items that are part of the measure. For example, across academic disciplines and types of four-year colleges and universities, more than eight in ten

Figure 4.3 Ethic of Caring High and Low Scorers by Academic Discipline/Field

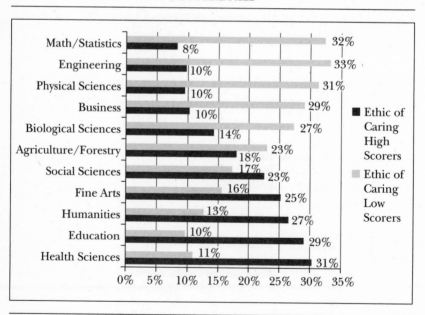

Source: 2012 Faculty Beliefs and Values Survey

faculty (85%) who responded to the 2012 Faculty Beliefs and Values Survey characterize themselves—at least to "some" extent—as "trying to change things in the world that are unfair." Across disciplinary affiliations, roughly one-quarter of faculty in the humanities (25%), social sciences (25%), and education (24%) place high personal priority on "trying to change things in the world that are unfair." By comparison, roughly one in ten, or fewer, in the biological sciences (12%), physical sciences (11%), business (10%), and math/statistics (9%) characterize themselves this way. Holding constant the core demographic variables of gender, race/ethnicity, and age, faculty in the humanities and in education remain notably more inclined than colleagues in other fields to endorse values and personal priorities that reflect an ethic of caring. Interpreted within Smart, Feldman, and Ethington's classification (2000) of academic disciplines based on Holland's personality-based career development framework (1973, 1997), this finding may be attributable to the comparatively more "social" type orientation of individuals who are attracted to these fields. In contrast, irrespective of their particular demographic characteristics, faculty in the physical sciences, biological sciences, and social sciences, along with those in math/statistics, engineering, and business, tend, on the whole, to be significantly less inclined with respect to ethic of caring considerations. Per Smart and his colleagues' classification scheme, individuals in these fields tend to be primarily "investigative" or "enterprising" types, who, in general, may be less inclined than their more "social" colleagues to give high priority to ethic of caring considerations.

In addition, just over half of four-year college and university faculty rate as at least "very important" the personal priority they place on "reducing pain and suffering in the world" (59%) and "helping others in difficulty" (54%). Roughly half place the same levels of personal emphasis on "helping to promote racial understanding" (49%) and "influencing the social structure" (47%). Substantially fewer, however (roughly one-quarter or less), characterize as "very important" the personal priority they place on "cleaning up the environment" (24%), "influencing the political structure" (21%), or "becoming a community leader" (18%).

"SPIRITUALITY" AND ETHIC OF CARING

Among high scorers on the Spiritual Self-Identification measure (that is, those who consider themselves a spiritual person "to a great extent," give high priority to integrating spirituality in their lives, and actively seek opportunities to grow spiritually), 28 percent also register as so-called high scorers on Ethic of Caring. Another roughly 60 percent of high Spiritual Self-Identification scorers score moderately on Ethic of Caring. The remainder (roughly 12%) of high scorers on Spiritual Self-Identification are low scorers on Ethic of Caring. On the whole, this latter group of faculty members tend to be middle aged (45–64 years old) white males who are social scientists, are politically conservative, consider themselves both spiritual and religious, and work at "other" (that is, non-Catholic, typically Protestant) religious colleges. Another subset of faculty (also roughly 12%) are low scorers on Spiritual Self-Identification but high scorers on Ethic of Caring. By and large, these faculty members tend to be men and women between the ages of thirty-five and forty-four who are politically liberal, consider themselves not spiritual and not religious, and work in the humanities and social sciences at nonsectarian liberal arts colleges.

Irrespective of whether faculty members' spiritual lives are intertwined with particular religious faiths, their descriptions of the meaning spirituality has to them often included ethic of caring undertones. Among these are recurrent references to "having love and compassion for others and ourselves," "being nonjudgmental," "living life with deep empathy for others," and "using love (compassion, caring, attentiveness) as the springboard for actions." In some cases, these descriptors were coupled with notions of "limiting selfishness and self-delusion," "developing readiness to help others," "encouraging sympathy and understanding toward others," and "showing resistance where necessary to uphold human dignity." Others offered that, for them, spirituality most fundamentally refers to "the capacity to transcend self-interest in order to act compassionately" and to be "forgiving of self and others." Those who embrace care-oriented conceptions of spirituality offer common characterizations that the spiritual dimension of life encompasses "operating with a moral compass," subscribing to "values of goodness, compassion, justice, self-awareness, responsibility to the greater good, non-harming, respect, and equality," and "being centered in a way that I can treat all others (and myself) with loving kindness and compassion." In the eyes of faculty who ascribe to a sense of spirituality oriented to an ethic of caring, such orientation also entails being cognizant that "compassion and understanding are the answers to most of the world's problems," which is supported by an underlying belief that "life is not about me."

ETHIC OF CARING AND FACULTY WORK

According to their responses to nationally normative surveys, the overwhelming majority of college and university faculty (roughly 98% across different types of institutions) consider it "essential" or "very important" to be a good teacher (see, for example, Lindholm, Szelélenyi, Hurtado, and Korn, 2005). However, those who are high scorers on Ethic of Caring are considerably more inclined to rate this an "essential" consideration (80%) relative to their colleagues who score moderately (67%) or low (55%). As depicted in Table 4.1, there are also pronounced differences in how those who are high and low scorers prioritize goals for undergraduate students. For example, whereas enhancing self-understanding and preparing for responsible citizenship are considered "essential" priorities for roughly half of high scorers, less than 15 percent of low scorers concur. Pronounced differences are also evident with respect to developing students' moral character, helping them develop personal values, and providing for their emotional development. Among these goals for undergraduates, facilitating students' search for meaning and purpose is considered "not at all" important by the largest proportion of those who score low on Ethic of Caring.

In describing how their own spiritual life relates to their work, faculty tend to highlight most prominently their work with students, often in the capacities of "being an encourager" and

TABLE 4.1 GOALS FOR UNDERGRADUATES BY HIGH AND LOW ETHIC OF CARING SCORES (PERCENTAGES)

	Essential		Very Important		Somewhat Important		Not at All Important	
	High	Low	High	Low	High	Low	High	Low
Enhance self-understanding	50.5	11.8	39.4	33.2	9.5	41.5	0.6	13.5
Prepare for responsible citizenship	49.4	13.5	41.3	37.6	8.6	38.4	0.7	10.5
Develop moral character	46.4	20.0	39.5	33.1	12.9	36.5	1.2	10.3
Help develop personal values	41.1	10.8	42.4	32.4	15.2	41.5	1.3	15.2
Facilitate search for meaning and purpose	37.3	10.6	37.6	22.2	21.2	38.1	4.0	29.1
Provide for emotional development	29.2	5.7	45.3	24.2	23.0	50.5	2.5	19.6
Instill community service commitment	27.1	3.1	43.4	18.5	26.7	47.1	2.8	31.3

Source: 2012 Faculty Beliefs and Values Survey

"helping students see the gifts and potential they have." Highlighting a perspective on success that is grounded in an ethic of caring, one professor remarked:

> For me, success is having the courage to defy convention and follow one's own path, but also not leaving other people behind in your journey. It's not enough to get to the mountaintop alone and be free and liberated and rich. You should "lift while climbing" as Marion Wright Edelson said at my college graduation. The more I live, the more important I think it is to do even more—you really need to go back down the mountain and help the people who are really suffering, who never get far out of the swampy plains at the bottom.

Reflecting on the connections between their spiritual and professional paths, others shared teaching-related perspectives that illustrate ethic of caring considerations:

> Simply put, the student/teacher relationship is a sanctified relationship. I am entrusted with helping my students learn and I need to deal with them honestly, fairly, and in sincere hope of them finding wholeness in their lives. I don't evangelize in the classroom at all—in fact, most students don't know I'm religious unless they see me at church. I feel called to be the best teacher I can be, and I answer to more than my department, college, and university. I've also reached a point in my life and career where I feel very blessed—I get to help young people learn about what I love most to do (creative writing). In this sense there is almost complete overlap between my professional life and my spiritual (religious) life, and I am grateful for that every day. I hope it shows up in my classroom . . . if it doesn't, then I'm not loving my job enough.

> I love my students and they know it. I do not feel that I am an especially good teacher. I suffer from personal difficulties. But when my students write a good essay or poem, when they achieve high proficiency in language learning, when they catch a fascination with Chinese language and culture—I feel a strong sense of reward. I have a sense of their inner spirit and essential self and yearn for their higher growth and development. I have a mission in my work to build people.

> I try to meet [students] where they are, help them find their own path, encourage them that their path is going to look different

than mine, and, above all, I want to work on making relations that are really rooted in an earthly, human, humble kindness and love, not fear.

In all of my interactions, I live by the idea: "One earns the right to speak into someone's life." This is accomplished by forming a real relationship, based on sincere interest and respect. This takes a significant amount of time and energy. As an instructor, mentor/ advisor, or researcher, I am to fully invest into those under my charge. Each person has to be treated with the dignity and respect due them as a fellow spiritual being.

Morality is central to my personal spiritual beliefs. In the classroom, there are always opportunities to teach morality in a broad sense (e.g., treating others as you want to be treated; being honest; fostering tolerance, empathy and compassion). I do not explicitly teach morality, and I do not teach it in a political, spiritual, or religious context. I teach it in the context of critical thinking and responsible citizenship. In this sense I cannot help but express myself spiritually in my professional life.

I take teaching as a spiritual exercise. I am not simply a transmitter of knowledge to my students. Rather, through teaching, I reveal who and what I am to my students. This exercise, of course, includes my spiritual aspect. In addition, a lot of teaching activities correspond to the great religions' spiritual exercise such as listening to others compassionately and patiently, no harming others, doing good to others without expecting anything in return, and being conscious of what I am saying, behaving, etc.

[The connection between my spiritual life and my professional life is reflected through] trying to teach people how to take care of themselves and help others do the same. We are given freewill to make choices and with education a person may make informed decisions. The choices we make impact more than we may ever know.

Who I bring to the classroom, myself, is completely integrated with spiritual beliefs. It is who I am. It guides the ethical principles I work within such as to help, not harm; guide, not berate; encourage, not destroy; facilitate, not dictate—all while maintaining a challenging, thought filled learning/research/ service environment.

Taken together, these perspectives on spirituality as it relates to teaching mesh well with Glazer's conceptualization (1999) of "sacredness," or the practice of "wholeness and awareness" in academic work. Characterized by "approaching, greeting, and meeting the world with basic respect," Glazer explains that sacredness as the ground of learning pertains to "rooting education in the practice of openness, attentiveness to experience and sensitivity to the world." From Glazer's vantage point, spirituality in education begins with questions: What is my experience? What is my effect? What are the interrelationships between myself and others? Are these being attended to? (pp. 11–12).

Highlighting these considerations, those who are heavily inclined toward living a life characterized by an ethic of caring also differ from their colleagues who are less inclined to do so with respect to aspects of their careers that they consider "essential." Beyond the critical importance of having "intellectual freedom," those who score high on Ethic of Caring also place comparatively greater emphasis on having a strong network of good colleagues, opportunities for teaching and for influencing social change, and mentoring others (illustrated in Figure 4.4). Referencing

FIGURE 4.4 "ESSENTIAL" CAREER CONSIDERATIONS BY ETHIC OF CARING SCORE

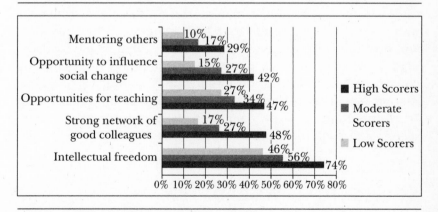

Source: 2012 Faculty Beliefs and Values Survey

aspects of academic work that transcend teaching, another faculty member offered that, at least in part, the spiritual aspects of his life that relate most directly to his role as an academic involve

> being careful not to tarnish or destroy a colleague with unkind, unnecessary criticism; being a "builder" of people/administration/process rather than a destroyer. Being a builder means that I must think critically, think honestly, be willing to take a risk and speak my thoughts peacefully, be willing to listen, valuing a person above "being right."

Further extending an ethic of caring approach to their work and lives, other faculty members underscored the linkages between who they consider themselves to be spiritually and how they approach their academic work and professional pursuits through their own efforts to be a "model" and/or "mentor" to others. This orientation includes facilitating the career pathways of junior colleagues by "helping them navigate the pressure cooker that is the tenure process" and through supporting colleagues' efforts toward "finding a balance in their life that recognizes they are more than just their work." Also reflected in this conceptualization is the spiritually based importance not only of helping others but also of remembering to exercise "self-acceptance" of one's own limitations, "self-care," and "self-compassion," especially in the midst of challenging periods of one's life. In keeping with the comparatively greater emphasis that high scorers on Ethic of Caring have with respect to living a life that "well integrates" their personal and professional pursuits and that enables them to serve others, high scorers also tend to place greater emphasis on "achieving congruence between my own values and institutional values." Among high scorers, 74 percent consider this an "essential" or "very important" priority, compared to 52 percent of moderate scorers and 26 percent of low scorers.

ECUMENICAL WORLDVIEW

As detailed previously, the eight-item Ethic of Caring measure addresses "caring" in the sense of a personal commitment to alleviate others' suffering. The Ecumenical Worldview measure, in contrast, is focused primarily on people's inclination to see the world as an interconnected whole and to feel a personal connection with—and acceptance of—all other beings. Eight of the twelve items that constitute the measure reflect explicitly a sense of connectedness: "feeling a strong connection to all humanity," "believing in the goodness of all people," believing that "all life is interconnected," and not only "having an interest in different religious traditions" but also believing that "love is at the root of all the great religions," that "we are all spiritual beings," that "non-religious people can lead lives that are just as moral as those of religious believers," and that "most people can grow spiritually without being religious." Also included are three items reflecting a personal commitment to act on this world-centric vision: "improving the human condition," "improving my understanding of other countries and cultures," and "accepting others as they are." Finally, the measure includes a self-rating on "understanding of others."

Relative to others their own age, more than two-thirds (67%) of faculty rate their understanding of others as at least "above average." Half or more also indicate that "to a great extent" they accept others as they are (55%) and that they agree "strongly" that all life is interconnected (50%). However, in keeping with the notably smaller proportions who indicate that, "to a great extent," they feel a strong connection to all humanity (31%) or that they believe in the goodness of all people (30%), just three in ten faculty consider it an "essential" personal priority to contribute to improving the human condition. Less than one-quarter (22%) consider it "essential" to improve their understanding of other countries and cultures.

Roughly three-quarters (73%) of faculty agree at least "somewhat" that we are all spiritual beings. More than one-third (36%) endorse that view "strongly." More than three-quarters (76%) of faculty also "strongly" endorse the notion that nonreligious people can lead lives that are just as moral as those of religious believers. Nearly four in ten (38%) express the same level of endorsement for the notion that most people can grow spiritually without being religious. Fewer than one-quarter describe themselves as having "great" interest in different religious traditions (24%) or agreeing "strongly" that love is at the root of all the great religions (23%).

FIGURE 4.5 ECUMENICAL WORLDVIEW HIGH AND LOW SCORERS BY SPIRITUAL/
RELIGIOUS SELF-IDENTITY

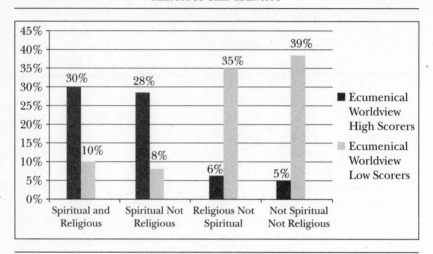

Source: 2012 Faculty Beliefs and Values Survey

Based on their patterned responses to Ecumenical Worldview items, 25 percent of faculty overall register as high scorers, 60 percent are moderate scorers, and 16 percent are low scorers. These proportions vary distinctively based on how faculty self-identify with respect to spiritual and religious self-conceptions. Those who self-identify as religious but not spiritual or as neither spiritual nor religious are considerably more likely than their "spiritual and religious" colleagues and their "spiritual but not religious" colleagues to register as low scorers on Ecumenical Worldview (see Figure 4.5). Across the individual Ecumenical Worldview items, the most pronounced response differences based on Spiritual Self-Identification score are evident with respect to the extent that faculty are inclined to endorse the notion that all life is interconnected and the degree to which they feel a strong connection to all humanity (see Figure 4.6).

Faculty inclinations to embrace an ecumenical worldview vary considerably depending on disciplinary affiliation, with those in

Figure 4.6 Prioritized Ecumenical Worldview Considerations by Spiritual Self-Identification

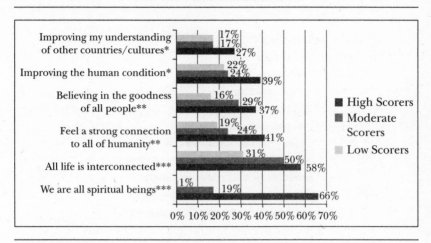

*Considered an "essential" personal goal
**Describes me "to a great extent"
***Agree "strongly"

Source: 2012 Faculty Beliefs and Values Survey

the health sciences, education, the fine arts, humanities, and social sciences comparatively more inclined, on the whole, to endorse an ecumenical worldview (see Figure 4.7). In these fields, however, additional analysis reveals that much of this difference is attributable to demographic characteristics, especially with respect to gender. Overall, 33 percent of women faculty (vs. 18% of men) register as high scorers on Ecumenical Worldview. Just 9 percent of women are low scorers, compared with 21 percent of men. Once gender and other demographic variables are taken into account, faculty members' affiliations with these particular disciplines/fields, in and of themselves, are insignificantly correlated with Ecumenical Worldview. As with Ethic of Caring, however, faculty affiliation in the physical and biological sciences as well as in math/statistics, engineering, and business correlates negatively with Ecumenical Worldview above and beyond faculty members' personal demographic characteristics. At least in part, this finding again may be attributable to the predominately "investigative" and "enterprising" (as opposed to "social" or "artistic") orientations

FIGURE 4.7 ECUMENICAL WORLDVIEW HIGH AND LOW SCORERS BY ACADEMIC
DISCIPLINE/FIELD

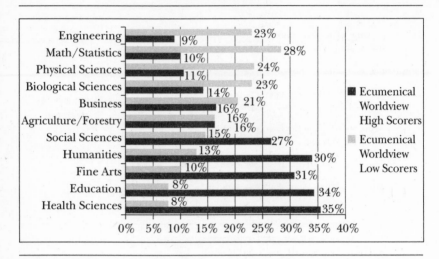

Source: 2012 Faculty Beliefs and Values Survey

of faculty who tend to work in these disciplines/fields (see Smart, Feldman, and Ethington, 2000). Irrespective of their particular disciplinary/field affiliation, African American and Hispanic faculty tend to be comparatively more inclined than other faculty to embrace an ecumenical worldview: nearly four in ten (39%) faculty who self-identify as African American or Hispanic register as high scorers on Ecumenical Worldview.

Overall, those who work at Catholic colleges are markedly more inclined than colleagues at other types of colleges and universities to register as high Ecumenical Worldview scorers, whereas public university faculty are the least likely overall to rate similarly (see Figure 4.8).

On the whole, those who score high on Ecumenical Worldview are also notably more likely than their low-scoring colleagues to say that they "frequently" question their assumptions and worldviews (33% vs. 14%) as well as their spiritual/religious beliefs (20% vs. 7%). High Ecumenical Worldview scorers are also considerably less inclined to believe that "the evil in this world outweighs the good." Whereas just 15 percent of high scorers "agree"

FIGURE 4.8 ECUMENICAL WORLDVIEW HIGH AND LOW SCORERS BY
INSTITUTIONAL TYPE

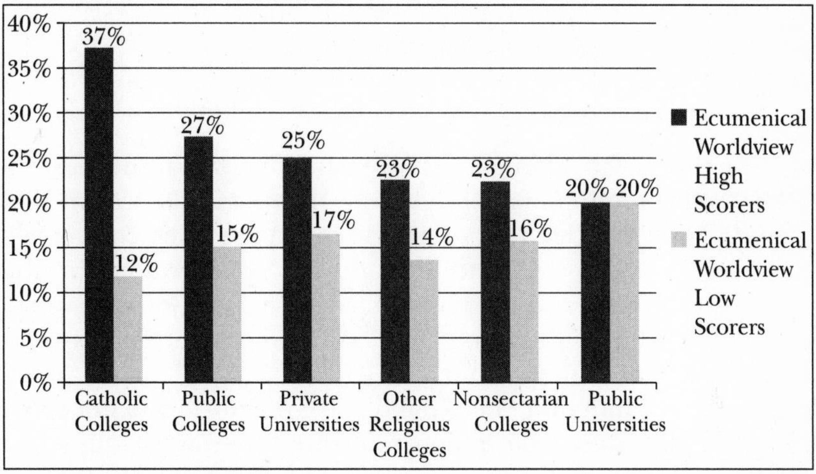

Source: 2012 Faculty Beliefs and Values Survey

with that notion, 26 percent of moderate scorers and 39 percent of low scorers endorse that perspective.

THE VALUE OF CONNECTEDNESS IN FACULTY MEMBERS' LIVES

As reflected in some of the faculty comments incorporated in Chapter Two, one prevalent criticism of "spirituality" is that it is too self-focused a construct, steeped in incessant American individualism, self-absorption, and the like. However, in descriptions of personal conceptions of spirituality, one of the most prevalent themes among those who self-identify with being spiritual centers around notions of "connectedness," "unity," and "interdependence" with others, the natural world, and the universe. A sustaining sense of interconnectedness not only among "all who are here currently" but also among "all who will come before us and will come after us" helps "dispel our sense of isolation and alienation" and "allows us to move from self-absorption to inclusion and connection." As one faculty member elaborated,

> Spirituality is the force that leads to a connection with others in my world and to the universe itself. Without appreciating the interconnectedness of all involved, it is easy to become self-centered and selfish. True spirituality means that I understand that there is more to life than the things I have or what I do. I reach beyond my mortal self to find the love, peace, and joy that transcends my personal understanding of the world itself.

For those who resonate with an ecumenical worldview, spirituality refers predominantly to "a way of being in the world" that reflects "aspects of life that pertain to human striving, connectedness, and compassion" and that reveals appreciation for the "beauty, goodness, and interconnectedness in and with the world and the universe." Believing that "we are spiritual beings on a human path, not human beings on a spiritual path" carries associated responsibilities for "helping to make the world a better place for all beings" and "continuing to evolve my consciousness and kindness and generosity to others, including non-human beings and nature." Maintaining "humility in the face of what is much greater than us, but also a confidence that we are here to make a difference, to make this world better" is also a core consideration. Another faculty member explained that spirituality

> is a conviction that one's life is part of a larger fabric of meaning; that this meaning is personal and moral, not just material; and that living in harmony with this meaning leads to both individual and social thriving.

Underscoring the importance of remaining open to, and respectful of, others' core values and beliefs, another professor offered additional perspective related to how one's spirituality enables that commitment:

> Being spiritual allows one to be strong in conviction while understanding and kind toward others of differing beliefs and convictions. A spiritual person allows others to believe what, how, and when they may.

Building on these themes, the following comments reflect commonly expressed sentiments regarding the perceived benefits of "living a life of conscience, goodwill, love and understanding" that stems from "feeling emotionally connected to others" and experiencing a "common bond/solidarity beyond traditional boundaries of family, tribe, race/ethnicity, country, and even species":

> A spiritual person is one who sees awesome beauty in all things created and organized by God—from the complexity and beauty of sub-atomic particles to the immensity of the expanding universe. Being spiritual drives one to be highly grateful and appreciative of life and all living things.

> The process of reflecting on my origin, beliefs, and interactions with people (and the environment) and trying to reconcile my desires against those of other people [helps enable me to be] a peaceful and helpful person to myself and as many other people as possible.

> Spirituality relates to the ability to love the world, the people in it, the environment, the animal kingdom . . . even those who are personal, political, or national enemies. That love helps you forgive yourself, forgive others, [and] offers the opportunity for growth and change and positive evolution.

Some faculty associate their spirituality with experiencing a sense of connectedness; others highlight the specific linkages between their personal sense of spirituality and nature or elements of the natural world. For these faculty, being "entwined" with nature, embracing its "awe inspiring beauty and power," and "cultivating a sustained connection with those forces" represent the core element of their spirituality and provides them with "peace, strength, and energy." Being "reflective, thoughtful, and appreciative of the gift of life," retaining a "sense of wonder at the world and all its creatures," "respecting and fostering the positive energy associated with the universe," and recognizing that "interconnectedness and compassion are at the center of what is" are especially critical spiritual considerations for those who embrace an ecumenical worldview. Faculty sentiments that elaborate on this theme are reflected through the following comments:

> For me, the diversity of life and its interconnectedness is awe-inspiring and it functions as a balm for my emotions and "spirit." Losing myself in the beauty and complexity of the natural world,

feeling its "rightness," and my insignificance in the face of its grandeur is the nature of my current "spiritual" experience.

Spiritual to me means "awe." It's that almost indescribable feeling that you get when you walk through the woods all alone or look out over the ocean as the sun sets. I'm not sure if there's something called "God" that has anything to do with that, and I don't think I'll ever find out, so I don't even try to seek the answer. But, I know that in those moments, I am filled with a sense of spiritual awe.

I am a scientist, a plant biologist. The wonders of living cells, evolved by natural processes including the laws of physics and chemistry, random events, and natural selection to a level that suggests (but is not) perfection, is inspiring. Likewise, the huge, integrated web of interactions of living things on just our little, insignificant planet taken in the context of the possibilities offered by an incomprehensibly large Universe invariably inspires awe in me that is the core of my spirituality.

TEACHING, LEARNING, AND ECUMENICAL WORLDVIEW

As viewed through an ecumenical worldview lens, spirituality pertains fundamentally to "living beyond a purely materialistic and physical plane" and to honoring and celebrating "the magic underlying life" and "this marvelous opportunity we have to move about in the world . . . to live." Included in those conceptions is a belief that spirituality "is the force that gives each of us our uniqueness but also connects each of us to others." Associated awareness reminds us that "we are all part of one whole" and necessarily "encourages acceptance and understanding of those who are different." As reflected in the following comments, that worldview has inevitable connections to how faculty conceive of their spiritual lives relative to their work as teachers.

For example, in talking about the teaching dimension of their work lives, faculty who resonate with an ecumenical worldview often noted that the values they try to help develop in their students are "closely tied to appreciation for the uniqueness of every person, and the dignity and respect each person deserves." Others explained the primary value of their work as teachers in the context of "the interconnectedness of all mankind . . . By improving the state of one person, I help to improve the state of all":

> I see teaching as a vocation. I don't know that I was "called" to it, but I do feel that teaching is a sacred trust. I feel deeply responsible to my students and that my job is not merely to teach them English or writing but rather to help them connect meaningfully and constructively with all the beings in their world. I believe it is my job to help them make the world a better place. As a teacher, I strive to make the world a better place and, sometimes, I believe I'm really doing that.
>
> My teaching seeks to increase my students' understanding of other cultures, other faiths, other points of view. I try to educate them to the difference between knowing and believing. I attempt to instill in them a respect for human beings regardless of whether they actually like the other person(s). I also hope they come to develop at least some degree of humility regarding their own knowledge and wisdom.
>
> Teaching is great way to walk the talk of concern for helping others improve their lives economically, politically, socially, and spiritually. I never indoctrinate but I can model respectful interest in viewpoints quite different from my own. I can model patience and compassion as undergraduates struggle with moral maturity and personal identity in a setting far from their childhood friends.

In keeping with their broader mind-set, high scorers on Ecumenical Worldview are considerably more likely than their lower-scoring colleagues to agree that "it is okay for spiritual/religious topics to be addressed in public colleges and universities as long as all worldviews are given representation." Whereas 44 percent of high scorers agree "strongly" with that statement, just 29 percent of moderate scorers and only 20 percent of low scorers believe similarly.

CHALLENGES TO CARING AND CONNECTEDNESS WITHIN THE ACADEMY

As illustrated by faculty comments featured in this and other chapters, academic work provides many potential avenues for engaging aspects of one's spiritual/religious life in personally meaningful ways. However, apart from "separation of church and state" concerns, there can also be considerable challenges. For example, in response to an open-ended item on the 2012 Faculty Beliefs and Values Survey that asked about tensions faculty may experience between their spiritual lives and their professional lives, faculty recurrently expressed the concern that "personal beliefs about the value of life and people and the need for connection and empathy" are "sometimes at odds with academic culture."

As noted earlier in this chapter, faculty members nearly universally consider being a good teacher a "very important" priority. Nationally normative data also show consistently that, for the overwhelming majority of faculty (roughly 90%), "being a good colleague" is also a "very important" pursuit (see, for example, Lindholm, Szelélenyi, Hurtado, and Korn, 2005). One of the historically embedded elements of academic careers is the notion of a "collegium of scholars" working together in service to knowledge and truth (Pelikan, 1992). Paralleling the perspectives expressed by earlier national faculty survey respondents regarding compelling factors for pursuing an academic career (see, for example, Lindholm, Astin, Sax, and Korn, 2002), Faculty Beliefs and Values Survey respondents tended generally to place high priority on the availability for "strong collegial networks." Within academic workplaces, "good colleagues" are also a key element that faculty seek and value (see, for example, Boice, 1992; Lindholm, Astin, Sax, and Korn, 2002; Rice, Sorcinelli, and Austin, 2000; Tierney and Bensimon, 1996; Trower, 2010; Whitt, 1991). Collegial relationships are known to impact job satisfaction (see, for example, August and Waltman, 2004; Bozeman and Gaughan, 2011; Rosser, 2004; Seifert and Umbach, 2008). Women and faculty of color—especially those who are new to their roles—especially tend to underscore the importance of a strong ethos of community, including mentorship and inclusion in professional and social networks (see, for example, Austin, Sorcinelli, and McDaniels, 2007; Gappa and Austin, 2010; Moody, 2001; Ponjuan, Conley, and Trower, 2011; Tierney and Bensimon, 1996).

Considered within an institutional context, collegiality refers to "opportunities for faculty members to feel that they belong to a mutually respectful community of scholars who value each faculty member's contributions to the institution and feel concern for their colleagues' well-being" (Gappa, Austin, and Trice, 2007, p. 305). Trower (2010) reported that, in marked contrast to previous generations of tenure-track faculty (for whom "autonomy in the workplace" was the single most important concern), today's young tenure-track professors care more about departmental climate, culture, and collegiality than they do about workload, tenure clarity, and compensation. Collegiality is important because, as Gappa, Austin, and Trice have noted, "when people feel they are included in [the institutional] community in explicit, implicit, and symbolic ways, they feel they are respected, that they belong, and that they have sufficient status" (p. 305). This sense of belonging tends to enhance individuals' satisfaction with work and their overall morale (Rice and Austin, 1988). Ultimately, campus communities that are characterized by mutual respect and caring benefit all faculty (see, for example, Rice, Sorcinelli, and Austin, 2000). Not surprisingly, it follows that a sense of community has also been identified as one of the prominent factors associated with the decision to remain at one's institution (Barnes, Agago, and Coombs, 1998).

Writing about workplace interactions in general (as opposed to specifically within academic contexts) as they relate to individuals' quest for meaning and engagement of the human spirit at work, May, Gilson, and Harter (2004) maintain that to the extent that interactions with colleagues "foster a sense of belonging, a stronger sense of social identity and meaning should emerge" (p. 15). To be sure, the benefits of behaving in a collegial manner are considerable. However, engaging in a consistently caring and compassionate manner with colleagues who are "unable or unwilling to reflect critically on issues that threaten the primacy of certain of their ideologies" and who sometimes have "harsh personalities" and exhibit "inappropriate behavior" and a more generalized "lack of grace" can test faculty members' "spiritual limits." As one 2012 Faculty Beliefs and Values Survey respondent offered,

> You can attempt to do the right thing, but some people are going to be self-serving. Let's face it . . . academics can be crazy. We've got a few in my department. I've learned that doing the right thing by them gets you more trouble and heartache, so I stay away from them . . . not very kind, but necessary for survival.

Certainly, interactions with particular colleagues may challenge faculty members' capacities to exercise care and compassion. More difficult for many faculty to contend with, however, is the general nature of "academic personalities" and a "professional culture that too often reinforces and rewards" behavior that is antithetical to their own spiritual values. For example, across disciplines and types of institutions, faculty recurrently noted that the academy "in many ways reinforces an ego-driven, self-centered practice . . . Institutional rewards and the whole academic system seem largely set up for promoting the individual in the tower." "Academic politics" coupled with professional inclinations to prioritize "self-interest over the greater good" and to "value argumentation, one-upsmanship, and power mongering over problem solving" can readily "pre-empt compassionate action and ethical decision making." Similarly, "academic pride" in conjunction with tendencies toward "shameless self-promotion" in "pursuit of professional glory" are, in the eyes of many faculty, directly antithetical to "spiritual humility" and "harmonious" collegial dynamics:

> Academia isn't always a place of compassion, respect or integrity. It's often a place where ego-driven intelligent individuals fight over ridiculousness just to be considered "right." This profession has a lot of insecure people in it which is why I compartmentalize my professional and social life.

> The academy can be a dark place. Academics can be self-serving narcissists. This is depressing, and depression is a bad state of mind for someone seeking spiritual joy or solace. I worry, too, that I'm not immune from the competitiveness and narcissism. I sometimes wonder whether I'm making a difference in the world or just greasing the wheels of things as they are.

> The bigotry of the academic world in its hubris and self-conceit [can cause tensions]. The arrogance of some in the academic community is so destructive and so distorting of the educational enterprise whose values are openness and critical thought within the bounds of mutual respect and expression.

Reflecting on a powerful cultural tension with respect to potential applications of "spirituality at work," one faculty member commented:

Professional and academic excellence usually promotes the individual. Spirituality is about losing the individual in the sea of people and beings past, present, and future.

Another noted,

Sometimes the rational approach to thinking makes me highly critical and skeptical. A spiritual life requires openness and trust. These are sometimes in tension.

While in many cases "aspiring to create harmony," faculty recurrently noted that they themselves "fall short" more often than they would hope when, in the midst of feeling "pushed," "pressured," and "generally overextended," their "own ego gets in the way":

I cannot be a good partner, mother, teacher, administrator, and scholar. The demands are too high. When I experience this level of stress, I cannot act lovingly and caringly in every situation. I become less patient with colleagues and students and family members who disagree with me, see situations different. I lose my temper. I make poor decisions that offend others or add to conflict from lack of time to make good decisions. The demands of professional and family life leave no time for my own spiritual development and that saddens me greatly.

I certainly don't live up to many ideals I hold sacred, but I also know how to apologize and try again and seek help from family and colleagues. Sometimes I exaggerate the importance of a project, and have to remind myself that I am much more like an ant carrying a grain of sand than a Mover and Shaker of the Universe; that we are all little "Who's" on a dust speck floating about in the morning of the world—though we are "Who's" and not "Nothings" . . . and there is a Horton who hears us.

Indeed, "reconciling the behaviors and attitudes of others who profess/preach one thing and do another" can create tensions for faculty. "Knowing I *should* speak up" in the face of "ethical and moral inconsistencies" or other "discriminating behavior" but struggling to "determine whether I *can* speak up without "too severely jeopardizing one's own institutional and/or professional well-being" is a struggle for many faculty. Elaborating on the notion that "professorial life is not always concerned with the good of the individual," other faculty members shared:

I worry that professional success requires us to overlook injustices done within the university (by administrators or colleagues) but my spirituality requires me to fight all injustice.

I have ethical issues within the academy where my university says one thing but does another; expands administration but cares little about teaching and research; rewards people with horrible selfish behavior so you feel there is no social justice.

My spiritual beliefs direct me toward honesty and social justice. These two things are in short supply in current corporatized academia.

Acknowledging the professionally and societally "privileged" roles they fulfill as full-time, traditionally appointed (that is, tenured or tenure-track) faculty, some faculty struggle too with a sense that they are "too removed" from the "real world" and the "tremendous challenges that many people face." Thus, like this professor, they experience occasional tensions between the professional path they have chosen and the priority that they feel they "should" be placing on "helping those with the greatest need":

My spiritual life has led me to value and acknowledge the inter-connectedness of all of humanity; yet, I struggle with the knowledge that in my professional life, I work primarily with people who are privileged in many ways and who do not recognize the ways in which their actions (or inaction) harms other people. I often wonder whether I would be serving my spiritual beliefs better by working with people who seek to resist oppression (their own and others'), rather than with people who are struggling to understand (or who want to remain ignorant of) their privilege.

For faculty who also serve in administrative roles and who thus, by definition, become "the enemy" in the eyes of some of their colleagues, additional tensions come into play:

My spiritual framework calls me to be collaborative and inclusive; many times, the politics of academic situations require self-preservation and self-advocacy, to the exclusion of other interests. As a department chair, I have to balance the "greater good" of collaboration with the "immediate need" of advocacy.

I went into education to teach and learn and work with others in a collaborative way. However, because I would qualify half of the

people in my department as "difficult personalities," acting as
chair has required that I deal with people on a level that I would
prefer to avoid. I do not like judging people in a formal way. I
dislike grading, although I can see the need for it. I dislike having
to review untenured colleagues who have troubling issues. And I
dislike having to deal with tenured faculty who drastically
misbehave but are guaranteed a job because academia is so
petrified of lawsuits. So I sometimes want to change jobs so I can
work with nicer people.

As an institutional leader, I often felt the tension between
compassion for an individual who was in some sort of difficulty,
and the welfare of the institution as a whole. Tenure and
misconduct cases have given me many sleepless nights.

There are times when what I believe I must do professionally
seems to me hurtful or harmful, which is a conflict for me. At
times, I feel that I must compromise with directives or policies
that are less than fully compatible with a spirit of care and
compassion for all; in much of what the administration does, care
for money and financial performance trumps care for persons and
principles, but I dare speak out only occasionally, and in keeping
my silence I feel conflicted.

Some faculty also struggle to find "common ground" in their
work with today's students, who they sometimes find to be both
"much more needy and much less able to connect" than the
undergraduates they used to teach. The "judgmental" activities of
"grading" and "gatekeeping" can also be at odds with faculty
members' values related to "inclusion," "empathy," "understanding," and "social justice." Also challenging for many is interacting
effectively with students who "don't like to question what they
think they believe," who "assert their beliefs as unquestionable,
even though they have not examined these beliefs themselves,"
or who otherwise "confuse beliefs with knowledge." Reminding
oneself of the "need to be gentle" and "to remain neutral" in
those circumstances, others offered:

I teach in a state university and work with many students who hold
deeply conservative and evangelical beliefs. On the one hand, this
means that I must distance my teaching from my views on
spirituality. On the other hand, my students view me suspiciously
as a purveyor of harmful, left-wing secularism.

Probably most of the tensions occur working with students with strong ideological bias, believing they have the "truth" and are seeing the world in black/white terms. I tend to see the world as ambiguous, open to multiple interpretations.

Having patience with myself in the face of fatigue and personal limitations on my ability to understand and reach students [causes tension]. I would like to establish positive, mutually respectful working relationships with them all, but this is not always possible.

Finally, in reflecting on the tensions and "disconnects" between "the best of who I can be" and the "realities" of professional life, some faculty also highlighted aspects of higher education's "changing landscape," which sometimes conflicts with their personal and professional values:

The intrusion of one-dimensional, corporate culture into higher education creates a sense of tension for me . . . Students are human beings, not "revenue units" . . . and one size does not fit all.

As academia moves increasingly to a for-profit model, there is increasing pressure towards micromanagement and "accountability." Trust is no longer in the university system, and this has created a climate of fear and judgment. My spiritual journey has taken me to a place where I am working to eschew judgment, because I have seen how empowering this can be. I often find myself having to revert back to old, fear-based ways of dealing with institutional demands . . . and having to continually do this often drains me, and sets me back in my spiritual growth.

As universities become more like business enterprises, we (institutions) have come to be more concerned with monetary concerns and with delivering a "product." On the other hand, as faculty and spiritual beings, our concern must be with facilitating the processes of growth that enable/empower our students to become better people. One of the slogans of my (religious) university is cura personalis (teaching to the whole person) and "people for other people." But the everyday decisions of administrators belie that mission.

Taken together, behavior and cultural tensions can conflict actively, and sometimes intensely, not only with the desire for "serenity and self-acceptance" but also with "openness and critical thought within the bounds of mutual respect and expression."

CHARITABLE INVOLVEMENT

The third caring and connectedness measure, Charitable Involvement, is the behavioral counterpart to Ethic of Caring. As adapted
from the CSBV Survey for the Faculty Beliefs and Values Survey,
the measure comprises four items, two of which involve volunteer
or community service work: "participated in community food or
clothing drives" and "performed volunteer work." The other two
items reflect other helping behaviors: "helped friends with personal problems" and "donated money to charity." Noddings (1984,
1989, 1992, 2002) has argued that caring about others is the foundation for our sense of justice, which in turn leads to caring for
others. In other words, "caring about" can be empty if it does not
culminate in "caring for."

Overall, 26 percent of four-year college and university faculty
are high scorers on Charitable Involvement, and 12 percent are
low scorers. The rest (63%) score moderately. Faculty who consider themselves both spiritual and religious are notably more
inclined to be highly involved in charitable activities compared to
their colleagues who characterize themselves as religious but not
spiritual, spiritual but not religious, or neither spiritual nor religious (see Figure 4.9). This finding is in keeping with the fact that
among U.S. adults more generally, religiosity predicts both secular
and religious volunteering (Putnam and Campbell, 2012). Putnam
and Campbell go on to explain, however, that the "religious edge
in civic engagement is not linked or limited to the Religious
Right" (p. 456). Indeed, religious individuals of both political
persuasions are more inclined than their secular counterparts to
be engaged civically and charitably. However, when it comes to
many measures of civic engagement, religiosity has a greater
impact for self-described liberals than for self-described conservatives. In other words, Putnam and Campbell observed greater
differences in activism between religious liberals and secular liberals than between religious conservatives and secular conservatives.
Differences in faculty responses to each Charitable Involvement
item based on Spiritual Self-Identification scores are illustrated in
Figure 4.10.

In general, women are also more likely than men to score
high on Charitable Involvement (33% vs. 20%). Overall, African

FIGURE 4.9 CHARITABLE INVOLVEMENT HIGH AND LOW SCORERS BY SPIRITUAL/
RELIGIOUS SELF-IDENTITY

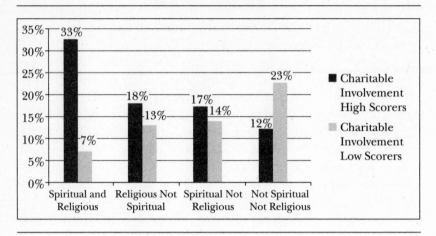

Source: 2012 Faculty Beliefs and Values Survey

FIGURE 4.10 "FREQUENT" PARTICIPATION IN SELECTED CHARITABLE
INVOLVEMENT ACTIVITIES BY SPIRITUAL SELF-IDENTIFICATION SCORE

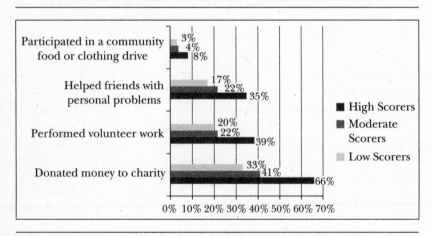

Source: 2012 Faculty Beliefs and Values Survey

American and American Indian or other Native American faculty—among whom just over one-third (35%) are high scorers—are also more inclined than their colleagues of other races and ethnicities to value, and partake in, charitable activities. This finding parallels broader higher education research that has long shown that women and faculty of color are more likely to participate in service activities and to otherwise give high priority to civic engagement (see, for example, Antonio, 2002; Antonio, Astin, and Cress, 2000; Hurtado, Ponjuan, and Smith, 2003; O'Meara, 2002).

Not unexpectedly given the moderate correlation between Charitable Involvement and both Religious Commitment (r = .31) and Religious Engagement (r = .33) and the comparatively higher proportions of conservative faculty who are also highly religious, those who self-identify as politically conservative are comparatively more likely to register as high scorers on Charitable Involvement (36%) relative to their middle-of-the-road (29%) and liberal (22%) colleagues.

Health science and education faculty are the most likely to register as high scorers on Charitable Involvement, whereas the lowest disciplinary representations among high scorers are evident in engineering, math/statistics, and the physical sciences (see Figure 4.11). In each of these disciplines/fields, significant correlations with Charitable Involvement remain even after faculty demographics are taken into account. As was the case with Ethic of Caring and Ecumenical Worldview, these findings may be explainable, at least in part, in terms of the types of individuals who are attracted to these various fields.

Finally, those who score high on Charitable Involvement generally are more represented within public colleges and in Catholic or "other" religiously affiliated colleges than in either private nonsectarian colleges or universities or public universities (see Figure 4.12).

As anticipated given our earlier analyses with college students, both Ethic of Caring (r = .29) and Ecumenical Worldview (r = .22) correlate modestly with Charitable Involvement activities, as does Spiritual Self-Identification (r = .29). However, irrespective of their spiritual/religious inclinations, those who are high scorers on Ethic of Caring and/or Ecumenical Worldview are more likely than their lower-scoring colleagues to also be high scorers on

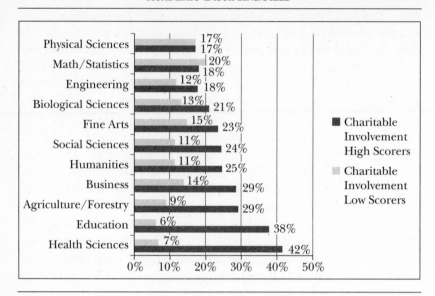

Source: 2012 Faculty Beliefs and Values Survey

FIGURE 4.12 CHARITABLE INVOLVEMENT HIGH AND LOW SCORERS BY INSTITUTIONAL TYPE

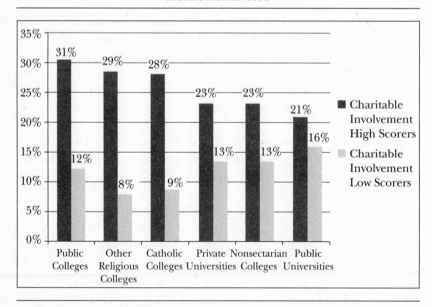

Source: 2012 Faculty Beliefs and Values Survey

Charitable Involvement. For example, 44 percent of high scorers on Ethic of Caring (relative to just 5% of low scorers) also score high on Charitable Involvement. Similarly, 39 percent of high scorers on Ecumenical Worldview (relative to just 6% of low scorers) are also high scorers on Charitable Involvement. Overall, roughly one-quarter of *low* scorers on Ethic of Caring (27%) and Ecumenical Worldview (23%) are high scorers on Charitable Involvement. Demographically, that population tends to be composed of faculty who are politically conservative and highly religiously engaged.

For faculty who are high scorers on Charitable Involvement, "being engaged in service to my broader community beyond the academy" provides a way to act on their ethic of caring and ecumenical worldview inclinations. Exemplifying the tension some faculty experience in association with having a "very privileged professorial role" within a work environment in which one can "easily allow oneself to become over-absorbed with self-importance," one professor explained:

> I find that my career puts me directly in touch with students and colleagues who are relatively well to do, so it is difficult to have a tangible impact on those who are oppressed or otherwise struggling except through charitable giving.

Other faculty emphasized the disconnect they experience between the value they place personally on charitable involvement and the comparatively limited emphasis their institutions place on community service "in the name of financial security, political considerations, or ego . . . in addition to the normal petty meanness of people in groups."

Faculty members' charitable involvement inclinations have implications both for the emphasis they tend to place on selected institutional priorities and their priorities for undergraduate teaching and learning. For example, findings from the 2012 Faculty Beliefs and Values Survey show that those who are high scorers on Charitable Involvement are also substantially more likely than their lower-scoring colleagues to place a higher priority on efforts to help promote a strong sense of community on campus and to place high value on "instilling in students a commitment to community service." Four in ten high scorers (42%) also view "preparing students for responsible citizenship" as a personally "essential" goal for undergraduate students, as compared to just over one-quarter (28%) of moderate scorers and 18 percent of low scorers on Charitable Involvement. High scorers are also more likely than their lower-scoring colleagues to give higher priority to participating in community action programs and becoming a community leader (see Figure 4.13).

These findings complement previously unpublished normative analyses that our Spirituality in Higher Education team conducted in 2007 that examined the interplay between faculty members' Spiritual Self-Identification and their endorsements of "civic-minded values" and "civic-minded practice." Those analyses showed that high scorers on Spiritual Self-Identification are markedly more inclined than low scorers to give higher priority to all of the individual items that constituted the Civic-Minded Values measure. As illustrated in Table 4.2, the largest percentage-

FIGURE 4.13 "ESSENTIAL" OR "VERY IMPORTANT" PERSONAL PRIORITIES BY CHARITABLE INVOLVEMENT SCORE

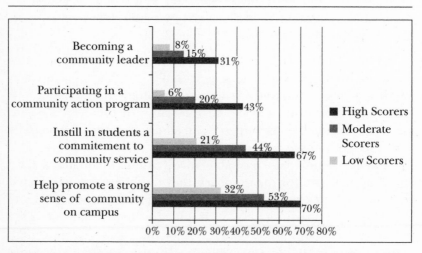

Source: 2012 Faculty Beliefs and Values Survey

point differences between high and low scorers were evident in
the value placed on instilling in undergraduate students a commitment to community service and preparing students for responsible citizenship, in *dis*agreement with including community
service as a part of a course on the basis that doing so is a poor

TABLE 4.2 INDICATORS OF CIVIC-MINDED VALUES AMONG HIGH AND LOW
SCORERS ON SPIRITUAL SELF-IDENTIFICATION (PERCENTAGES)

Civic-Minded Values Indicator	*Spiritual Self-Identification High Scorers*	*Spiritual Self-Identification Low Scorers*
Goals for Undergraduates[1]		
Prepare for responsible citizenship	77.5	49.3
Instill a commitment to community service	69.0	19.1
Personal Objectives[1]		
Influence social values	51.7	26.8
Influence the political structure	26.8	12.9
General Opinions[2]		
Including community service as part of a course is a poor use of resources	58.0	21.4
Individuals can do little to change society	52.0	29.2
General Opinions[3]		
Colleges should encourage students to be involved in community service activities	49.5	14.8
Colleges have a responsibility to work with their surrounding communities	39.7	12.0
Colleges should be actively involved in solving social problems	22.8	10.7

[1]Percentage who indicated "essential" or "very important"
[2]Percentage who "disagree strongly"
[3]Percentage who "agree strongly"
Source: 2004–2005 HERI Triennial National Survey of College Faculty

TABLE 4.3 INDICATORS OF CIVIC-MINDED PRACTICE AMONG HIGH AND LOW
SCORERS ON SPIRITUAL SELF-IDENTIFICATION (PERCENTAGES)

Civic-Minded Practice Indicator	Spiritual Self-Identification High Scorers	Spiritual Self-Identification Low Scorers
Activities[1]		
Engaged in public service/professional consulting without pay*	59.2	47.8
Used scholarship to address local community needs	56.1	31.2
Advised student groups involved in service/volunteer work*	47.1	28.9
Collaborated with the local community in research/teaching*	46.0	31.0
Taught a service learning course*	23.0	16.7
Hours per week[2]		
Community or public service	27.5	56.9
Teaching practice[3]		
Community service as a part of coursework	10.7	2.3

[1]Percentage who indicate "yes"
*in past two years
[2]Percentage who indicate "none"
[3]Percentage who use selected method in "all" or "most" of their courses
Source: 2004–2005 HERI Triennial National Survey of College Faculty

use of resources, and in the beliefs that colleges should encourage students to be involved in community service activities and that colleges have a responsibility to work with their surrounding communities.

As shown in Table 4.3, with respect to Civic-Minded Practice, high scorers on Spiritual Self-Identification were also considerably more inclined than their less spiritual colleagues to engage civically. The most notable difference between high and low scorers was evident with respect to the proportions who spend at least "some" time each week involved in community or public service activities. Stark contrasts were also evident with respect to using one's scholarship to address local community needs, advising student groups involved in service/volunteer work, and collaborating with the local community in research/teaching.

After controlling for demographic, disciplinary, professional practice, and institutional variables, Spiritual Self-Identification remains a significant correlate of both civic minded values and civic minded practice. For both measures, the "citizenship climate" of the institution also figured prominently. In other words, faculty who work at institutions that they characterize as giving priority to (1) developing a sense of community among students and faculty, (2) developing students' leadership ability, (3) helping students learn about how to bring about change in American society, (4) creating and sustaining partnerships with surrounding communities, and (5) providing resources for faculty to engage in community teaching and research tend to be more inclined themselves both to embrace civic-minded values and to engage in civic-minded practice. This holds true irrespective of institutional type (college or university) or control (public, private, faith based). Although liberal faculty were found to be more likely to endorse civic minded values, they were not necessarily more inclined than their conservative colleagues to engage in civic minded practice. Finally, in further keeping with current Charitable Involvement findings, once other potentially influencing variables are held constant, women faculty across academic discipline/fields along with faculty at large in the health sciences tend to be more inclined toward both civic-minded values and civic-minded practice.

Conclusion

Taken together, faculty members' ethic of caring, ecumenical worldview, and charitable involvement inclinations are the manifestations of what can be considered "external" spirituality dimensions. These aspects of spirituality are important in that they have the potential to "lift us beyond ourselves and our narrow self-interests" and to help us "see our deeper connections to one another and to the world beyond ourselves" (Conger, 1994, p. 17). This sense of connectedness in our lives, including our work, is essential for wholeness (Hoppe, 2005). To be sure, interpersonal dynamics that unfold between colleagues create a powerful context in which work meanings are composed (Wrzesniewski, Dutton, and Debebe, 2003).

As illustrated through faculty members' own voices, opportunities for expressing care and compassion and for cultivating meaningful connections with colleagues and students are plentiful within faculty roles. For some, the caring and connectedness dimensions of their work as teachers, researchers, and service providers within institutional, disciplinary, and local community contexts are among the most compelling. Yet, as addressed in this chapter, caring, compassion, and widespread commitment to cultivating community are sometimes in short supply on college and university campuses, and it can be difficult within various professional contexts to act on these values consistently. Indeed, potentially more challenging to contend with than the philosophical reluctance of most faculty to engage in what one professor referred to as "designated spirituality time" within the academic workday are our own and others' ego-driven, self-promoting, self-protecting, and self-preserving thoughts and actions. As addressed in the next chapter, for colleagues whose religious faith is a centrally important element of their lives, the academy can be a sometimes especially unwelcoming professional home.

CHAPTER FIVE

RELIGIOUS FAITH AND PERSPECTIVES

Religiousness generally involves devotion to, and practice of, some kind of faith tradition. It also typically involves membership in a community of fellow believers and participation in the rituals of the faith. In recent decades, there has been a decline in religious self-identification within the United States. Nevertheless, the vast majority of Americans (80%) continue to identify themselves as religious, and 56 percent of the overall U.S. adult population indicates that religion plays a "very important" role in their lives (Kosmin and Keysar, 2008; Pew Forum on Religion & Public Life, 2012). Religious self-identity is not exclusive, however, to those who are members of particular religious faiths. For example, only 54 percent of Americans belong to a religious organization such as a synagogue, mosque, or church (Beal, 2008). Moreover, among U.S. adults who are *not* affiliated with any particular religion, 41 percent indicate that religion is at least "somewhat" important in their lives. For 16 percent of the unaffiliated, religion plays a "very important" life role. Among the most notable differences between the most religious Americans (those in the top 20%) and the least religious (bottom 20%) is how spiritual they consider themselves to be. Reaffirming that for many, if not most, Americans, spirituality and religion go hand in hand (see Chapter Two), 80 percent of those who are most religious describe themselves as "very spiritual," whereas just 4 percent of the least religious do (Putnam and Campbell, 2012).

The 2012 Faculty Beliefs and Values Survey queried faculty members in regard to their religious denominations, Evangelical self-identification, belief in God, perspectives on the relationship between science and religion, and inclinations toward religious/social conservatism. The questionnaire also included items that constitute four scales that our Spirituality in Higher Education research team developed through our previous study of college students: Religious Commitment, Religious Engagement, Religious Struggle, and Religious Skepticism. Those measures, along with consideration of faculty members' religious preferences and perspectives, are the focal point of this chapter.

RELIGIOUS PREFERENCE

In keeping with the approach that our Spirituality in Higher Education research team took in analyzing students' religious preferences, faculty preferences were classified into nineteen different categories, including twelve major Christian denominations, "Other" Christian, Unitarian, Jewish, Hindu, Islamic, Buddhist, and "None." (An "'Other' Religion" response option was also available—accounting for about 9 percent of the faculty, which is not considered here because of ambiguities in interpretation.) The religious preference accounting for the highest percentage of respondents to the 2012 Faculty Beliefs and Values Survey is "None" (29%). Roman Catholics make up the next largest proportion (15%), and another 18 percent selected one of the mainline Protestant faiths: Episcopalian, Presbyterian, Methodist, or Lutheran. The remaining most sizable groups are "Other" Christian (8%), Baptist (4%), and Jewish (4%). (Table 5.1 summarizes these results.) Roughly 16 percent of faculty consider themselves Evangelical Christians, with the following groups showing the highest percentages: Baptist (73%), "Other" Christian (62%), and Church of Christ (53%).

Largely paralleling our Spirituality in Higher Education research team's earlier student analyses, there are two clear clusters of faculty religious preferences. The first—involving Mormons, Baptists, and "Other" Christians—is highly spiritual and highly religious, and expresses very little religious skepticism. This group also tends to endorse religiously/socially conservative views, such as "people who don't believe in God will be punished." The second group—comprising Episcopalians, Buddhists, Hindus,

TABLE 5.1 FACULTY MEMBERS' RELIGIOUS PREFERENCES

Religious Preference	Percentage
None	29.4
Roman Catholic	15.0
"Other" Religion	8.8
"Other" Christian	8.3
Episcopalian	5.0
Methodist	4.6
Jewish	4.4
Presbyterian	4.4
Lutheran	4.1
Baptist	4.0
Unitarian	2.5
Buddhist	2.2
Latter-day Saints (Mormon)	1.7
United Church of Christ	1.6
Quaker	1.0
Eastern Orthodox	0.7
Hindu	0.5
Islamic	0.4
Seventh-Day Adventist	0.2

Source: 2012 Faculty Beliefs and Values Survey

Jews, Unitarians, and members of the Eastern Orthodox church—
tends to score low on religiousness, high on Religious Skepticism,
and high on Ecumenical Worldview and Ethic of Caring.

On the whole, those who indicate "None" as their religious preference tend, not unexpectedly, to score high on Religious Skepticism and low on Religious Commitment and Engagement.
However, roughly one-third (32%) of faculty who indicate no religious preference score moderately on Religious Commitment, and
18 percent score moderately on Religious Engagement. Predominately, those who are religiously unaffiliated also tend to score at
least moderately high on Equanimity, Ethic of Caring, Ecumenical

Worldview, Spiritual Quest, and Religious Struggle. On each of these measures, roughly 20 percent of those with no religious preference register as high scorers.

College professors are more likely than other adults in the United States to identify as religiously unaffiliated. However, in parallel with Putnam and Campbell's earlier findings (2012) regarding those who are comparatively less attuned to religion, the most recent report from the Pew Research Center's Forum on Religion & Public Life (2012) features the rapid rise of the "Nones," or the religiously unaffiliated, as a continuing trend (up from just over 15% of U.S. adults to just under 20%). Generational differences account for part of this shift. Today, for example, 32 percent of adults under thirty years of age indicate "None" as their religious preference, compared to just 9 percent of those who are sixty-five or older. This trend has also been most pronounced among whites.

Not unexpectedly, those who are religiously unaffiliated generally tend to have less positive views of religious institutions. It is important to note, however, that much like many of their professorial counterparts, religiously unaffiliated adults within the broader U.S. population are not uniformly secular, nor are they broadly hostile to religion. One-third, for example, say that religion is at least "somewhat" important in their lives. Two-thirds believe in God, and more than half describe themselves either as a religious person (18%) or as spiritual but not religious (37%) (Pew Forum on Religion & Public Life, 2012). Davie (1990) characterized this phenomenon of being largely unattached to organized religion but not altogether disregarding religious beliefs and predilections as "believing without belonging" (see also Lim, MacGregor, and Putnam, 2010).

BELIEF IN GOD

Overall, 54 percent of four-year college and university faculty say that they believe in God. However, there are marked differences in the prevalence of belief among faculty in different disciplines. Whereas roughly three-quarters or more of faculty in the health sciences, education, agriculture/forestry, and business are believers in God, fewer than half of those in the biological sciences,

FIGURE 5.1 BELIEF IN GOD BY ACADEMIC DISCIPLINE/FIELD

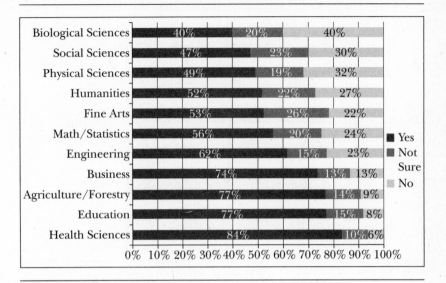

Source: 2012 Faculty Beliefs and Values Survey

social sciences, and physical sciences endorse the existence of God. Fine arts faculty are comparatively more likely than their colleagues in other disciplines to be unsure of their belief in God. (Figure 5.1 summarizes these results.) Irrespective of disciplinary affiliation, two-thirds or more of those employed at faith-based institutions express belief in God. By comparison, half or fewer of those employed by nonsectarian private colleges or public universities say they believe in God (see Figure 5.2). The most pronounced faculty demographic differentiations with respect to belief in God are related to political views: nearly three-quarters or more of those who espouse self-described middle-of-the-road or conservative/far right political views endorse the notion of God, compared to only slightly more than four in ten faculty who characterize their political views as liberal/far left (see Figure 5.3).

Describing the tensions between their spiritual/religious lives and their work as academics, those who "gain spiritual strength

FIGURE 5.2 BELIEF IN GOD BY INSTITUTIONAL TYPE

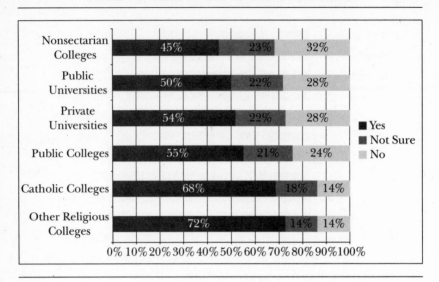

Source: 2012 Faculty Beliefs and Values Survey

FIGURE 5.3 BELIEF IN GOD BY POLITICAL VIEWS

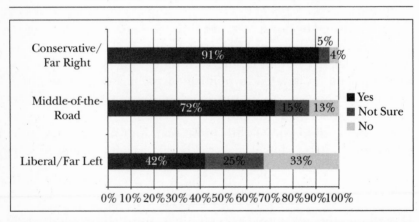

Source: 2012 Faculty Beliefs and Values Survey

by trusting in a higher power" (53% of faculty overall) often reported challenges related to working in environments where "many of my colleagues deny the existence of things beyond their knowing." Within a profession described often by religious believers as one "dominated by atheists" and "intolerant secularists" who believe that "only deluded or uneducated people or people who are weak and afraid believe in God," there is a contingent who are particularly "eager to proselytize their views on secularism" and who actively "mock," "belittle," "ridicule," and otherwise behave "disrespectfully" toward those who do believe in the existence of God or other higher power(s). Echoing the sentiments of many of their God-believing colleagues who lament the inclinations of some of their nonbelieving colleagues to "promote their atheistic beliefs by way of derision" are these elaborated comments:

> A former colleague made the comment that only stupid people believe in God. I believe in God and I'm not stupid.

> There are numerous colleagues I've had who think a person's intellect is seriously in question if they believe in God, so professional and personal relationships with them are difficult at times.

> Most of my colleagues, I think, might be classified as dogmatic atheists and it is consequently difficult to discuss my own views on a life of the spirit which they tend to see as contrary to living a life of the mind.

Both within secular colleges and universities as well as in the broader disciplinary and professional associations that are central to the work lives of many faculty, the "open hostility" to religious faith coupled with what is experienced to be the "widespread disbelief" that "one can believe in god, practice a religion, and also be a true intellectual" creates tension between individuals' personal and professional lives. As one faculty member elaborated,

> My relationship with God is such a big part of who I am. It is central to who I am. But I feel I must close that off and only show part of myself to the people I work with professionally. It makes it difficult to feel whole while at work.

Others offered similar perspective:

Sometimes it is difficult to be a Vatican II Catholic in a department with loud voices proclaiming that religion is the cause of all
evil in the world. It is difficult to be seen as intellectually
dishonest for believing in God by people whose knowledge of
religion is quite shallow.

Like many universities, many faculty at my university think those
who believe in God and creation are ignorant and inferior. It is
difficult to speak up about faith when you are untenured as some
senior faculty are so intolerant they would use this as a reason to
deny tenure.

I have experienced intolerance (or closed mindedness) to faith. I
am very tired of "scientists" not being open minded to the
existence of a higher power, and claiming that those who do
believe in this existence are narrow-minded. As a person who
enjoys research and science, I find this very oppressive and closed
minded.

Just over half of faculty express belief in God, but many elect
to keep that belief "silent" when working among colleagues who,
particularly in selected disciplinary and institutional segments of
U.S. higher education, openly denigrate believers in God or other
higher power(s) and otherwise denounce religious (or spiritual)
commitment and engagement.

RELIGIOUS COMMITMENT

Religious Commitment is an "internal" measure comprising twelve
attitudinal and belief items. Specifically, the measure reflects the
individual's self-rating on "religiousness" relative to others who
are the same age, as well as the degree to which he or she seeks
to follow religious teachings in everyday life, finds religion to be
personally helpful, and gains spiritual strength by trusting in a
higher power. Also reflected is the individual's experience (or
lack thereof) of feeling loved by God. Finally, the measure includes
items that query the extent to which people's spiritual/religious
beliefs "give meaning and purpose to my life," "lie behind my
whole approach to life," "are one of the most important things in
my life," "help define the goals I set for myself," "provide me with

strength, support, and guidance," and "have helped me develop my identity." Such orientations are resonant with Allport's conception (1950) of intrinsically motivated religiosity, whereby religion serves as the overarching reference point from which other aspects of life are perceived and understood.

As illustrated in Table 5.2, overall, more than three-fourths of faculty agree at least "somewhat" that their spiritual/religious beliefs have helped them develop their identity. Fully two-thirds say that those beliefs provide them with strength, support, and guidance. For more than half, spiritual/religious beliefs help

TABLE 5.2 INDICATORS OF FACULTY MEMBERS' RELIGIOUS COMMITMENT (PERCENTAGES)

	Agree Strongly	Agree Somewhat	Disagree Somewhat	Disagree Strongly
My spiritual/religious beliefs:				
Have helped me develop my identity	44.8	32.6	8.6	13.9
Provide me with strength, support, and guidance	37.2	28.5	11.9	22.3
Give meaning and purpose to my life	36.6	27.1	13.9	22.4
Are one of the most important things in my life	35.8	22.1	17.7	24.4
Help define the goals I set for myself	31.7	29.9	14.8	23.6
Lie behind my whole approach to life	31.0	26.3	16.8	25.9
I find religion to be personally helpful	30.2	27.0	13.9	28.9
I gain spiritual strength by trusting in a higher power	29.6	23.2	12.9	34.2

Source: 2012 Faculty Beliefs and Values Survey

define personal goals, lie behind their whole approach to life, and give meaning and purpose to their lives. Similar proportions find religion to be personally helpful and say that they gain spiritual strength by trusting in a higher power. For more than one-third of college and university faculty, their spiritual/religious beliefs are one of the most important things in their lives.

Just under half of faculty consider it either "essential" (22%) or "very important" (24%) to follow religious teachings in their everyday lives. Nearly two-thirds (64%) of faculty say that, to at least "some" extent, they feel a sense of connectedness with God or other higher power that transcends their personal self. Just over one-third (35%) feels that way "to a great extent." About four in ten faculty (39%) say they "frequently" feel loved by God. All in all, 32 percent faculty rate themselves "above average" on religiousness relative to others their age.

In their overall responses to items comprised by the Religious Commitment measure, 31 percent of four-year college and university faculty register as high scorers on Religious Commitment and 25 percent register as low scorers. Much higher proportions of Mormons (89%), Baptists (80%), Church of Christ members (70%), Seventh-Day Adventists (68%), and "Other" Christians (70%) obtain high scores. Overall, 47 percent who are high scorers on Religious Commitment consider themselves Evangelicals. Roughly one-third (31%) of those who are highly committed religiously also say that, to a "great" extent, they are committed to introducing others to their faith (16% of Religious Commitment high scorers are "not at all" inclined in this way). Among Evangelicals, 41 percent report that they are greatly committed to introducing others to their faith; 8 percent say that they are "not at all" inclined to do so. Faculty with the lowest levels of religious commitment—all less than 12 percent high scorers— include Buddhists (11%), Jews (9%), Hindus (7%), Unitarian/Universalists (5%), and faculty members whose religious preference is "None" (1%).

On the whole, African American and Hispanic faculty are comparatively more likely than colleagues of other races/ethnicities to register as high scorers on Religious Commitment. More than half (54%) of African American faculty (along with 37% of Hispanic faculty) are high scorers on Religious Commitment compared with just 31 percent of white non-Hispanic faculty and 28 percent of Asian faculty. For African Americans in particular, the church is the longest-standing and most resilient social institution. Traditionally, the church was also the only black-controlled institution of a historically oppressed people and continues to serve as a "mobilizing force for civic activism" (Putnam, 2000, p. 68). Faculty who self-identify as LGBT are the least likely demographic group to resonate with having a strong religious self-identity and a strong, accompanying commitment to religious faith and active engagement. Just 16 percent register as high scorers on Religious Commitment; 32 percent are low scorers.

As illustrated in Figure 5.4, and in keeping with our own and others' prior research, there are also stark contrasts in the extent to which faculty are religiously inclined and otherwise committed to religious beliefs based on their political orientations (see, for example, Gross, 2013). Whereas 67 percent of faculty who are politically conservative "agree strongly" that they find religion to be personally helpful in their lives, just 39 percent of those who

FIGURE 5.4 Religious Commitment High and Low Scorers by Political Views

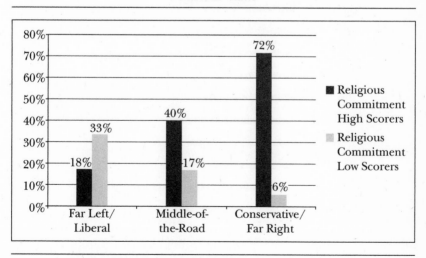

Source: 2012 Faculty Beliefs and Values Survey

are politically moderate and 18 percent who are liberal indicate
the same. The relative proportions who "disagree strongly" with
that sentiment are also pronounced: 38 percent among liberals,
compared to 18 percent of those whose political beliefs are
middle-of-the-road and just 6 percent of conservatives.

Within the general adult population, women tend to be more
religiously inclined than men (see, for example, Gallup, 2002;
Newport, 2012; Putnam and Campbell, 2012; Stark, 2002).
However, somewhat different patterns are evident among women
faculty. Although female faculty are indeed less likely than their
male colleagues to be *low* scorers on Religious Commitment (23%
vs. 28% of men), they are also somewhat less likely overall to be
high scorers (30% vs. 33% of men). This is particularly evident
within selected disciplines/fields. Figure 5.5 shows the relative
proportions of high and low scorers on Religious Commitment
based on academic discipline/field. In eight of these disciplinary

FIGURE 5.5 RELIGIOUS COMMITMENT HIGH AND LOW SCORERS BY ACADEMIC
DISCIPLINE/FIELD

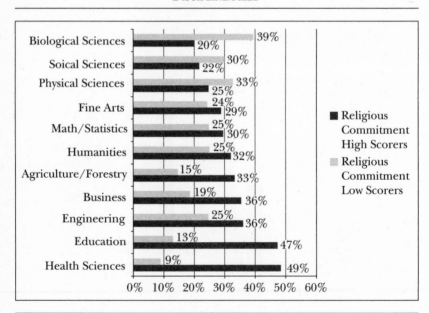

Source: 2012 Faculty Beliefs and Values Survey

groupings, significantly lower proportions of women than men registered as high scorers on Religious Commitment, ranging from a 3 percentage-point difference in the social sciences to a 12-point differential in the humanities. Only in the health sciences (which include a notable contingency of predominately female Nursing Department faculty) and in education (also skewed heavily toward female faculty) were women more likely than men to register as high scorers on Religious Commitment (see Table 5.3). However, even when gender, age, and race/ethnicity are held constant, significant positive correlations between Religious Commitment and education or health sciences affiliation still remain. Correspondingly negative correlations also persist within physical sciences, biological sciences, and social sciences. These findings reflect patterns similar to those identified with respect to selected spirituality measures addressed in previous chapters. Generally speaking, openness to spiritual/religious issues tends to be more prevalent in disciplines/fields

TABLE 5.3 Gender Differences in Faulty Members' Religious Commitment

Academic Discipline/ Field	Percent High Scorers		Percent Low Scorers	
	Men	Women	Men	Women
Health Sciences	42.1	49.7	15.8	7.8
Education	44.6	49.2	15.5	10.8
Business	39.7	27.9	20.5	15.1
Humanities	38.2	25.9	25.2	24.8
Engineering	37.3	31.0	26.1	20.7
Fine Arts	32.3	23.4	23.4	24.9
Math/Statistics	32.1	23.3	26.1	20.5
Physical Sciences	27.0	18.1	33.0	31.9
Social Sciences	24.1	21.1	31.1	28.5
Biological Sciences	22.0	17.3	43.6	32.5

Note: There were not enough female respondents within agriculture/forestry to make valid gender comparisons.
Source: 2012 Faculty Beliefs and Values Survey

that are more person oriented (versus subject oriented). As reflected in some of the faculty comments included in this chapter, there may also be a normative tendency for faculty to view their disciplinary subject matter and predominating styles of academic inquiry as explaining—or even explaining away—the validity of spiritual/religious claims and orientations.

◦◦◦◦   ◦◦◦◦

Irrespective of their particular faith traditions or beliefs, religiously committed faculty—especially those in disciplines where "faith is sometimes considered hogwash"—highlighted common tensions they experience. These tensions, elaborated by the following comments, often stem from colleagues' gratuitous presumptions about "who you are . . . or who you 'should' be . . . based on what you study":

> In Physics there are few religious people. The tension comes
> from the fact that most people assume that I am not religious or
> spiritual.

> There is a pointed skepticism, and in many cases outright
> derision, by fellow academics, particularly in my field and related
> fields (social sciences/sciences). I wouldn't say I'm "in the closet,"
> but I don't always speak up when my colleagues assume I am
> atheist just like they are.

For many, especially those who are untenured or those who feel marginalized within the academy, "cohabitating peacefully" in a "liberal academic environment where faculty proudly wear their atheist and agnostic badges" and don't "respect or appreciate my beliefs" means "keeping quiet about my religious life" and "silent about my religious views." To do otherwise, let alone challenge dominant views, would potentially result, some fear, in retribution:

> The academics at my college are dedicated to secularism and any
> form of spirituality is considered the mark of an unintelligent
> person. Professors have started ugly rumors about me and some
> are active in their campaign to intellectually discredit me.
> Students are likewise tormented for professing any sort of
> religious or spiritual belief.

Many of my colleagues (even those I consider close friends) would be appalled and "defriend" me because of my conservative Christian beliefs, as I have seen them do to others.

A lot of assumptions are made by many faculty that serious academics do not believe in traditional Christian beliefs. I have never suffered professionally from being a Christian but I have had to listen to a lot of condescending remarks made by colleagues who don't realize that someone who believes some of the things they are denigrating is sitting right there . . . and then I have to decide what, if anything, to say.

Other tensions originate from disciplinary colleagues' strong convictions that "all aspects of life can be explained in purely physical (and psychological) terms" coupled with "a lack of openness to different points of view" and "suspicion" of those whose perspectives "deviate from unquestioned norms." Echoing the refrains of many religious faculty, one professor explained:

It is not an easy thing to be spiritual/religious and a scientist. It seems as though it is viewed by others as weak, inconsistent, or just plain stupid.

Others elaborated:

As a scientist, many (but not all) of my colleagues either don't believe in God or organized religion or are actively contemptuous, or hateful, of those who have any kind of spirituality in their lives. I am not very religious or observant and I certainly don't try to force my spiritual beliefs on anyone else. But there is this feeling one gets that some scientists don't think you can be a good scientist and still have religious beliefs or participate in religious activities.

[The primary tension I experience between my spiritual and religious life relates to] colleagues (especially in the biology field) who are hostile to or make fun of religion, making me feel that, as a practicing Christian, I'm some kind of minority group who has to keep her mouth shut at times to avoid conflict or ridicule. Students are more comfortable with such practices and likely to discuss them.

Sociology tends to be very secularly orientated, in spite of (or because of) a long history of sociologists trying to deal with the subject matter. There is distrust in some circles of anyone claiming

to have any faith and also claiming to be a good sociologist. This
is particularly true of those that hold to the philosophy that
"doing sociology" should be "value-free." Interestingly, there are
many sociologists who declare themselves as "humanist," "feminist"
or "Marxist," that is declaring other value systems rather than
religious ones.

My secular university, especially my department, has sufficient
numbers of people openly hostile to anything religious or
spiritual. There is also a dismissal in my field—psychology—of
things spiritual, assuming that they cannot be studied scientifically
and hence are "beneath" or outside of the purview of psychology.
Of course, nothing is further from the truth, and for psychology
to truly be a science of behavior [it] must do a much better job of
studying and understanding religion and spirituality in people's
lives.

The tensions are not inherent in the material that makes up my
field, which actually tends to confirm my spiritual life and beliefs.
The tensions come from my colleagues and from a deep seated
hostility to these beliefs within the broader academic community
today.

Faculty from markedly different disciplines highlighted other
tensions that originate largely from central features of the predominating academic and/or disciplinary culture:

The academic life is the life of the mind. As a choreographer-artist
and performer, the denial of embodied knowledge in traditional
academic environments is at odds with my artistic-spiritual
life. Academic institutions are about making distinctions—between
disciplines—and argument as opposed to synthesis. My experience
as an artist is the life of the body-mind. Heart-centered, intuitive
ways of learning are not necessarily valued.

As a Buddhist, I believe in "let go" and "nothing lasts" so I try to
take things less seriously, especially with things that are beyond my
control or involve others. I can only control myself and my
thoughts and actions. But to "let go" can contradict my responsibilities as a faculty member. There are expectations for me to
deliver evidence of my performance in different areas. Also, I
cannot teach business students that "nothing lasts" so they should
"let go" because of the expected business mentality of being
proactive and trying to avoid problems—"there is always a solution
and you always need to take action" mentality.

As would be expected, faculty who are employed at faith-based institutions are comparatively more likely than their colleagues at nonsectarian private and public colleges and universities to register as high scorers on Religious Commitment. Whereas more than one-third of those employed at Catholic colleges and nearly half of those employed at "Other" (primarily Protestant) religiously affiliated colleges are high scorers on Religious Commitment, fewer than one-quarter of their colleagues at nonsectarian colleges and at public universities (which also have the highest overall proportions of low scorers on Religious Commitment) are high scorers (see Figure 5.6). Even within those environments, some religiously committed faculty—many of whom have elected to work at those faith-based institutions *because of* their own beliefs and values—marvel at the "open disregard" for the institution's religious connections that some of their nonreligious institutional colleagues' express:

> I chafe that some faculty members at my church-related institution regard our connection with the church as something unsavory. It puzzles me that someone who feels that way would accept a position at a church-related college.

FIGURE 5.6 RELIGIOUS COMMITMENT HIGH AND LOW SCORERS BY INSTITUTIONAL TYPE

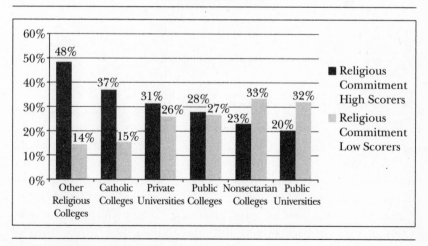

Source: 2012 Faculty Beliefs and Values Survey

For some faculty—irrespective of their particular faith tradition—the "realization" that being religious (or spiritual) is considered in many, if not most, academic circles to be "un-academic," "unprofessional," or "intellectually primitive" causes them to feel "mocked, even though I am not vocal about my beliefs." For religious faculty, the academy's "hostility not only to conservative, narrow religious beliefs, but also to the most open, progressive forms of religion" can be both "frustrating" and "saddening." Reflecting on the "commitment of many in the academy to a critical, disrespectful attitude towards religious life," one faculty member noted that Christians in particular are "the last group remaining that it is politically correct to joke about and denigrate in public forum." Some faculty who are of "minority" religious faiths—who shared, for example, that they are "a Muslim living in a country where Muslims are seen as the enemy" or explained that, as a Buddhist, "I do not feel comfortable explicitly expressing my beliefs in an environment which is dominated by those who are nonreligious, Christian, or Jewish"—expressed that colleagues' "misunderstanding" or "mistrust" of their faith can make it difficult to feel a true sense of belonging within their academic workplaces. As one professor elaborated:

> If you aren't a member of a major religion, it's not too cool to talk about it. That was particularly true on the southern east coast. If, as a white person, I wasn't Christian or Jewish, it was absolutely mindboggling to people. If I said, I'm a Pagan Buddhist, it wouldn't even compute, or it would be, "You must worship the devil." There is less of that where I am now but, still, many academics are completely skeptical of faith or practice of any kind, so I am careful of what I speak, where.

RELIGIOUS ENGAGEMENT

Religious Engagement is an "external" measure that represents the behavioral counterpart to Religious Commitment. It contains seven items, six of which address the frequency with which the individual attends religious services; prays; attends classes, work-shops, or retreats on matters related to religion/spirituality; engages in religious singing/chanting; reads sacred texts; and does other reading on religion/spirituality. The proportion of "close friends who go to church/temple or other house of worship" is also included.

Table 5.4 shows the frequencies with which faculty report that they engage in various religiously oriented practices. Praying is the most common daily practice (29%); roughly half (51%) say that they pray at least once per week. Roughly one-third engage at least weekly in reading sacred texts (37%), religious singing or chanting (37%), and doing other reading related to spirituality and religion (31%). Roughly one-quarter (27%) engage in meditation weekly. About four in ten faculty (38%) also attend religious services "frequently" (23% say they do so "occasionally"). For fully one-third of faculty, "all" or "most" of their friends go to church, temple, or other houses of worship.

Considering patterns of faculty responses to items comprised by the Religious Engagement measure, just 25 percent of faculty members overall are high scorers on Religious Engagement; 35 percent are low scorers. Largely paralleling the denominational findings on Religious Commitment, the most highly engaged faculty include Mormons (91%), Church of Christ members (78%), Baptists (67%), Seventh-Day Adventists (58%), and "Other"

TABLE 5.4 FACULTY ENGAGEMENT IN SELECTED RELIGIOUS PRACTICES (PERCENTAGES)

	Daily	Several Times/ Week	Once/ Week	Monthly	Less than Monthly	Not at All
Prayer	28.8	15.6	6.9	4.0	7.3	37.3
Reading sacred texts	10.0	13.8	12.8	7.2	17.8	38.5
"Other" reading on spirituality or religion	5.3	14.0	11.3	14.0	22.7	32.8
Meditation	3.6	10.8	12.6	7.2	20.7	45.0
Religious singing/ chanting	3.5	11.9	21.1	5.0	9.1	49.4

Source: 2012 Faculty Beliefs and Values Survey

Christians (63%). The least engaged with respect to proportions of high scorers on the Religious Engagement measure are Hindus (10%), Jews (9%), Buddhists (6%), Unitarian/Universalists (3%), and, as would be expected, those with no religious preference (0%). Among faculty who are highly engaged religiously, just over half (53%) consider themselves Evangelicals.

For all faculty, religious engagement levels are lower than commitment levels. As would be expected, the demographics of religiously engaged faculty parallel closely those reported for religious commitment earlier in this chapter. In other words, those who are most religiously committed also tend to be most religiously engaged. Faculty at public universities and nonsectarian colleges tend to be the least religiously engaged, and Catholic college faculty display the most balanced split between high and low scorers. Disciplinary differences largely parallel those for religious commitment, with the exception of education faculty, who, although among the most highly religiously committed (47% high scorers), are among the least likely to be highly religiously engaged (19%). Once the potentially overriding influence of demographic characteristics has been accounted for, the remaining positive and negative disciplinary correlates with Religious Engagement are identical to those noted earlier in this chapter for Religious Commitment. That is, on the whole, education and health science faculty (irrespective of their gender, race/ethnicity, or age) tend to be more religiously engaged than their counterparts in other fields. Physical, biological, and social science faculty are comparatively less religiously engaged.

FAITH CHALLENGES IN THE ACADEMY

For religiously engaged faculty, one frequently reported tension between their spiritual/religious lives and their professional lives is an often unspoken institutional expectation that they be available to work on Saturdays and Sundays when they have commitments to attend religious services. For many faculty, particularly those who are not Christian, institutional calendars and dates for disciplinary conferences "often tend to be scheduled without consideration of holy days." In addition, and in keeping with perspectives addressed earlier in this chapter, faculty who are religiously engaged—especially in terms of religious service attendance—note the associated insinuations by colleagues that they must then either be "gullible morons" or "social climbers." One faculty member's remarks illustrate how some faculty attempt to "justify" or "qualify" their religious practice to colleagues, and the resulting internal tensions:

> Sometimes the Unitarian/Universalist church seems "hokey" to me and doesn't satisfy my analytical needs (but often, it does). I worry that when colleagues hear I go to "church" they will make assumptions, so I often add "the church with Buddhists and pagans and atheists that doesn't use the 'G' word much," or some such. Then at times I might feel I have denied or dishonored spirit itself, when in truth I am a grateful devotee.

Those who actively practice their faith and who are also progressive or liberal in their social views and political beliefs sometimes feel like "outsiders" in both their academic and faith communities:

> Most of my colleagues are not very religious, and they tend to see my practices/beliefs as simplistic. Conversely, my church friends see me as the crazy liberal person who believes in full inclusion.

> Colleagues and students who are "true believers" do not respect my views as having a place in the church. I also am at pains to explain how I as a feminist can continue to stay in a patriarchal religious tradition. Thus, sometimes this is a struggle about integrity. Nevertheless, I believe that some are called to exercise a prophetic role vis-a-vis the institution when it is harming others or not causing their human flourishing. I accept this "call" reluctantly—it does cause tension.

> I consider myself a progressive, liberal, Christian. Because I am pro-choice, support gay marriage, incorporate tolerance and diversity into my classroom, believe in evolution, etc., a lot of academics assume I must not be Christian. I experience a lot of antagonism from academics towards Christians, until they find out I am a Christian. I've had academics say intelligent people can't believe in God, that Christians are ignorant bigots, etc. The tensions come from both sides—my professional life, and my religious life, where other religious people don't understand how I can be "liberal." I consider myself progressive and feel my religious beliefs inform my political and professional values.

However, all too often people make assumptions about me based on my political views or my religious views, without asking how I reconcile both. The tension comes more from the assumption that my political/professional values automatically mean I must not be Christian. It can be difficult to explain to someone that the ignorant assumptions they are making about Christians are offensive to me.

Overall, 15 percent of college and university faculty say that within their workplaces, they experience discrimination at least "occasionally" based on their spiritual/religious beliefs (2% report "frequent" discrimination). Among those who are high scorers on Religious Engagement, 25 percent experience at least "occasional" discrimination (3% "frequent") based on their beliefs. At public colleges and universities, that "occasional" discrimination figure among those who are highly religiously committed rises to a high of 35 percent (including 5% who experience such treatment frequently). Evangelicals at public universities report the highest levels of "occasional" discrimination based on their spiritual/religious beliefs (39%, including 4% who experience such treatment "frequently").

Prior research has shown that across academic disciplines and demographic characteristics, college and university faculty tend to hold particularly strong negative feelings toward Evangelicals. Specifically, Tobin and Weinberg's profile (2007) of the religious beliefs and behaviors of college faculty showed that 53 percent of faculty have "cool/unfavorable" feelings toward Evangelical Christians, leading Mormons by 20 percent as the "least liked" religious group. Only 30 percent characterized their feelings toward Evangelical Christians as "warm/favorable." Evangelicals who completed the 2012 Faculty Beliefs and Values Survey are well aware that a significant proportion of their colleagues are, at best, "cynical and dismissive" about their faith and that, at the extreme, there is "a lot of anger and hatred toward Evangelicals." The "openly strong bias" against Evangelicals in the academy tends to affirm the inclinations of some academics to "openly" and, in some cases, "relentlessly" "question the intellectual abilities and commitments" as well as the "professional ethics" of those who have strong Evangelical faith. Such "derision" leads some Evangelicals to "mask my religious identity in professional settings" and to otherwise "compartmentalize" their personal and professional lives. The following elaborations address in more detail the sentiments shared by other self-characterized Evangelicals:

> As a so-called "evangelical Christian," I find that some of my colleagues stereotype me as intolerant, inflexible and conde-scending. Those who get to know me realize this is not the case, but the media view of evangelicals (like the media view of Muslims) tends to slant toward the extreme, which does not benefit either religious group.

> It seems that those who are non-spiritual think it is appropriate to denigrate spirituality, especially evangelical spirituality. I don't bring my spiritual life into my teaching that much because, given the nature of my courses, it is not that relevant. But I have seen anti-religious or anti-spiritual faculty act like it was their duty to bring their anti-spirituality into the classroom and even evangelize for their non-spirituality.

> Many of my non-Christian colleagues have ostracized me because I chose to work at a Christian college. In their view, it is difficult, even impossible, to be a thoughtful scholar and a Christian at the same time.

> As a Christian academic, I often find that the academy seems willing to extend grace and charity to anyone with the exception of Christians (particularly evangelicals) who are often viewed in terms of the flat, unfair stereotypes so pervasive in the popular media. The Academy recognizes non-Christian scholars as scholars and teachers foremost whose religious views do not undercut their work. This is not true, in my experience, of their views of Christian scholars, particularly evangelical scholars. Sadly, most non-Christian academics seem to believe that Christian beliefs are a detriment to the life of the mind.

Some Evangelicals feel relatively "out of place" not only in their academic communities but also in their faith communities, given their pursuit of a profession known for its liberalism. As one faculty member offered:

> As an Evangelical Christian who teaches geography, I feel pinched on both sides. I teach about the reality of climate change, about how our earth is old and evolving, and I point out sharp inequities

in life chances because of the sociospatial structuring of society. Students, friends, and family members with Evangelical Christian beliefs sometimes question my own Christian convictions because of my "liberal" stances regarding politics and those sorts of issues. On the other hand, I have some colleagues who are deeply hostile towards Evangelical Christians and at times openly mock Christians and discriminate against people of faith in job searches. For example, in one tenure-track search where I was the external member of the search, candidates with undergraduate degrees from Christian schools were automatically eliminated from consideration, even when they came from really strong schools. I see that my secular colleagues can be much less guarded and more transparent about their beliefs when they teach and do research.

RELIGIOUS SKEPTICISM

The *Religious Skepticism* measure that our Spirituality in Higher Education research team developed comprises nine items, including such beliefs as "the universe arose by chance," "in the future, science will be able to explain everything," "whether there is a Supreme Being doesn't matter to me," "and "it doesn't matter what I believe as long as I live a moral life." The measure also reflects *dis*belief of the sentiments that "what happens in my life is determined by forces larger than myself" and that "while science can provide meaningful information about the physical world, only religion can truly explain existence," as well as *dis*belief in the notion of life after death. The final item reflects the belief that "religion and science are in conflict, and I side with science."

In many respects, Religious Skepticism is the antithesis of Religious Commitment and Religious Engagement. Whereas the latter two are based on a belief in the truth of particular theological propositions, Religious Skepticism is grounded in the belief that these same propositions are in error. As addressed earlier in this chapter, colleges and universities are the professional home to many who are not particularly inclined toward religious commitment and engagement and who, in some cases, are actively opposed to such belief. Indeed, fully three-quarters of four-year college and university faculty who hold traditional (full-time tenured or tenure-track) appointments are at least moderately skeptical. In total, slightly more than one-third (34%) register as high scorers on Religious Skepticism. Another four in ten (41%) are moderate scorers, and 25 percent are low scorers.

As would be expected, those who consider themselves neither spiritual nor religious are the most likely to be religiously skeptical, with nearly nine in ten registering as high scorers and none registering as low scorers. Similarly, 99 percent of "spiritual but not religious" faculty score at least moderately on Religious Skepticism. More surprisingly, nearly four in ten "religious but not spiritual" faculty are also high scorers, and fully six in ten faculty who identify, at least to some extent, as both spiritual and religious exhibit at least moderate levels of religious skepticism (see Figure 5.7).

Demographically, the largest proportions of highly skeptical faculty are those who characterize their professional interests as "very heavily in research" (55%), who are politically liberal (44%), and who identify as LGBT (42%). On the whole, male and female faculty are similarly inclined with respect to indicating high levels

FIGURE 5.7 RELIGIOUS SKEPTICISM HIGH AND LOW SCORERS BY SPIRITUAL/
RELIGIOUS SELF-IDENTITY

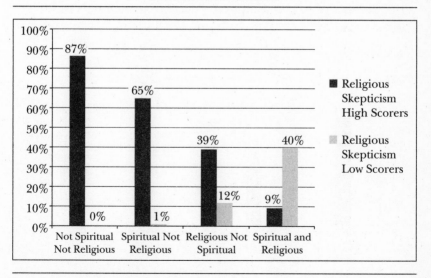

Source: 2012 Faculty Beliefs and Values Survey

of religious skepticism. Across disciplines, however (and in keeping with Religious Commitment and Religious Engagement patterns), female faculty are more likely than their male colleagues to be moderate scorers on skepticism (44% vs. 38%) and less likely to be low scorers (23% vs. 28%). On the whole, African American faculty and those who are politically conservative are the least likely to register as high scorers on Religious Skepticism (10% and 6%, respectively). Roughly one-quarter of those who consider themselves politically moderate are high scorers on Religious Skepticism; just over one-third are low scorers (see Figure 5.8).

The highest proportions of highly religiously skeptical faculty (roughly 40%) are employed at public colleges and universities and at nonsectarian colleges. At private universities, approximately one-third (35%) are high scorers on Religious Skepticism, as are roughly one-quarter or less at Catholic or "Other" faith-based institutions (illustrated in Figure 5.9).

Across institutional types, faculty in the biological sciences are considerably more likely than their colleagues in other disciplines/

FIGURE 5.8   RELIGIOUS SKEPTICISM HIGH AND LOW SCORERS BY
POLITICAL VIEWS

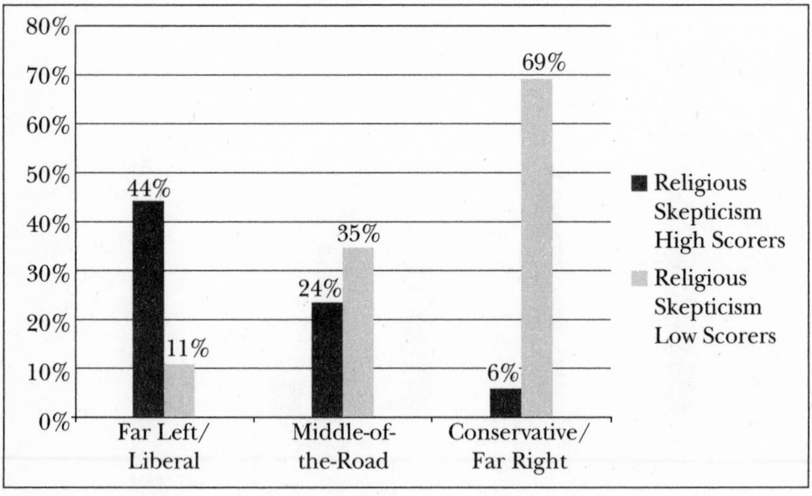

Source: 2012 Faculty Beliefs and Values Survey

fields to be religious skeptics, with just over half (53%) registering as high scorers. More than four in ten physical sciences faculty (43%) also score high on Religious Skepticism. Engineering faculty, however, are the most likely to score at least moderately on Religious Skepticism as reflected by the fact that just 10 percent are low scorers, compared to 15 percent of biological sciences faculty and 17 percent of social sciences faculty. In keeping with their high levels of religious engagement and commitment, health sciences and education faculty are the *least* likely to score high on Religious Skepticism (15% and 18%, respectively). (These results are illustrated in Figure 5.10.)

Once faculty members' personal demographic characteristics are held constant, both the significantly positive correlations between physical, biological, and social sciences affiliation and Religious Skepticism and the significantly negative correlations between education and health sciences affiliation and Religious Skepticism persist. Given the relatively consistent generalized patterns of spiritual/religious inclinations and disinclinations among faulty in different disciplines/fields, these findings are to be expected. The most "balanced" distributions of high and low scorers are found in business and agriculture/forestry, where

FIGURE 5.9 RELIGIOUS SKEPTICISM HIGH AND LOW SCORERS BY
INSTITUTIONAL TYPE

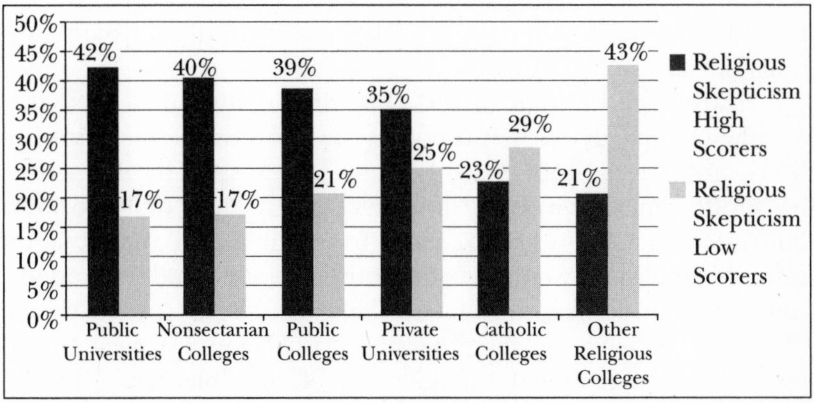

Source: 2012 Faculty Beliefs and Values Survey

Figure 5.10 Religious Skepticism by Academic Discipline/Field

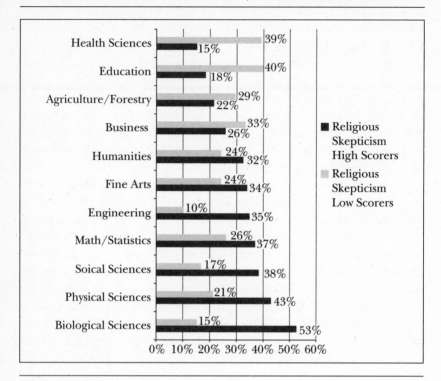

Source: 2012 Faculty Beliefs and Values Survey

roughly one-third of faculty are high scorers and approximately one-quarter are low scorers.

As addressed earlier in this chapter, faculty who self-identify as religious, particularly those who work in nonsectarian institutions and in disciplines or fields where faith is viewed with "scorn" or "indifference," can experience tensions in their daily work. As illustrated in Chapter Two, apart from the belief that religion (and spirituality) are embraced by those who are "muddleheaded," some religiously skeptical faculty take an openly active stance against those who are religious or spiritual, employing a "social justice" rationale based on rejection of the "bigotry," "intolerance," and general "backwardness" of religious believers, especially those who are "dogmatic":

FIGURE 5.11 "MOST RELIGIOUS PEOPLE ARE HYPOCRITES"

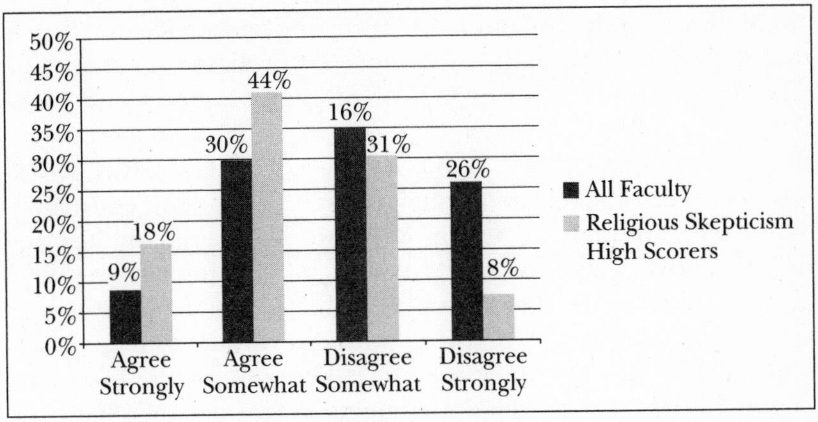

Source: 2012 Faculty Beliefs and Values Survey

Most people use the term "spiritual" or "religious" to define a state of self-righteousness and judgment. Many religious views are in their end point highly destructive. Many organized religious have intolerance and supremacy at their core, and I think that is extremely dangerous.

Those who are highly skeptical are also more (although certainly not uniformly) inclined to endorse the view that "most religious people are hypocrites who don't practice what they believe" (Figure 5.11). High scorers on Religious Skepticism are also less likely than their colleagues as a whole to say that their "spiritual/religious beliefs have been formed through much reflection and searching" (24% vs. 43%). Those who are highly skeptical are also considerably more likely to disagree "strongly" with that statement (34% vs. 14%).

PERSPECTIVES ON SCIENCE AND RELIGION

Nearly half of those who score high on Religious Skepticism conceptualize the relationship between science and religion as one of "independence"; 12 percent consider there to be a "collaborative" association between the two—essentially, each can be used to support the other. By comparison, the dominant view among both moderate and low scorers on Religious Skepticism is that the relationship between science and religion is one of collaboration. More than one-half of moderate scorers and more than three-fourths of low scorers endorse such a conceptualization. Most others (39% of moderate scorers and 16% of low scorers) view science and religion as independent constructs. Those who are high scorers on Religious Skepticism are also the most likely to view science and religion as being in conflict (39%) and to characterize themselves as siding in favor of science. A very small percentage of those who are moderately skeptical embrace the same perspective (4%). Very few faculty both conceptualize science and religion as being in conflict and characterize themselves as siding in favor of religion; just 3 percent of low scorers on Religious Skepticism and 1 percent of moderate scorers endorse that perspective (see Figure 5.12).

As expected, there are notable variations in faculty perspectives on the relationship between science and religion based on academic discipline/field. Those in applied fields, such as education, the health sciences, agriculture/forestry, and business, tend, on the whole, to be considerably more likely than their disciplinary colleagues to endorse a collaborative conceptualization of the relationship between science and religion. In contrast, faculty in the biological, physical, and social sciences are notably more inclined to view science and religion as independent. There are faculty in every discipline who view the two constructs as being in conflict and who describe themselves as favoring either science or religion. Exclusively science-oriented biases are most prevalent within engineering, math/statistics, and the biological sciences, whereas strong religion-oriented biases are most prevalent (albeit reflecting a very slim percentage of faculty) in health sciences (see Table 5.5).

Relative to their colleagues as a whole, faculty who are high scorers on Religious Skepticism also tend to be the most likely to say that believing in supernatural phenomena is foolish (69%) and that trying to discover the purpose of existence is futile (49%). Those who are highly skeptical also say that, to a "great"

FIGURE 5.12 PERCEIVED RELATIONSHIP BETWEEN SCIENCE AND RELIGION BY
RELIGIOUS SKEPTICISM SCORE

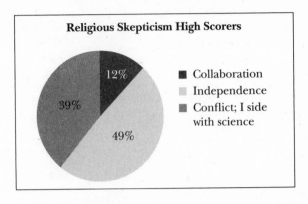

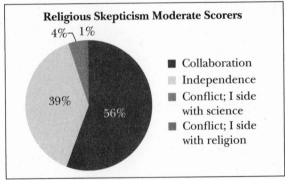

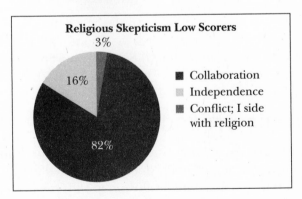

Source: 2012 Faculty Beliefs and Values Survey

TABLE 5.5 RELATIONSHIP BETWEEN SCIENCE AND RELIGION BY ACADEMIC
DISCIPLINE/FIELD (PERCENTAGES)

	Collaboration	Independence	Conflict (Consider Myself on Side of Science)	Conflict (Consider Myself on Side of Religion)
Education	63.7	28.3	6.4	1.7
Health Sciences	62.6	28.1	5.2	4.1
Agriculture/ Forestry	60.0	30.9	7.3	1.8
Business	56.2	29.3	13.0	1.4
Humanities	48.9	36.8	13.8	0.5
Fine Arts	47.7	34.4	16.8	1.0
Engineering	44.6	33.2	21.8	0.5
Math/Statistics	41.7	36.3	21.0	1.0
Social Sciences	40.1	41.8	17.9	0.3
Physical Sciences	37.6	43.0	18.6	0.8
Biological Sciences	27.0	48.9	23.8	0.3

Source: 2012 Faculty Beliefs and Values Survey

extent, they believe in nothing beyond the physical world. Asked to characterize their current views about spiritual/religious matters, high scorers on Religious Skepticism were most likely to indicate "not interested" (51%) or "secure" (39%).

RELIGIOUS STRUGGLE

Religious Struggle is a composite measure of the individual's responses to seven survey items: feeling unsettled about spiritual and religious matters; feeling disillusioned with religious upbringing; struggling to understand evil, suffering, and death; questioning religious/spiritual beliefs; having felt angry with God (within the previous two years); having felt distant from God (within the previous two years); and disagreeing with family about religious matters.

On the whole, college and university faculty do not tend to be heavily engaged in religious struggle. The largest proportion (49%) score moderately on Religious Struggle, and just 10 percent are high scorers. The remaining 42 percent are low scorers. Clear-cut variations in the proportions of high scorers based on disciplinary and institutional contexts tend to be minimal, as do notable demographic differences. However, one exception to that pattern is LGBT faculty, 15 percent of whom register as high scorers. Also noteworthy is that once demographic characteristics are controlled for, faculty in the humanities, fine arts, and social sciences remain more likely than their colleagues in other disciplines/fields to experience religious struggle. As is true of all the disciplinary/field-based differences addressed in this and previous chapters, the comparatively greater propensity toward spiritual struggling among faculty in these fields warrants additional study. These findings may be at least partially attributable to the selective mix of personality styles among faculty who are drawn to these fields, coupled (especially, in some cases, within the social sciences) with the specific subject matter that is the focal point of an individual's academic work.

Aggregated faculty responses to Religious Struggle items show that, within the past two years, nearly three-quarters of faculty have at least "occasionally" struggled to understand evil, suffering, and death. Roughly half have at least "occasionally" disagreed with family about religious matters, questioned their own religious/spiritual beliefs, and felt distant from God, and slightly over one-quarter indicate having at least "occasionally" felt angry with God (see Table 5.6). Overall, 48 percent of faculty say that, to at least "some" extent, they feel unsettled about religious and spiritual matters (9% feel this way to a "great" extent). Four in ten feel at least somewhat disillusioned with their religious upbringing (12% to a "great" extent).

Provided the option of marking all relevant descriptors, those who are high scorers on Religious Struggle are most likely to describe their current views about religious/spiritual matters as conflicted (50%), seeking (47%), and doubting (26%). Nearly half (45%) are high scorers on Spiritual Quest.

TABLE 5.6 INDICATORS OF FACULTY MEMBERS' RELIGIOUS STRUGGLE
(PERCENTAGES)

	Frequently	Occasionally	Not at All
Struggled to understand evil, suffering, and death	22.2	51.8	26.0
Felt distant from God	14.5	38.3	47.2
Questioned my religious/ spiritual beliefs	14.0	39.7	46.3
Disagreed with family about religious matters	11.8	45.8	42.4
Felt angry with God	3.1	23.7	73.2

Source: 2012 Faculty Beliefs and Values Survey

Conclusion

Writing about how, within U.S. society, religion divides and unites us, Putnam and Campbell (2012) contend that "people are driven to (or repelled by) religion for many reasons—some spiritual, some intellectual, some emotional, some transcendent, some sociological, some liturgical, and some political and moral" (p. 133). Increasingly, they go on to explain, "Religion in America . . . is a domain of choice, churn, and surprisingly low brand loyalty" (p. 148). Unlike the studies conducted by Putnam and Campbell and the Pew Research Center's Forum on Religion & Public Life (2012), the 2012 Faculty Beliefs and Values Survey administration was not designed to evaluate patterns of faculty religiosity over time. However, the profile of faculty members' religious faith and perspectives presented in this chapter does reveal relatively clear distinctions with respect to how members of this faculty cohort differ among themselves on indicators of religious commitment, engagement, skepticism, and struggle. Overall, where overlap exists in the particular types of questions asked, these findings largely affirm earlier accounts of the religious beliefs and behaviors of college professors (see, for example, Gross and Simmons, 2007; Tobin and Weinberg, 2007). Essentially, although not to the same extent as the broader

U.S. adult population, most faculty (and some more strongly than others) embrace religious identity, beliefs, and behavior to at least some extent.

As addressed in this chapter, the tensions and occasional discrimination that some religious faculty encounter within their academic workplaces reflect some of the key challenges that religiously oriented faculty may experience in striving to create a life where personal and professional aspects are fully integrated. This is particularly true for Evangelical faculty, faculty of "minority" faiths, and faculty of any faith within particular disciplinary (physical, biological, and social sciences) and institutional (non-faith-based) contexts. The challenges and sometimes clearly oppositional encounters experienced by faculty whose religious faith is a core aspect of their lives are not necessarily surprising given the evolution of higher education in the United States and, particularly, what Smith (2003) describes as the "secular revolution" in which safeguarding freedom from religious pressures became a unifying theme among members of the academy.

Indeed, considerations of spiritual and religious forms of diversity are often less prominently prioritized than other diversity-related considerations within college and university environments. However, they represent a critical point of focus with respect to cultivating academic work environments that are characterized by the mutual respect, collegiality, and social support that the overwhelming majority of faculty say they value highly. As Sandage, Dahl, and Harden (2012) explain, spiritual and religious forms of diversity are "among the most sensitive due to the activation of ultimate concerns and ideals" (p. 59). At the same time, the very nature of the issues they relate to can provide valuable opportunities for enhancing intercultural development and competence in academic workplaces.

CHAPTER SIX

EQUANIMITY

Equanimity can be equated with a dynamic state of internal equilibrium, or mental and emotional balance. Internally, equanimity is characterized by a sense of calmness and peace. Outwardly, equanimity is reflected by an individual's poise, especially under pressure. As detailed in *Cultivating the Spirit* (Astin, Astin, and Lindholm, 2011b), equanimity plays an important role in the quality of people's lives because it shapes how they respond to their experiences, especially those that are potentially stressful or anxiety producing. Those who are able to remain clear minded and otherwise at ease in the midst of turmoil are also more resilient in the face of adversity and more adaptable to major and minor life changes. Writing particularly about college students, Astin and Keen (2006) contend that, ultimately, the capacity to "frame and reframe meaning . . . in the face of ambiguity, uncertainty, and change and, in particular, in the face of dislocating challenge" while maintaining "a deep sense of composure and centeredness" is a critical determinant of the quality of one's life (p. 4). The same can be said for college faculty. For example, in describing her personal conception of spirituality, one faculty member offered:

> Being spiritual to me means being mindful of the many wonders life has to offer. It is very easy to get caught up with the "harriedness" of everyday life and the constant stress of feeling behind, inadequate, and tired. Being spiritual means "stopping" and truly experiencing what is before you and being grateful for having had the good sense to do so.

Other faculty noted that it is the spiritual dimension of our lives that most directly "reflects our humanity"—essentially, it is the "most real part of me" that "keeps the rest of my being (physical, mental/intellectual, and emotional) together and centered." As some faculty elaborated, being "fully present and attentive" and "remembering to take time each day to find peace within myself" takes "hard work and persistence." That effort, however, has the potential to offer tremendous reward not only with respect to being better able to find "awe and sacredness" in the midst of otherwise seemingly "mundane" activities but also with respect to cultivating a sense of equanimity in one's personal and professional lives. For some, retaining "reasonable detachment from and perspective on life" is also a primary consideration for sustaining a state of centeredness and calm in the midst of life's inevitable trials and tribulations. Others define the essence of their life success in terms of equanimity, including one faculty member who equates success in life with the degree to which one can maintain "unruffled peace and serenity in the face of all that confronts you."

The Equanimity measure that our Spirituality in Higher Education research team developed comprises five items. The first two query how often ("frequently," "occasionally," or "not at all") the individual—per his or her own estimation—is able to find meaning in times of hardship and feels at peace, or centered. The other three items ask respondents to indicate the extent to which ("to a great extent," "to some extent," or "not at all") each of the following descriptors are personally characteristic: "I feel good about the direction in which my life is headed"; "I see each day, good or bad, as a gift"; and "I am thankful for all that has happened to me."

Overall, 32 percent of faculty register as high scorers on Equanimity. Another 58 percent are moderate scorers; 10 percent are low scorers. Generally speaking, those who characterize themselves as both spiritual and religious are comparatively more likely to score high on Equanimity than colleagues who consider themselves spiritual but not religious, religious but not spiritual, or neither spiritual nor religious (see Figure 6.1). However, regardless of their spiritual/religious self-identity (or lack thereof), those who score high on the Spiritual Self-Identification measure are

FIGURE 6.1 EQUANIMITY HIGH AND LOW SCORERS BY SPIRITUAL/RELIGIOUS SELF-IDENTITY

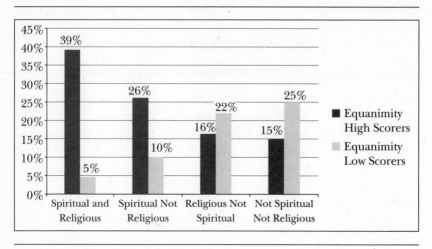

Source: 2012 Faculty Beliefs and Values Survey

considerably more likely to be high scorers on Equanimity (47%) than their colleagues who are moderate (26%) or low (15%) scorers.

In keeping with previous findings on college students, the Equanimity measure for faculty is correlated relatively strongly with Spiritual Self-Identification ($r = .42$). Figure 6.2 illustrates variations in how faculty members who are high, moderate, and low scorers on the Spiritual Self-Identification measure respond to the individual items that constitute the Equanimity measure. The greatest response disparities are evident between the proportions of low and high scorers who see each day, good or bad, as a gift; have been able to find meaning in times of hardship; and who are thankful for all that has happened to them.

Parallel to Astin and Keen's college student findings (2006), the Equanimity measure for faculty correlates relatively strongly with other clusters of items that reflect the faculty members' degree of religious commitment ($r = .44$) and religious engagement ($r = .38$). The spiritual and religious inclinations of faculty who obtain high scores on Equanimity are further evidenced in the substantial correlations of Equanimity with such variables as

FIGURE 6.2 EQUANIMITY INDICATORS BY SPIRITUAL
SELF-IDENTIFICATION SCORE

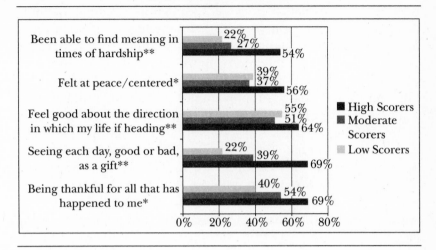

*"Frequently"
**"To a Great Extent"

Source: 2012 Faculty Beliefs and Values Survey

"feeling connected to God/Higher Power" (r = .48), "believing in the sacredness of all life" (r = .39), and "seeking opportunities to grow spiritually" (r = .39). Additional positive correlations are evident between Equanimity and the faculty member's degree of charitable involvement (r = .28) as well as the value a faculty member places on "becoming a more loving person" (r = .31), "knowing my purpose in life" (r = .31), "attaining inner harmony" (r = .25), and "improving the human condition" (r = .23).

Not surprisingly, there tends to be a relatively strong correlation between one's sense of Equanimity and the feeling that one's life has a clear sense of direction (r = .41). Faculty with high scores on Equanimity also tend to report that they are comparatively more optimistic (r = .36), resilient (r = .23), and socially self-confident (r = .21) than others their age. Equanimity is also modestly (negatively) related to feeling that one's life is filled with stress and anxiety (r = −.19). Faculty members' sense of equanimity tends to be bolstered, at least in part, by having a supportive network of friends and family outside of academe (r = .27).

Faculty engagement in spiritual/religious practices such as prayer (r = .31), reading sacred texts (r = .30), doing other reading on religion or spirituality (r = .28), religious singing/changing (r = .28), self-reflection (r = .25), and meditation (r = .25) also tend to equate with higher levels of equanimity.

Demographically, higher proportions of African American (49%) and Hispanic (38%) faculty register as high scorers on Equanimity (compared, for example, to 32% of non-Hispanic whites and 31% of Asians). Overall, women are more likely than men to be high scorers (35% vs. 30%). Although marital status does not differentiate high scorers, having children does; 34 percent of those with children are high scorers, compared to 27 percent of those without children. Reaffirming that, for most people, it takes time and experience to develop the maturity to approach life with a sense of inner calm and quiet confidence, faculty who are sixty-five years or older are more likely than their younger colleagues in every age group to score high on Equanimity (39% vs. 29% of those under thirty-five years old). On the whole, political conservatives are also substantially more likely to register as Equanimity high scorers (50% vs. 34% of those who are politically moderate and 27% of liberals).

With respect to contextual associations, faculty at nonsectarian colleges and public universities are less likely to register as high scorers on Equanimity, whereas those at faith-based institutions are, in the aggregate, the most likely to be high scorers (see Figure 6.3).

Looking across academic disciplines/fields, faculty in most applied fields, particularly those in the health sciences and education, are markedly more inclined than colleagues in math/ statistics, engineering, and the physical, social, and biological sciences to be Equanimity high scorers (see Figure 6.4). Once the potential effects of faculty demographic characteristics are held constant, no significant negative correlations between disciplinary/ field affiliation and Equanimity remain. In other words, there is no particular academic discipline/field in which faculty at large are necessarily low scoring on Equanimity indicators. Upon holding demographic characteristics constant, however, significant positive correlations between affiliation with the education, health science, and business fields remain. Why, exactly, this is so

FIGURE 6.3 EQUANIMITY HIGH AND LOW SCORERS BY INSTITUTIONAL TYPE

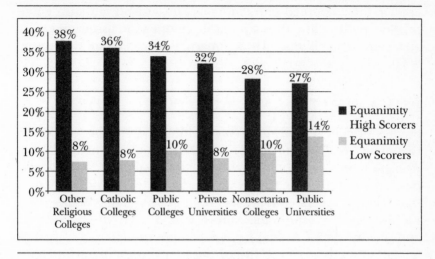

Source: 2012 Faculty Beliefs and Values Survey

FIGURE 6.4 EQUANIMITY HIGH AND LOW SCORERS BY ACADEMIC
DISCIPLINE/FIELD

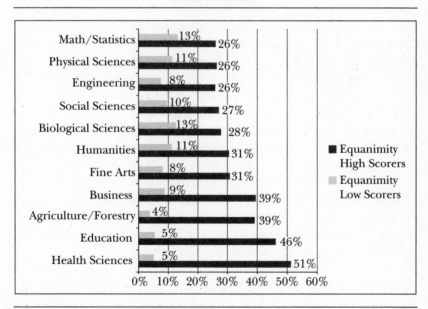

Source: 2012 Faculty Beliefs and Values Survey

is unclear. Common among these three fields, however, is an applied focus coupled with tendencies toward "social" and "enterprising" personality types among those drawn to associated work and study (see Biglan, 1973; Smart, Feldman, and Ethington, 2000).

EQUANIMITY AND ACADEMIC WORK

Studies of college and university faculty have shown recurrently that many are drawn to academic work through strong, and often primary, desires not only for intellectual challenge, growth, and discovery but also for the relative independence and autonomy that faculty careers enable (see, for example, Finkelstein, 1984; Lindholm, 2001; Lindholm, Astin, Sax, and Korn, 2002; Sorcinelli and Austin, 1992). As one faculty member interviewed as part of an earlier study noted, "One of the best things about my job is the ability to do *what* I want, *when* I want, and *how* I want." Closely linked to a strong personal desire for autonomy is an expressed passion for the "spirit of individuality" and "sense of personal independence" that faculty work affords. Also attractive is the "boundless freedom" within academic contexts to pursue intellectual puzzles and lines of research inquiry that are "inherently interesting" and "personally engaging." The value of "pursuing knowledge for its own sake" and "having a flexible schedule" also tend to be featured prominently as appealing characteristics of faculty work. Opportunities specifically for teaching and research as well as "being around different, interesting people" also tend to be featured prominently both as initial motivations for pursuing academic work and as sustaining features that make professorial work appealing (Lindholm, 2001). As illustrated in Figure 6.5, these same aspects were also viewed as "essential" considerations among 2012 Faculty Beliefs and Values Survey respondents. Other "essential" considerations—albeit for notably smaller proportions of faculty—include opportunities for mentoring others (18%) and influencing social change (15%).

Another prominent theme with respect to the attractiveness of professorial careers is the opportunity for pursuing intrinsically meaningful work (see, for example, Austin, Sorcinelli, and McDaniels, 2007; Rice, Sorcinelli, and Austin, 2000). Overall, more than

FIGURE 6.5 "ESSENTIAL" ASPECTS OF AN ACADEMIC CAREER

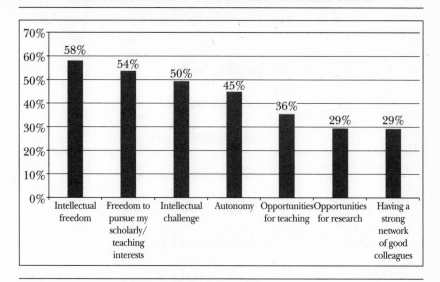

Source: 2012 Faculty Beliefs and Values Survey

seven in ten faculty (78%) who responded to the 2012 Faculty Beliefs and Values Survey say that "to a great extent" they are grateful to be involved in the type of work they do and that their work adds meaning to their lives (74%). Similar proportions say that "to a great extent" they are passionate about their work most of the time (74%) and experience joy in their work (71%). Underscoring the inherent autonomy of traditional faculty roles, roughly two-thirds say that "to a great extent" they have intentionally focused their career in personally meaningful ways (67%). Roughly half or more indicate that they are fulfilling a calling through their work (56%) and that they see connections between their work and the betterment of society (49%). Just under half (45%) of faculty say that "to a great extent" they are comfortable expressing their whole selves authentically at work. If given the opportunity to retrace their steps, less than one-third (30%) would choose to work at a different institution. Even fewer (18%) would choose a different profession entirely. Faculty who score high on the Equanimity measure are two to three times more

FIGURE 6.6 FACULTY WORK PERCEPTIONS (AGREE "TO A GREAT EXTENT") BY
EQUANIMITY SCORE

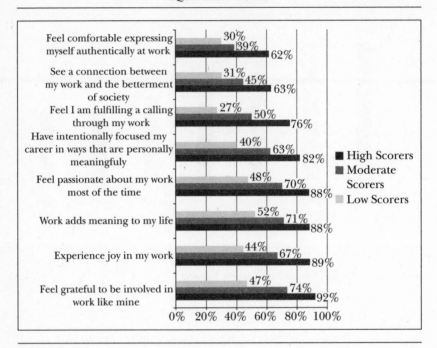

Source: 2012 Faculty Beliefs and Values Survey

likely than their low-scoring colleagues to respond affirmatively
to each of these items (see Figure 6.6).

CONTRIBUTORS TO FACULTY MEMBERS' SENSE OF EQUANIMITY

For many high scorers on Equanimity, "centeredness in my professional life comes from my spiritual life." Work environments that
are characterized by acceptance, collegiality, and respect for the
multifaceted aspects of faculty members' lives (that is, environments that reflect a strong ethic of caring and a predominately
ecumenical worldview among faculty) can contribute to promoting equanimity. For many faculty, healthy work-life integration
and values congruence are also key.

VALUES CONGRUENCE

The degree of congruence that exists between the fundamental characteristics of individuals, including their values, and the fundamental characteristics of their workplaces is an important consideration in determining person-organization fit (see, for example, Kristoff, 1996; O'Reilly, Chatman, and Caldwell, 1991; Posner, 1992). Faculty self-perceptions of the fit between themselves and their institutional work environments are predicated on a complex set of relationships between their personal values, needs, and attributes and the corresponding values, needs, and attributes of their academic units and the broader campus environment. High scorers on Equanimity are more likely than their lower-scoring colleagues to indicate that they experience close alignment both between their work and personal values ($r = .27$) and between their own values and the values of the college or university that employs them ($r = .23$). For example, whereas roughly three-quarters (76%) of those who score high on Equanimity report that, "to a great extent," they experience close alignment between their work and personal values, markedly lower proportions of moderate scorers (56%) and low scorers (34%) report the same. Relative to their lower-scoring counterparts, notably higher proportions of faculty who score high on Equanimity also "agree strongly" that they experience congruence between their own values and the values of their employing institution (illustrated in Figure 6.7).

Overall, more than eight in ten faculty (86%) say that achieving congruence between personal and institutional values is at least "somewhat" important to them, including 38 percent who view such congruence as "very important" and another 13 percent who consider it "essential." For these individuals, a "high quality work life necessarily entails the alignment of personal, professional, and institutional values and priorities." Knowing that "one's core values can be expressed" and that the "enactment of those values will be respected, appreciated, and rewarded" is also an important consideration. Describing the type of workplace he most appreciates, one faculty member explained:

> It is [an environment] that is in harmony with one's deepest held identity and the values and meanings operating with that identity.

Figure 6.7 Experience Congruence Between Own Values and Institutional Values, by Equanimity Score

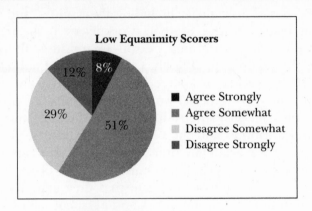

Low Equanimity Scorers

8%
12%
29%
51%

- Agree Strongly
- Agree Somewhat
- Disagree Somewhat
- Disagree Strongly

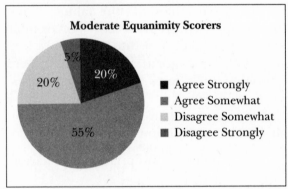

Moderate Equanimity Scorers

5%
20%
20%
55%

- Agree Strongly
- Agree Somewhat
- Disagree Somewhat
- Disagree Strongly

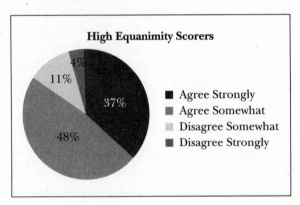

High Equanimity Scorers

4%
11%
37%
48%

- Agree Strongly
- Agree Somewhat
- Disagree Somewhat
- Disagree Strongly

Source: 2012 Faculty Beliefs and Values Survey

Institutional "compatibility with one's deepest values and clearest goals in life" is important in that it serves to reaffirm for faculty the "work I do and the person I am." Not surprisingly, when faculty are not "pushed to compromise personal values" and do not feel a need to "sacrifice my sense of self" while at work, they are considerably more inclined to "wake up every morning wanting to go to work." When faculty can engage in activities that are a "reflection and outgrowth" of their personal values, and when they can engage with institutional colleagues who not only "share and contribute to my values, perspectives, and commitments" but also "respect and accept individual differences," they tend to experience their personal and professional lives as being more "well integrated." The inevitable occasional tensions between work and life are also perceived as "less stressful." Within the workplace, that sense of integration also contributes to feeling both "compelled" and "empowered" to contribute more fully.

In part, the level of congruence that develops depends, at least in part, on processes that orient newcomers to a given work environment, including organizational socialization, or the process by which individuals "acquire the attitudes, behavior, and knowledge needed to participate as an organizational member" (Van Maanen and Schein, 1979, p. 210). Organizational members are socialized through four distinct processes: developing work skills and abilities, acquiring appropriate role behaviors, adjusting to the work environment and its norms, and learning organizational values (Feldman, 1983). Although socialization is typically viewed as a tool for indoctrinating new organizational members, it is important to remember that socialization is an ongoing and dynamic process. For example, as individuals progress through their careers, they often assume different roles and escalating responsibilities that necessitate periods of learning and adjustment. Moreover, because the actors and external forces that affect workplaces and the people within them are not static, socialization may recur over the course of one's organizational affiliation as the needs, expectations, and values of the institution's constituencies change and the sociohistorical context evolves over time. Supportive colleagues can play an important role in facilitating socialization processes and, as described in the next section, also contribute to promoting equanimity.

Supportive Colleagues

As discussed in Chapter Four, collegiality is a core element of academic work, one which, for many faculty, is both a compelling motivation for pursuing professorial work and a source of work-related satisfaction over the course of their career. As shown in Figure 6.8, compared to their lower-scoring counterparts, faculty who are high scorers on Equanimity are more likely to report that "to a great extent" they have departmental colleagues who value their teaching, research, and service contributions; who care about their well-being; and who generally respect the expression of diverse values and beliefs. In explaining her conception of a high-quality workplace as one where "each member of the community feels like he or she is doing valuable work, is appreciated for that valuable work, and is grateful to others for the valuable work that they perform," one faculty member noted:

FIGURE 6.8 COLLEAGUE PERSPECTIVES (AGREE TO "A GREAT EXTENT") BY EQUANIMITY SCORE

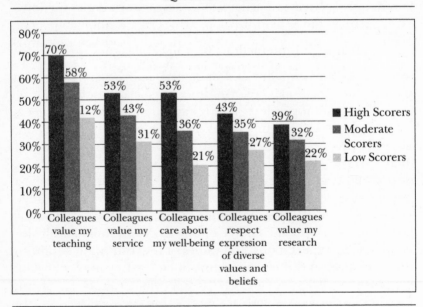

Source: 2012 Faculty Beliefs and Values Survey

I really like my colleagues in every corner of the university and will move chairs with the physical plant staff, teach PE with the coaches, fund raise with administrative staff, attend lectures with the science faculty, choreograph for the fine arts faculty, talk politics with the economists, and talk about child-raising and community matters with so many fine colleagues.

"Active," "engaged," and "enthusiastic" colleagues who "respect," "hear," "support," and "help" each other, who are "friendly" and "want to help you succeed," and with whom you can be "authentic" and otherwise enjoy a "sense of camaraderie" contribute significantly to faculty members' own quest to "learn and grow" and contribute significantly to creating what many faculty characterize as a high-quality institutional work environment. One faculty member elaborated:

A high quality work environment is one where you experience academic freedom, share an appreciation for colleagues' work and have colleagues who are collaborative and with whom you can discuss research projects and other issues of an academic nature. It is also important to have leadership that appreciates the work of the members of the department, is open to suggestions, and objective in assigning duties and awarding perks.

"Being able to combine my personal and professional life by having meaningful interactions with my colleagues on both personal and professional matters" contributes to the "enjoyment" that some faculty experience in their institutional work environments and supports faculty efforts to establish and sustain a positive work-life balance. Especially in challenging economic times when institutional resources are in short supply, the value of a "team oriented environment" that is characterized by generally "positive and upbeat attitudes from colleagues ('can do' spirit rather than complaining and negativity)" can be especially instrumental in promoting faculty members' sense of equanimity. As one faculty member noted,

While I don't need to be friends with all my colleagues, having several good friends that I work with is important to me. And PLEASE less work gossip and rumor mongering!!!!!!

More than two-thirds (68%) of faculty who score high on Equanimity, compared to just under half (48%) of low

Equanimity scorers, also agree "strongly" that, within their academic careers, they have had at least one mentor whose influence has had a lasting impact.

Taken together, these sentiments from 2012 Faculty Beliefs and Values Survey respondents echo previous research findings pertaining to the central roles that collegiality and community play in promoting positive faculty outcomes within academic work environments (see, for example, August and Waltman, 2004; Austin, Sorcinelli, and McDaniels, 2007; Bozeman and Gaughan, 2011; Ponjuan, Conley, and Trower, 2011). Indeed, as was also highlighted in Chapter Four, for many faculty—especially those who are new to their roles and, particularly within that subset, women and faculty of color—knowing that colleagues value their presence, perspectives, and contributions can contribute to enhanced spiritual well-being as reflected, at least in part, through one's sense of equanimity.

HEALTHY WORK-LIFE INTEGRATION

"Feeling overwhelmed by all I have to do" and "feeling that my life is filled with stress and anxiety" are common faculty laments; just 13 percent of Faculty Beliefs and Values Survey respondents (primarily very senior faculty) say that they "never" experience such emotions. The higher education literature prominently features issues related to potentially stress-inducing aspects of faculty work (see, for example, Berrett, 2012; Eddy and Gaston-Gayles, 2008; Hendel and Horn, 2008; Lindholm and Szelényi, 2008) and to the value of establishing (and sustaining) a healthy degree of work-life integration, or balance (see, for example, Gappa, Austin, and Trice, 2007; O'Meara, Teroksy, and Neumann, 2008; Philipsen, Bostic, and Mason, 2010).

Exemplifying the struggle that many faculty experience in trying to balance multiple priorities, one 2012 Faculty Beliefs and Values Survey respondent explained:

> My professional life and schedule are incompatible with being centered and calm. I am so busy that I can't imagine how to find time to do most self-care or to be introspective in the way I need or want to. I can seldom find time to read and going to church every week to sing is an act of defiance against the culture we live

in. I find there is little time for gratitude, for rejoicing or worship in community. I believe the institution does everything it can to support my development in these areas but the life I lead . . . not enough money, teaching full-time, trying to make art, and to have a career, taking care of my parents and two children, my husband and myself working full time, is impossible. Once I was in the midst of it I don't know how to give any of it up . . . can't live without making my art, want to be a successful teacher, can't tell my parents I don't want to take care of them or give my children back but I feel trapped because the lifestyle often feels like it is killing me spiritually and physically. I just repeat to myself over and over again that I love all that I do, but it is just too much. I also try and remember gratitude for having a job and children. I just hope that it doesn't kill me before or as soon as I retire.

Others offered similar insights:

I constantly have to make choices between what I could call the ordering of my loves and identities. Should I be a good professor and work more on this paper or a good parent and spend more time with my children? Should I be a good professor and spend additional time talking to students or should I be a good husband and hurry home to help or spend time with my wife? Should I spend more time engaging in writing that may make a contribution to the political life of our nation or should I spend more time and energy devoted to serving my church? I'm constantly having to make decisions about the ordering of my loves and identities.

I am a good citizen, good wife and mother, and a valued colleague who contributes both intellectually and professionally to my department and students. I am happy in all aspects of my world, but wish I had more time to balance work/home demands.

Refrains of "too much work and too little time" were commonly expressed, as were associated concerns related to how, within academic culture, "busyness" is "assumed to reflect professional seriousness and value." The "compulsory workaholism we seem to be expected to model for our students" coupled with personal struggles to balance "ambition and the drive to succeed versus calm and selflessness" were also commonly noted:

Research universities tend to reward faculty for behaving in self-centered ways, constantly striving to achieve, acquire, and seek

> recognition and to be unbalanced—devoting more time and energy to work, which leaves less time for family/friends/ community involvement and less time for rest and renewal. This is contrary to my understanding of the goals of a spiritual life.
>
> My professional life demands of me a dedication of time and energy that conflicts with my personal and religious values. I feel that in order to succeed professionally, one needs to worship the profession as a god in itself.

As explained in Chapter Three, many professors view their work as a calling. Although there are many potential benefits associated with that conceptualization, one potential downside is vulnerability to viewing one's work as being of ultimate importance in one's life (Dik and Duffy, 2012). Dik and Duffy explain that passion for one's work, coupled with perceiving that work to have considerable importance and value and feeling enhanced positive regard for oneself when engaged in those professional pursuits, can lead to workaholism.

To be sure, faculty who score high on Equanimity are not immune from feeling overwhelmed or experiencing stress and anxiety in the midst of juggling multiple and sometimes competing personal and professional responsibilities. However, high scorers on Equanimity are less inclined than their lower-scoring colleagues to report feeling overwhelmed "to a great extent" (27% vs. 39% of moderate scorers and 48% of low scorers). High equanimity scorers are also less likely to "frequently" feel that their lives are filled with stress and anxiety (18% vs. 32% of moderate scorers and 47% of low scorers). By extension, those who score high on Equanimity are less likely than their lower-scoring colleagues to say that "to a great extent" they do not have adequate time to give their personal and/or professional responsibilities the attention that each deserves. Reflecting their capacity for establishing and sustaining a healthy degree of work-life integration, or balance, high Equanimity scorers are also less likely to report that they "need to work an unhealthy amount to succeed" in their careers and are more likely to report that they achieve a healthy balance between their personal and professional lives (see Figure 6.9). As reflected by the relative proportions of high, moderate, and low Equanimity scorers who indicate "not at all" versus

FIGURE 6.9 WORK-LIFE INTEGRATION PERSPECTIVES (AGREE "TO A GREAT
EXTENT") BY EQUANIMITY SCORE

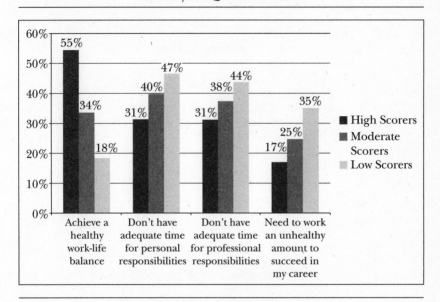

Source: 2012 Faculty Beliefs and Values Survey

"to a great extent," high Equanimity scorers are also less inclined
to feel that success in their professional lives has come at significant expense to their personal lives (Figure 6.10).

Work-life integration (or, as it is often called, work-life balance)
is a central issue for many faculty, and those who are high scorers
on Equanimity consider establishing and sustaining balance to
be an essential consideration in determining how "successful"
they are in life. The following comments offer additional perspective on the "doing my work well, but not so much so that it's all
consuming" sentiments that were commonly expressed by high
scorers:

> Success in life is finding a sense of balance and contentment, and
> being able to devote time and energy to the nurturing of family
> and others close to you. If everyone spent that time, the world

FIGURE 6.10 PROFESSIONAL SUCCESS HAS COME AT THE EXPENSE OF PERSONAL SUCCESS, BY EQUANIMITY SCORE

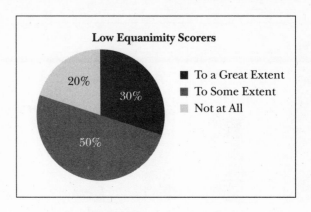

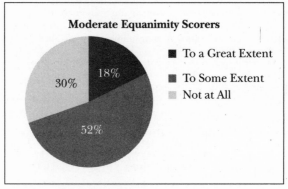

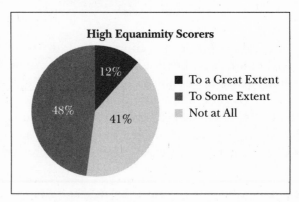

Source: 2012 Faculty Beliefs and Values Survey

would be a much better place. I feel successful because I have been able to draw a line that allows me to feel fulfilled in both.

If one defines success in life as success in my field, I am less successful than I could have been in terms of research/scholarly productivity because I have had such high teaching loads. On the other hand, I feel that I have been successful in life in terms of fulfillment and joy, less stress and anxiety, better health, and a richer (not in monetary terms) personal life. That is, I have struck a better work/life balance than my colleagues at research extensive institutions, so in that regard I have been more successful in life, if not in career.

Success in life is different for each individual. Personally, I measure success as being able to complete what I set out to do; having goals that I have set and accomplished throughout my life but also balancing work with all the rest. Most importantly success is balance. Keeping in mind the trinity—body, mind, and spirit, success is when I have balance and health in all three areas.

Success in life occurs when you have priorities to better yourself and others around you. It requires the setting of goals and a constant balancing act between work, time with family, community service, church obligations, and rest and relaxation. While monetary rewards are important to get through the demands of life, they should not be the top priority and should be shared with others in need. A successful person is one who is respected professionally and personally, and is sensitive to the concerns of others and tries to help in that regard.

ADDITIONAL PERSPECTIVES ON LIFE SUCCESS

Overall, fully two-thirds of respondents to the 2012 Faculty Beliefs and Values Survey agree to at least "some" extent that "compared with most others my age, and with my training, I have been more successful." However, only one-third of faculty members say that success in their professional lives has come "not at all" at the expense of their personal lives. Half say that professional success has "to some extent" compromised success in their personal lives; 17 percent say this is true "to a great extent." As noted earlier, many faculty members—particularly those who register as high scorers on Equanimity—consider a personally determined degree of integration, or balance, between one's personal and professional pursuits to be a critical consideration in determining how successful one is in life. Not unexpectedly, tangible indicators are featured prominently in faculty members' responses, primarily in terms of "a reasonably well paying job" that enables them to provide a "safe home" and "security" for themselves and their families. Many also defined their success in part (or whole) by extrinsic measures that are gauged in terms of "recognition," along with determinations of "how much" and "how many" relative to their peers.

High scorers on Equanimity were more inclined than their lower-scoring colleagues to take time near the end of an already very long survey not only to share their thoughts on life success but also to define "success" in primarily intrinsic ways, noting more materialistic considerations as secondarily relevant (if at all). As one professor shared:

> To be truthful, at times I am aware of appearances and measure what I own against what others own and the prestige of my institution compared to others, but I try not to let this be the sole determinant of my actions. I try to keep this part of my personality in perspective, because I have found that [prioritizing such comparisons] will most likely make me miserable.

In no small measure, faculty who score high on Equanimity tend to characterize success as a life personified by "balance and harmony," "freedom from anxiety," richness of engagement," and "constant growth." Being able to "look forward with excitement and backward with satisfaction" and feeling reasonably confident that you have "done little harm and some good" resonated broadly as core elements of a successful life. As one professor noted, "If today is an improvement relative to yesterday and tomorrow is looking even better, then I am okay." Indeed, "not agonizing about success" and focusing instead on living a life that reflects consistently "the best of who I am and who I can be" contribute to a sense of "groundedness" that enables one to "withstand with grace" the trials and tribulations one inevitably encounters over the course of a career and a lifetime.

Faculty often framed their success-related responses in terms of questions that, if answerable in the affirmative, reaffirm a sense of personal and professional contentment and inner peace. Two of these questions serve as frames for addressing how faculty who enjoy a strong sense of equanimity in their lives view success.

"AM I USING WELL MY TALENTS AND EXPERIENCES?"

One recurrent theme in response to the question, "How do you define success?" centered around considerations related to "finding a match between one's passion and talent and someone else's need," "contributing to my world," and "having a sense that the world values my service." Having the "opportunity to serve others through vocation and avocation" and to "build a legacy that passes on to others" through "reaching out," "supporting," "encouraging," "mentoring," and, ultimately, "making even a small positive difference" in the lives of those whose paths intersect with one's own is a "privilege" for those who measure their success based on how well they have contributed to "enhancing the well-being of others and the planet as a whole." Others' elaborations capture commonly shared sentiments:

> I believe that success relates as much, or more, to inner satisfaction than to wealth. True success is measured in using wisely the gifts one has been given. Success is measured in how we love and encourage others to succeed in a satisfying way. Nothing is more satisfying than to know that we have been a positive influence on the lives and well-being of others. Its greatest realization is to know that we have helped someone be the person they were meant to be . . . personally, spiritually, and professionally.

> For me, there are various measures. I think finding what your passion is and following it—sharing it with others and seeing it make an impact in some way is success. It is also success to see one of my students grow and go on and make a difference in the world. I don't measure success by having a well-paying steady job, although it is nice to have that. If I can share nothing through my job, if I don't impact the world around me in some way and if I don't grow through my job then I don't consider that success. I think success also is reflected in the impact one has on those around you for the better: Do I make a difference? Do I have friends and colleagues who depend upon me or are

better because of their work with me . . . and am I better because of them?

I measure success by the number of lives I feel I have changed. If a student comes into my office and I am able to help them, I feel successful. When I discuss a topic in class and I see the light bulb come on for the students or I see them capture the big ideas in their papers or assignments, I feel successful. When I see students graduate who would not have been able to get a college degree because I created an online program and mentoring system for non-traditional students, I feel successful. When I visit a town anywhere in the state and I find out that one of my graduates is teaching successfully there where before there was an unqualified teacher in that early childhood program, I feel successful. When I see master's students mentoring each other and helping each other in different parts of the state, I feel successful. When I assist in influencing state government policies on behalf of young children and families or write materials for the state that become permanent documents that influence change, I feel successful. Whenever I see change in the social good, I know I am successful.

Commenting specifically about his work with students, another professor remarked:

When I die, I want many students to remember that they learned important things in my class. I'd love for them to think every once in a while in their future life, my prof is guiding me here.

"AM I FULFILLED?"

The second prominent success theme focused on considerations related to how "content," "satisfied," and "at peace" faculty feel when reflecting on their lives and careers. In large part, college and university faculty who score high on Equanimity base their consideration of themselves as successful on *how* they live. "Success is not so much a thing . . . success is really in the way you live now . . . the process of how you live." Noting that she dislikes the term *success* "because it implies some sort of finish to a process," one professor elaborated:

I hope to continue to grow, to be more loving and to be more authentic and to do so in a way that facilitates others also becoming more loving and authentic. I don't think that process ever ends or can be called "successful," so much as it either is going in that general direction, or not.

Living a life that is "true to my beliefs and values," knowing when faced with challenging circumstances that "I am doing the right thing rather than the easiest thing," and being "comfortable with who I am, what I have accomplished, and how I am able to give back to society" were among the most frequently noted foundational elements for "feeling fulfilled in my work and personal life":

> All I have ever wanted was to be in an occupation in which I felt fulfilled personally, spiritually, and intellectually. I have that. I only ever needed to make "enough" money. I make just that, though I do wish it were more. I have wanted to feel happiness, peace, and an active contentment in myself. That is also something I have and continue to manifest regularly. I am content, but actively so . . . meaning that I am conscious of the present, and look for ways to improve upon it to make the future at least the same, if not better.

> Whatever you take on, you have courage, generosity, and faith (in yourself and others). That applies to marriage, raising children, and your career. No matter your failures, you can hold your head up and be proud of your attempts. You have to be able to recognize when you do and when you do not have control over outcomes. Success is the result of how you feel about your own struggle to overcome your weaknesses, forgive others their weaknesses, and use whatever strengths or talents you have to help your family, your colleagues, your community. You may fall flat, but you get right back up and try again.

> Success for me is being able to fall asleep at night without a knitted brow. To be able to wake up each day happy to greet a new day . . . and, throughout each day, to be in harmony with others . . . friendly, courteous, caring . . . also to be productive and fruitful in the work I do . . . not wasting time or opportunities.

"Finding a good fit between myself and my institution," "feeling that where you are is where you're supposed to be," and "being able to pursue your dreams and work toward realizing your potential while having a sense that things are going well" are often key considerations for feeling professionally fulfilled:

For me, professional success has been finding precisely the fit between myself and my institution. I am at the right place, with students who are getting something from me—even though it might be very different things depending on the students. I enjoy my days, mostly reading old books and talking about them with students and colleagues. I am suspicious of people with high ambitions and a strong drive for excellence. I usually suspect that they are insecure and need some kind of validation. I am concerned when institutions utilize such people as models for productivity.

As illustrated through the following remarks, for most faculty—not unexpectedly—determinations of life success are based not only on the state of one's professional life but also on the degree of fulfillment in one's personal life:

> I measure my success by not wishing to change most of what has happened. My choice to be an artist has given me everything that is good and beautiful in my life including my husband, my home, a satisfying career as an artist, the ability to experience the world, and a wonderful place to teach, enabling me to share my insights with, and to be informed by, my students.

> I consider that my life is now is a "success." In my work, I feel as though I am doing what I am called to do in the place that I am called to be. My work is intimately integrated with who I am, and the beliefs that matter most to me, and are the foundation of my life. Outside my work, between good friends, an outstanding church, volunteer activities and hobbies, and with the bedrock of my faith, I am deeply content, in a way that transcends the ups and downs of whatever my day to day circumstances happen to be.

> I feel I am successful because in everything I have done in my professional and personal lives, I have been able to keep my integrity, my values, my priorities. I have raised children who as adults personify the values which are integral to living with social awareness, compassion and responsibility. I have been able to instill in most of my students the ability to look critically but appreciatively at society. I feel successful as a mother and teacher because of this.

As noted earlier, the degree to which faculty feel that they have used their "talents" to nurture the development of their students is a key determinant of success. Indeed, among many faculty who have a considerably strong sense of equanimity, the quality of their relationships—both within the context of their academic work and beyond—is also a primary determinant of success. As one faculty member offered, "I measure my life with the yardstick of being a good friend, colleague, and partner." "Knowing I am there for my family," sustaining "loving, respectful relationships with family, friends, colleagues, and students," and, for parents, "raising happy, healthy children . . . helping them grow into productive, happy, well-balanced adults" are critical considerations for determining one's life success:

> If the people closest to me . . . family, friends, colleagues, students . . . find me to be a graceful, loving, responsible person . . . I consider myself a success.

> I measure success in life by having a career that makes me happy and provides for my and my family's needs, having a loving and supportive family and network of friends and belonging to a great spiritual community. I may not have been the most successful by other measures (reputation—in terms of publishing) or making more money, but that's fine by me.

Finally, for those who are high scorers on Equanimity, fulfillment also stems directly from a sense of "personal satisfaction in knowing I'm doing the best I can toward realizing my potential." Am I, for example, "constantly learning new things and challenging my own beliefs?" Included in such a process-oriented approach to life are "setting and achieving . . . or exceeding . . . the goals I have set for myself," "being able to make stepping stones of obstacles and stumbling blocks along the way," and being "secure in what I do and how to proceed." Doing "meaningful work I enjoy" and, through the conduct of that work and one's broader life "earning the respect of colleagues, administrators, students, friends, and family," provide a cornerstone for success irrespective of potentially perceived professional "shortcomings":

> I am not as successful professionally as I'd like to be; I have published a book, but with a small press, and I am not at all well-known in my field. However, I've had a good deal of success in my teaching, and I feel respected and valued at my institution, which is extremely important. I also have the time and freedom to be a parent and a friend, which is extremely important to me. So

while I often wish I were a better/more prominent writer and had more success in my writing career, I do feel that success in my personal life and here at my institution are equally important.

Ultimately, as one professor offered,

Success for me means knowing that I would do the same things, even if I didn't get a check. I get up each morning saying, "Thanks, God, I get to go to work" . . . not "Oh, God, I have to go to work."

PERSPECTIVES SHARED WITH JUNIOR COLLEAGUES

When asked what advice they would offer to faculty colleagues who are less advanced in their academic careers, associate and full professors who are high scorers on Equanimity offered recommendations for developing and sustaining a meaningful faculty career that centered around six themes: be true to yourself, seek mentoring, contribute wholeheartedly, value your students, practice balance, and maintain perspective while enjoying the journey.

BE TRUE TO YOURSELF

In framing their responses, many faculty acknowledged that today's academic labor market is markedly more challenging than it was at the time most now tenured and senior faculty were beginning their own academic careers, and that the higher education enterprise is in the midst of much ongoing change. As one faculty member noted,

Watch out! You're going to be expected to do more and work harder than those in the past.

Especially in light of these considerations, faculty encouraged their junior colleagues—especially those just starting out—to "make sure this is what you've been called to do," that you are "doing what you love" and are "committed to the long term . . . not just sticking to the path you know best" or that "others have urged you to follow." In short, although "it may seem riskier," "pursue your dreams and don't let others dictate them to you." Others elaborated:

Make your choices based not on what people and the culture around you (including academic culture) tell you is what is most important in life. Make your choices based on what actually is most important in life.

Conduct your life being true to yourself first. Worry less about what others think you should do.

Find the path that suits you rather than finding the path that moves you along in your career.

Make sure you know who you are or else you will become the person that others expect you to be. Remain authentic and true to yourself. Don't give the answers/responses that you think people want to hear but only the ones that you feel are truthful and accurate about who you are.

Find a ballast point on which to place your identity, because the academy can be rough on the psyche.

Don't let the "process" remove your focus on the reason you do what you do.

In making career decisions,

"Trust yourself."

"Avoid getting caught up in academic vanity."

Remember that whatever your field, apart from "working hard," "your success will come in part from your passion . . . let your passion shine."

"Don't be trendy; focus on what truly interests you."

"Do your best to integrate all your values into your academic work."

"Avoid the trap of trying to please somebody else too much in order to be accepted" because "over the long haul, your heart has to be in it."

For example, "write about the stuff you're really connected to" because "counting the number of articles you have written will be a short-lived source of pride." As others commented:

Learn the system and its expectations, but know yourself well enough to develop personal integrity. Make the tough choices about what really means the most to you, and then pursue your own values with grace and tolerance of others.

Remember who you are. Work out of that not for advancement, but for joy.

Go where your passion is leading you! Having a meaningful profession takes discernment, planning, risk, and commitment.

Make sure you want the carrot at the end of the stick . . . and make sure you know what that carrot is.

In terms of institutional work life, faculty encouraged doing one's best to "find a place that fits with you," that "matches your own vision and calling," one "that you understand and that understands you" and "where you can be yourself authentically":

Figure out what kind of academic you want to be, and what kind of life you want to lead both professionally and personally. Do your best to adjust the standards of your institution to your own, rather than vice versa. If you cannot be an academic where you are on something close to your own terms, look for another job or another career.

Be sure that you find an institution where there is congruence between your goals and values and those of the institution. Do not generate unnecessary stress for yourself by being at a place where there is constant friction between institutional values and your own. Try to find a place where you can enjoy your colleagues rather than always operating in tension with them. Do not allow faculty "refuse-niks" to undermine satisfaction and fulfillment in what you do.

Others advised:

"Go with the flow, but try to follow the flow that most interests you."

"If your current institution does not share your values" or if your job otherwise does not "allow you to live meaningfully, be bold and look for one that does."

"If you're not happy, change your life."

"If you enjoy what you are doing, hang in there."

Remember that "it takes a lot of dedication and hard work to be effective," so "be patient, especially with yourself."

"Find what you love and what you are good at" and "spend the most time developing this aspect."

"Take one step at a time" and "learn and hone your skills."

"Be authentic in your work and pursue integrity above praise and approval."

"Don't compare yourself to others, but be the best you can be where you are."

"Focus on who you are more than what you do" and "become comfortable with who you are."

"Don't be afraid of hard work . . . go after it."

Take time as well, though—"especially when you think you don't have the time"—to "take care of yourself."

"Stay grounded in a supportive, engaged community outside of work."

Ultimately, in all you pursue, "be the best you can be and your world will be good."

SEEK MENTORING

Overall, roughly six in ten faculty (61%) agree "strongly" that over the course of their career they have had at least one mentor whose influence has had a lasting impact. Another quarter (27%) say that this is "somewhat" true. There are relatively few empirical studies on the mentoring of professors (see, for example, de Janasz and Sullivan, 2004). However, mentoring has been associated with a variety of positive outcomes, including greater job satisfaction, higher compensation, more positive attitudes about one's work environment, and higher organizational commitment (see, for example, Fagenson, 1989; Higgins and Kram, 2001; Johnson and Ridley, 2004). For those who feel that they have been mentored well, there tends to be resolute agreement that having an "effective" mentor who "respects you," with whom "you share values," and "can talk honestly with about your challenges"—who is willing to "support you emotionally," "give you honest advice for growing," and "help smooth the way"—can make a "tremendous difference in your career success and satisfaction." As one respondent underscored:

> Always find a mentor, and ask for their help and advice. Even the most advanced faculty member is learning every minute

something new . . . even if they do not admit it. Do not feel like you are on an "island" with no one to assist you. If you choose to do that, it is your choice.

Others concurred:

To do good work, you need to have faith in your own insights but you also need someone older and smarter to help guide you.

Find a good mentor. Observe folks who are really good at what they do and find out why. Don't be afraid to ask for help from more experienced colleagues.

Find a person that you admire—someone to whom you can relate. Listen, observe and learn from them.

The importance of life-level connection with colleagues who share one's passion for teaching, for research, and for discussion about life's ups and downs cannot be over-emphasized. Academia can be a lonely place unless one seeks out the help and reassurance of others.

Faculty encouraged colleagues who are less advanced in their careers to "observe folks who are really good at what they do and find out why." "Surround yourself with those who are positive, caring, hard workers who can pull you along with them," and "stay away from the negative people who are primarily ego-centric about their work." In short, strive to "emulate" and "solicit advice" from "those you admire not only because of what they have achieved professionally, but for who they are." As one faculty member shared:

I'd offer the same advice I was given almost ten years ago, find a person who has the LIFE (not just career) you want and use that person as a model.

Others advised:

Try your best to find mentors at your institution and others whose advice you (at least think) you can trust so that they can help you find stability in your knowledge of your discipline and in the politics of your institution. Try to find a balance between fearing that your colleagues are all just self-serving enemies and assuming that they are all benevolent friends. You have to decide for yourself which ones truly fit either of those descriptions.

Observe the behaviors and choices of people who seem satisfied/ healthy in their personal and professional lives. Seek out their input when making professional choices, in addition to those of an academic advisor who might be more knowledgeable about your research area.

Seek out a mentor who has considerable successful experience and who can offer sage advice about strengthening one's teaching, research, and service while carving out significant room for a meaningful personal and family life.

Most important, "don't be afraid to ask for help from more experienced colleagues!" As one professor reminded, "All the giants in the field have trodden through that path and you are not alone."

Contribute Wholeheartedly

Lamenting what they perceive to be the comparatively "selfish and greedy" inclinations of many young faculty, as compared to those of their own generation who "worked very hard to make the department a better place and the institution a better institution," some senior faculty encouraged their more junior colleagues to focus more on "playing well with others," "taking an interest in your college/university community," and "remembering it's not all about you." Others elaborated:

Make all that you do about someone other than yourself. Your job is not you; it is created by you for others' benefit.

Remember how privileged you are to have made it this far. Be grateful and not too self-important!

Appreciate those who have laid the foundation for you. You are not independently successful. Your success is based on lots of people investing in you. Learn from those around you. You may think you know it all . . . but, surprise, nobody knows it all.

Acknowledging pressures to "do what's needed to earn tenure and promotion," contend with what can be "brutal politics" and "toxic situations," and "play the academic game," faculty who enjoy a high level of equanimity in their own lives nonetheless strongly encouraged their more junior colleagues to "not get too hung up on status." "Refuse," as well, to "play the political games that faculty try to impose" and remember that "not all administrators are from the evil side of the universe." Stay focused too on "always seeking to do your best for the students and the institution." As one faculty member noted,

> Although you may very well get ahead in your career by making the right friends and sucking up to [others], it is not an honorable way to advance your career.

Others added:

> Being competitive and self-centered is a waste of energy. Being collaborative and helpful to others is the more important use of time and energy because it is so much better to have many people succeed together than for one person to "succeed" alone. In fact, there is no such thing (in my opinion) of succeeding alone; that would be a contradiction in terms and yet, I have known people who are extremely competitive, constantly comparing themselves to others . . . [As a result] they really have no peace and, consequently, they can't serve their students or others very well.

> Build good professional relationships; take the time to get to know your colleagues; be supportive and collaborative rather than competitive. Identify your professional strengths, and use those strengths to contribute to the goals of the department and the institution in your own unique way. You will be successful in your work. Don't worry about whether the university appreciates you or you are getting paid what you are worth. Just focus on the work you love.

"Putting character before reputation," "respecting, helping, and treating others well," "telling the truth kindly," "collaborating more," and "building meaningful relationships with students and colleagues" will ultimately go further in creating the foundation for a meaningful career than will "seeking creative ways to get others to serve your interests":

> Be a good colleague! Show commitment to the well-being of your department, your students, your co-workers, and your institution. You ought not allow personal priorities (in teaching, research, or professional advancement) to contribute to a climate of dissatisfaction in your workplace. You will gain more professionally from a workplace that is supportive and caring; indeed, in the

long run, you will build enduring relationships that increase in value over the years of a career.

Make sure your colleagues know what you are really about. People can't guess what's inside your mind, so talk to them . . . show them who you are.

Underscoring the importance of not just "building one's own reputation" but also "investing in the lives of your students," "making the most of where you are," and contributing significantly to the "betterment of your home institution," others advised:

Show up every day ready to work and make a positive contribution. We all value faculty who teach with care and diligence, are excited by research and ideas, and are willing to collaborate and share. Absolutely resist the temptation to see teaching as an impediment to doing research; they are, in fact, synergistic.

Try new challenges, look for new ways to work in your field, never reject a chance to work on an interesting project, committee, or new area.

Commitment and motivation are key. If you work hard for the good of the other, contribute for the good of the whole, you will be appreciated and recognized.

Get to know your colleagues in other disciplines. Serve on committees. If you want the college to go in a certain direction, you need to make the effort to steer it there.

Learn to listen and show up. I am a firm believer in the idea that 75 percent of the good things in life are the result of just showing up . . . for the meeting, for the conference, as a volunteer, to ask the question, to help get "it" done.

Finally, within the context of focusing "more on what you can contribute than what you may receive," senior faculty suggested that when you are faced with the inevitable challenges of navigating the course of any career, "Stop whining. Roll up your sleeves and work harder." "Do your best any moment of anything you are asked to do" and "contribute actively" toward making life in your department "both honest and caring." Important too:

Recognize that colleges and universities are rarely places of daring, but with persistence and integrity you can make a difference in this matter.

Keep pushing. Get reinvigorated or engaged. Rediscover afresh the life of the mind beyond the bureaucratic aspects of higher education.

Don't be eaten alive internally by focusing on all the injustices that still remain as they may be related to your less advantageous position. As real as they are, they too are subject to revision. Essential change does not happen overnight.

Someday, maybe soon, you'll be running things. If you don't like things the way they are, be ready for the moment when change becomes possible, on a grand scale.

Value Your Students Highly

Apart from acknowledging the "undeniable importance" of working toward "being an expert in your field" and "mastering your subject matter," faculty who score high on Equanimity are particularly inclined to underscore the importance of strengthening your teaching through "working on skills that make you a better person" and "enhancing your own natural teaching style to make it more effective in meeting the needs of your students":

> The academy is a wonderful place. We are here for our students first. Do your best for them, not for yourself.

> If, when university politics or interpersonal relationships in the department get crazy, you stay focused on the students . . . on their learning . . . on being the best teacher for each of them at their particular point of development . . . the rest will seem much less important and will fall in to perspective.

> Along these same lines,

"Think about the impact of your work on the lives of your students."
"Foster a curiosity about your students as individuals."
Be "patient" and "positive" in your interactions with your students.
"Ask lots of questions."
"Show up fully in the classroom."
Be "creative in your attempts to help students learn."

As one professor noted, "Learn to know and value your students, because they are the individuals you have been called to serve." And, in your work with students, "listen, learn, teach . . . but don't preach":

> The secret of effective teaching is simple: love and nurture your own knowledge and love your students. There is no formula. Adaptation of your ever-growing knowledge and expertise to the needs of the next group of students requires continual reconfiguring. Context is everything.

> Nobody cares how much you know until they know how much you care. If you care about your students and their development deeply, it will make all the difference.

> Demonstrate that you actually care about your students' lives and futures. If you don't do that, you will be losing your most frequent and meaningful chance to make a difference in the lives of others.

> Remember that you have an enormously positive influence on your students, so make sure that you teach them about your mistakes, not just about [your subject matter].

Critical too is "accepting your students where they are" rather than "where you wish they would be":

> Students are never as prepared as you want them to be. What you are teaching is never as easy for students as you think it should be. Enjoy the students who want to interact with you whether they are high or low performers.

> Value all your students, not just the smartest or most assertive. Make no assumption about who is in that lecture hall, laboratory, or studio with you. You will be surprised when, in later years, you discover who was most influenced by your teaching.

> Be aware that the students in your class are indeed someone else's kids, and they are not unlike your own kids. Keep that in mind when you complain about them.

Observing that "today's students are different than those of the past" and that "future students will be different than today's students," senior faculty noted that if you are not "open-minded and willing to adapt," consider changing your career. "Times change, so too must educators." What doesn't tend to change is that "the more you can inspire students, the more rewarding teaching becomes."

PRACTICE BALANCE AND STRIVE FOR WORK-LIFE INTEGRATION

As detailed earlier, faculty encouraged their more junior colleagues to "contribute wholeheartedly." At the same time, however, they also acknowledged that "institutions can be greedy" and underscored the importance of "giving all you can, but knowing your limitations." "You can't be all about work . . . so be sure to set clear boundaries to avoid burnout." Appreciate that you will "need to make sacrifices . . . take responsibility for the evolution of your career . . . consider personal goals as carefully as professional goals . . . and, before making choices, always count the costs as well as the benefits":

> Do your best to manage your time to focus on what is important. Rather than obsessing with "finding a balance in work and life" make that happen yourself by focusing.

> Decide what you're willing to sacrifice; you can't have it all, despite the commercials. Every choice to do something is a choice not to do something else. Throw the Superwoman cape in the laundry now and then. If you're not wearing it, no one expects you to perform as if you were.

> Learn what your limits and boundaries are and learn how to say, "No, thank you." Live with integrity. The needs of an institution are limitless, so make sure you only take on what you can do while remaining productive and happy yourself. What is good for you is good for everyone else. You will be respected if you take care of yourself, and you will be valued if you only do what you can do. Everything will teach you something.

Noting that "how you manage your time is your own business," senior faculty advised their junior colleagues:

"Do not tell everyone what you do all the time . . . and do not devote your life to the job . . . or place all of your self-worth on your career."

"Set boundaries so you develop your career in a way that allows balance between personal and professional goals . . . do not let academic pursuits get in the way of being fully human."

"Seek to achieve balance between work and the whole rest of life that is not work."

Acknowledge that there is "more to life than the life of the mind . . . taking care of relationships is critical," as is "making sure to use parts of your brain that have nothing to do with your career."

Others noted,

Remember there is no such thing as a workaholic job. We choose whether to live in balance or not get rid of what's unimportant.

Be judicious in organizing your time. Be sure to carve out personal time (family, reading, walking, sports, political engagement, volunteering) so that you never feel completely swallowed up by what can be a thankless profession.

At the end of the day, it does not matter how many journal articles or books you have published, if you have missed important moments with your family.

The job will one day end and if you wrap up your entire existence and meaning into your career, then there seems to be nothing left after you have retired. Developing professionally is important, but it should not be the all-consuming aspect of your life.

Make sure you feed your soul . . . strive for some kind of balance in your life and make sure you do what you need to stay healthy (physically, mentally, emotionally) for the long haul.

There will always be a tension between your personal life and your professional life and you will have to occasionally put one out of balance for the short run and then readjust. The important thing is to readjust and to make personal time for yourself with an outlet that fits your needs and keeps in mind all aspects of your health. If you are balanced, you will have the energy to do anything.

MAINTAIN PERSPECTIVE . . . AND ENJOY THE JOURNEY

Many who offered perspectives on career and life to junior colleagues emphasized the importance of "taking a long view" and of being sure, at every stage, to "pace yourself," "persevere," "be resilient . . . bounce, don't break." Remember as well to "learn to appreciate the good things you have achieved" and "learn to be happy where you are and with what you have." Another senior professor noted:

> What will matter most about your career when looking back after 20, 30, or 40 years may not be what seems to matter most at 5, 7, or 10 years. How you deal with setbacks and mistreatment has more to do with your long run success than whether or not you are treated fairly at every turn. Whining and playing the victim will not advance your career or help others respect you. It is easy to wallow in self-pity, but will only lead you in a downward spiral.

Reflecting on their own career paths and lessons learned along the way, others advised:

> At every step, I wanted to reach higher, and thought that I'd be happy once I arrived at the next level. But that was never the case until I realized what a blessed life I have, and that being a professor—no matter where you teach—is a pretty special type of life.

> Pursue what you love with the integrity to follow where it leads. Love the questions more than the answers. Become obsessed and passionate and curious. Cross disciplinary boundaries. Don't identify too strongly with a profession and its standard presuppositions. Care as least you can about fame and position.

> Do not listen to gossip. Do not judge others who are being judged by your circle of friends. Give everyone a chance . . . try to be open-minded politically . . . try to keep in mind how privileged you are. Some of the slights you feel are not really serious impediments or barriers in your success. Don't go around looking for evidence that you are being victimized.

Underscoring that, ultimately, "attitudes have more to do with professional success than training or ability," senior faculty commonly urged their less experienced colleagues to be more "process oriented than goal driven." "Continuing to be a student your whole career," "focusing on the big picture," "being open to criticism and change," and "enjoying your learning experiences" will "serve you well in building a career you are proud to look back on":

Seek advice along the way from people you respect, work steadily and hard, and you'll get where you want to go, even if it seems impossibly distant at the moment. It's easier to say from a point of achievement that the work itself matters more than the benchmarks you aim for, but it really is true—you have to do work you like and like your work.

Above all else, "despite the stress and occasional red tape, enjoy your work." "Do what you love and what you think is right . . . work hard and be creative . . . keep growing, and keep in touch with the bigger world . . . and things will work out." "Be grateful for every day . . . Before you know it, you will be ready to retire."

Conclusion

This chapter has profiled the associations between faculty members' sense of equanimity and aspects of their professorial work lives. Values congruence, supportive colleagues, and work-life balance or integration were featured prominently in faculty members' comments that addressed equanimity-related work connections and tensions. Those who score high on Equanimity tend to define success in terms of the answers to self-reflective questions related to whether they are using their talents and experiences well and the extent to which their pursuits lead them to feel fulfilled. Reflecting back on their own career and life experiences, high scorers on Equanimity offered perspective to junior colleagues centered around the value of being true to oneself, seeking mentoring, contributing wholeheartedly, valuing students highly, and practicing balance and striving for work-life integration.

For many faculty, there can be deeply embedded tensions among personal needs for autonomy, independence, and interdependence. For example, faculty participants in a previous study (Lindholm, 2001) underscored nearly unanimously the importance of having the freedom and privacy to explore the types of work that interest them; maintaining flexibility in setting their schedules; and sustaining the generally loose ties they have with their institution, their respective academic units, and their institutional colleagues. Also apparent, however, was a longing for a more meaningful sense of connectedness within the campus community.

Taken together, the faculty perspectives on equanimity and academic work offered in this chapter, along with those shared regarding the value of connectedness and collegiality (see Chapter Four), reaffirm those earlier findings. Indeed, for many faculty, the value of establishing a "sense of space" within their institutional work environment that is uniquely their own— neither too distant nor too connected with their departmental and institutional colleagues, and where they feel comfortable, respected, and genuinely appreciated for being themselves— should not be underestimated. This is particularly true among those who are less well established in their academic careers and who, regardless of their career stage, are members of historically underrepresented groups within the professoriate. Collegiality and connectedness also tend to be given high priority by faculty who view themselves and their colleagues as institutional citizens who, by definition, have a collective responsibility for creating the character of their units and, by extension, the larger university (Lindholm, 2001).

Beyond the availability of sufficient time, space, and resources to support their teaching and other scholarly work (seemingly always in short supply today), faculty also tend to highlight the importance of institutional colleagues who help stimulate their thinking and offer a sounding board for discussing ideas and dilemmas. Positive collegial exchange can be especially important in that it provides confirmation that one's thinking is sound, one's ideas are interesting, one's approach is reasonable, and one's work is meritorious. Such support, arguably a function of both intellectual exchange and emotional reassurance, offers what many participants in my earlier study (Lindholm, 2001) described as an essential form of reinforcement not only for sustained creative endeavors but also for their sense of belonging within departmental and other institutional contexts. Associations between social-emotional support and faculty well-being, including the spiritually oriented quality of equanimity, tend to be especially important for assistant professors, women, and minority faculty. For these individuals whose representation is less prevalent (especially, in the case of women and minority faculty, within selected fields) and who sometimes hold nonnormative beliefs, values, and approaches to scholarly work, the availability of social-emotional support can help mediate potential feelings of marginality and isolation within the institutional work environment.

CHAPTER SEVEN

HIGHER EDUCATION AND THE LIFE OF THE FACULTY SPIRIT

Spirituality, as we defined it over the course of the Spirituality in Higher Education project, is a multifaceted quality. It involves an active quest for answers to life's "big questions"; a global worldview that transcends ethnocentrism and egocentrism; a sense of caring and compassion for others coupled with a lifestyle that includes service to others; and a capacity to maintain one's sense of calm and centeredness, especially in times of stress. The spiritual and religious measures that have served as focal points for this book, along with accompanying professorial perspectives, help illustrate the degree to which four-year college and university faculty resonate personally with the spiritual/religious dimension of life; how their associated values and beliefs may impact their personal and professional lives; and the implications those orientations may have for students, colleagues, and others with whom they interact. This chapter summarizes key findings, highlights associations between faculty members' spiritual inclinations and undergraduate teaching and learning, and considers more generally faculty members' attitudes about various applications of spirituality within college and university contexts.

SPIRITUALITY AND RELIGION IN THE LIVES OF COLLEGE FACULTY

Beal (2008) advises that we must take care both to "avoid gross generalizations about religion in America" and to "remember that behind every sweeping distinction and statistic are very particular local persons and groups whose stories are in many ways absolutely unique, even when they have much in common with others" (pp. 27–28). The same counsel holds true when considering the spiritual and religious lives and perspectives of college and university faculty.

As reflected in their responses both to the 2012 Faculty Beliefs and Values Survey and HERI's 2004–2005 Triennial National Survey of College Faculty, roughly 80 percent of traditionally appointed four-year college and university faculty who teach undergraduates consider themselves spiritual. Two-thirds describe themselves as religious. However, as detailed in Chapter Two, the personal meaning that spirituality has for faculty, along with the degree to which the spiritual/religious dimension of life and associated values, beliefs, and behaviors are centrally important to them, varies tremendously. In part, these variations are based on demographic differences. For some faculty, including many faculty of color (most notably African Americans and Hispanics), spiritual epistemologies play a central role both in their work with students and in navigating their academic lives (see, for example, Aguirre, 1987; Berry and Mizelle, 2006; Denton and Ashton, 2004; Dillard, 2006; Dillard, Abdur-Rashid, and Tyson, 2000; Fernandes, 2003; Shahjahan, 2004a; 2004b; 2005; 2010; Turner, 2002; Umbach, 2006). Quest inclinations, which were the focal point of Chapter Three, vary widely by academic discipline and also have implications for how faculty view their work and its role in their lives. The extent to which faculty members' internally focused spiritual inclinations tend to translate to externally focused ethic of caring and ecumenical worldview orientations also varies depending not only on personal characteristics, perspectives, and experiences but also on institutional and disciplinary contexts (Chapter Four).

As illustrated through perspectives shared in Chapters Two and Five, some who consider themselves traditionally religious have reservations about the term "spirituality" and thus are reluctant to embrace it fully in characterizing their own identities. Many atheist and agnostic faculty also have strong opinions about the damaging societal influences of religious adherence and, by extension, generally negative impressions of those who are "believers." Perhaps presuming that their disciplinary and/or institutional colleagues certainly must think and feel as they do (or perhaps simply not caring one way or the other), some of these faculty feel unequivocally justified and otherwise entitled to make their opinions clearly known. Especially when these faculty are powerful senior members of their academic communities, such behavior can have especially alienating and fear-inducing effects for spiritually and/or religiously inclined colleagues whose own careers within the academy are not as well established or otherwise secure.

SPIRITUALITY AND FACULTY WORK

The majority (82%) of respondents to the 2012 Faculty Beliefs and Values Survey indicated that their spiritual life and professional life are at least "somewhat" integrated. Of these, 30 percent reported that the two are "tightly" integrated. The rest (18%) view the two as "completely separate." Roughly two-thirds (64%) *disagree* that "the spiritual dimension of faculty members' lives has no place in the academy." Within all types of four-year colleges and universities and across academic disciplines/fields, at least half the faculty share that perspective. (Figures 7.1 and 7.2 summarize these findings.)

Faculty members' ethic of caring, ecumenical worldview, and charitable involvement orientations relate directly to Ashford and Pratt's *transcendence of self* dimension (2003), which reflects an individual's capacity for, and willingness to, expand his or her boundaries to encompass other people, causes, nature, or belief in a higher power, and leads to a sense of connection. Writing about those within the academy whom he characterizes as having "relational spiritualities," Bennett (2003) explains that these individuals are "no less committed to the enlargement and extension of learning" than other academics. However, in the course of their work, they also emphasize "openness and community rather than exclusion and separatism." Those who embrace so-called relational spiritualities—similar to those who embrace an ethic of caring and an ecumenical worldview—are also more inclined to view students as "potential colleagues in the quest for learning" and to "value the invitation to grow that attending to and caring for others involves" (pp. 12–13). Especially in light of the myriad challenges facing higher education and society at large today,

FIGURE 7.1 *DI*SAGREE THAT THE SPIRITUAL DIMENSION OF FACULTY
MEMBERS' LIVES HAS NO PLACE IN THE ACADEMY, BY INSTITUTIONAL TYPE

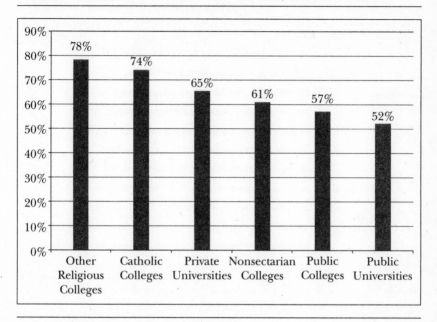

Source: 2012 Faculty Beliefs and Values Survey

such an orientation on the part of faculty may be especially instrumental in reaffirming a commitment to contribute fully to the
well-being of their students, colleagues, institutions, broader
scholarly communities, and society at large.

Prior research has shown that people are more inclined to act
"spiritually" (that is, demonstrate concern, care, and compassion
for others) when they believe in and embrace a purpose larger
than themselves (see, for example, Dehler and Welsh, 2003). As
illustrated through faculty comments incorporated in Chapters
Three, Four, and Six, academic work affords many possibilities for
exercising an ethic of caring and fostering interconnectedness.
On the whole, 87 percent of faculty (including 78% at public
universities) also agree at least "somewhat" that their institution
"allows for personal expression of spirituality." Moreover, across
different types of colleges and universities, 56 percent of faculty
(including 37% of public university faculty) express a similar level

FIGURE 7.2 *DI*SAGREE THAT THE SPIRITUAL DIMENSION OF FACULTY
MEMBERS' LIVES HAS NO PLACE IN THE ACADEMY, BY ACADEMIC
DISCIPLINE/FIELD

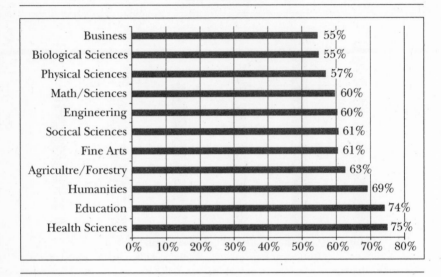

Discipline	Percent
Business	55%
Biological Sciences	55%
Physical Sciences	57%
Math/Sciences	60%
Engineering	60%
Social Sciences	61%
Fine Arts	61%
Agricultre/Forestry	63%
Humanities	69%
Education	74%
Health Sciences	75%

Source: 2012 Faculty Beliefs and Values Survey

of concurrence that "most people at this institution are interested in spirituality." However, what Bennett (2003) has referred to as the "prestige economy" of higher education, coupled with the "insistent individualism" of academic culture, "encourages exclusiveness rather than relationality" and "self-protection rather than openness to the other." Such an environment "works against internal integration and separates personal from professional lives," ultimately promoting institutional fragmentation, compromising inner vitality, and eroding the human spirit (p. viii).

Reflective, at least in part, of that individualistic orientation is the fact that although 64 percent of faculty *dis*agree that the spiritual dimension of faculty members' lives has no place in the academy, 58 percent also say that "my colleagues' spiritual lives are not a matter of concern to me," and 49 percent say that "my students' spiritual lives are not a matter of concern to me." Also telling, as highlighted especially in Chapters Four and Five, is the fact that the most common tensions between their spiritual and professional lives that faculty experience relate to their interactions with colleagues. The perspectives on success and thoughts offered to junior colleagues on building a meaningful career by faculty who register as high scorers on Equanimity (Chapter Six) provide insights into how academic communities might begin to work more purposefully toward creating and sustaining the types of work environments that enable faculty to live more fully integrated lives.

Faculty members' sense of equanimity equates, to a considerable extent, with Ashford and Pratt's *holism and harmony* dimension (2003), which pertains to the synergistic integration of various aspects of oneself and one's life, leading to a sense of coherence. This dimension and the *transcendence of self* dimension together reflect an ongoing journey of exploration and discovery that is associated with authenticity, balance, and perspective. Spirituality, of course, does not offer a "ubiquitous solution" to coping with the complexities of life, organizationally or otherwise (see, for example, Dehler and Welsh, 2003, p. 115). However, cultivating a capacity to maintain an internal sense of balance and calm in the midst of challenging circumstances plays an important role in spiritual well-being. "Time pressures," including "lack of personal time," are a significant source of stress for over 80 percent of faculty (see, for example, Lindholm, Szelényi, Hurtado, and Korn, 2005). Given the many responsibilities of today's faculty, the tight academic labor market, rising institutional performance expectations for granting promotion and tenure, and intensifying "accountability" expectations, it is not surprising that when forced to make difficult decisions, many faculty will forego focusing on their own spiritual enrichment and personal renewal in favor of meeting professional expectations and familial responsibilities. Indeed, faculty views shared in the 2012 Faculty Beliefs and Values Survey in regard to the multiple and often competing demands of personal and professional commitments reaffirm Astin and Astin's earlier finding (1999) that time is a major constraint for faculty in attempting to find space in their lives for reflection and spiritual renewal.

The inherent tensions of balancing work, family, and personal needs can be especially challenging for young women faculty (see, for example, Astin and Davis, 1985; Smith, 2000). Underscoring the significance of time, Menges and Associates (1999) found that time management is one of the most crucial variables related to the personal and professional welfare of new faculty. Given the popular view that faculty work is characterized by a good deal of autonomy, it is perhaps ironic that new faculty who leave their institutions in search of other jobs within or outside of academe often do so to "gain more control" over their lives. It makes intuitive sense that faculty who are unable to establish and maintain a healthy balance among work, family, and personal growth and renewal will feel fragmented. Over time, this lack of coherence is likely to impact faculty negatively on multiple levels, including their physical health, psychological well-being, and effectiveness in their roles as parents, teachers, scholars, and colleagues. Institutional efforts to help faculty develop (and sustain) a sense of equanimity by being true to themselves, seeking mentoring, practicing balance, and maintaining perspective as well as to establish healthy institutional work environments will no doubt serve everyone well.

Ashford and Pratt's third dimension of spirituality at work (2003) is *growth*, oriented around self-development and self-actualization leading to realization of one's aspirations and potential, resulting, ultimately, in a sense of completion. Growth relates most directly to the spiritual quest orientation addressed in Chapter Three. For faculty who resonate with a quest orientation, meaning-making and striving toward becoming one's best self are central features of their spirituality. Spiritual quest has been identified as an important factor in the process of meaning-making and transcendence, key components of adult development.

Although the search for meaning and purpose spans generations, the relative emphasis placed on quest-oriented considerations changes throughout different periods of life. For example, McLaughlin (1998) credits baby boomers with the rising interest in expressing one's spirituality at work and attempting to lead more integrated lives. He posits that many of that generation's members have now reached a stage in their lives where they have achieved a level of affluence that frees them to seek avenues for greater self-actualization, authenticity, and wholeness in their lives. Their current stature within work organizations (as senior-level colleagues and administrators) also enables them to bring a sense of legitimacy to addressing related issues within the workplace.

The seminal research that Astin and Astin (1999) conducted on issues of meaning and spirituality in the lives of college and university faculty revealed that although most faculty wanted to engage in conversations about these issues, their institutions provided few, if any, opportunities for such dialogue. Some faculty felt that frank, collegial discussion of such issues was hampered by the inherent cultural and structural constraints imposed both by their profession and their institutional work environments. What Weathersby (2000) calls the "rational academic paradigm" may indeed interfere with faculty's being spiritually present in their work and, by extension, may make it difficult for them to effectively facilitate student development in this realm. Stockton and Associate's analysis (2000) of attitudes toward spirituality among faculty and administrators at public universities revealed a common theme of "curiosity tempered with caution." Although there was an identified need for more open dialogue, faculty and administrators alike were unclear as to how best to engage in such conversations given issues of terminology, worry about being perceived as proselytizing, concern about First Amendment issues, and fear of isolation and labeling. In his thoughtful presentation and analysis of individual and institutional concerns related to dealing with spirituality and religion on campus, Edwards (2006) encourages "careful candor" as a means of helping academic communities become more open to considering what he refers to as the "perilous potential" of religion on campus.

As highlighted here and detailed throughout this book, the values and beliefs faculty bring to their work, and how they experience their work, have implications for their own personal and professional growth and development as well as for how they engage with and, ultimately, impact others. One population that faculty are known to have an important influence on is, of course, undergraduate students.

SPIRITUALITY AND UNDERGRADUATE TEACHING AND LEARNING

As young adults refine their identities, formulate adult life goals and career paths, and test their emerging sense of independence and interdependence, they often grapple with issues of authenticity, meaning, and purpose. Our Spirituality in Higher Education research team's earlier analyses of the spiritual development of undergraduate students showed that many students are eager to explore the inner dimension of their lives and to understand what others think, feel, and experience within that realm. Indeed, undergraduates often expect their college experience to facilitate that discovery process. These findings support the call of other scholars to (1) view spiritual considerations as legitimate concerns within our campus communities and (2) amplify the importance placed on spiritual growth, authenticity, and meaning (see Braskamp, Trautvetter, and Ward, 2006; Chickering, Dalton, and Stamm, 2006).

The undergraduate experience offers students many opportunities to explore issues of spirituality as they engage with others who embody various beliefs and practices. As detailed in *Cultivating the Spirit,* engagement with diverse people, cultures, and ideas helps students better understand, and value, multiple perspectives. Exposure to new and diverse perspectives is also instrumental in challenging students to examine and clarify their personal beliefs and values.

Our longitudinal research showed that, specifically with respect to academically oriented avenues for supporting students' spiritual growth and development, offering students opportunities to study abroad, take interdisciplinary coursework, and engage in course-based experiential field studies (otherwise known as "service learning" courses, which are designed to engage students in community service as part of an academic course) can contribute significantly to students' spiritual development. Participation in cocurricular experiences that are designed to attend to students' "whole" development and prepare them for work and community life—including leadership training, membership in student organizations, community service, and participation in student governance—can also be instrumental in facilitating students' spiritual growth. Indeed, most of the programs and practices that contribute to undergraduate students' spiritual development also promote many traditionally desired outcomes of higher education, such as academic performance, leadership development, self-esteem, satisfaction with college, and motivation for further education (Astin, Astin, and Lindholm, 2011b).

Through the course of our earlier study, we also found that when faculty directly encourage students to explore questions of meaning and purpose, students are more likely to show positive growth in spiritual quest, equanimity, ethic of caring, and ecumenical worldview. Similarly, if faculty attend to students' spiritual development by encouraging discussion of religious and spiritual matters, by supporting students' expressions of spirituality, and by acting themselves as spiritual role models, students show more positive growth in the same four spiritual qualities, as well as in charitable involvement (Astin, Astin, and Lindholm, 2011b). Other research provides additional insights regarding the instrumental role that faculty can play in fostering students' spiritual growth. For example, faculty members' incorporation of student-centered or developmental pedagogies—such as class discussions, cooperative (small group) learning, service learning, student-selected course topics, and reflective writing and journaling—have been found to enhance affective learning outcomes, including interpersonal development (see, for example, Astin, 1993; Braskamp, Trautvetter, and Ward, 2006; Chickering, Dalton, and Stamm, 2006; Duerr, Zajonc, and Dana, 2003; Keen and Hall, 2009; Lattuca, Voigt, and Faith, 2004; Nash and Murray, 2010; Sax and Astin, 1997).

Most recently, Piehl (2013) found that faculty members' use of developmental classroom teaching methods (especially when they specifically involve spirituality-related discussion or meditation/contemplation) was predictive of enhanced spiritual outcomes related to meaning-making, spirituality as quest, and moral care for others. These effects were evident even after statistically controlling for students' precollege and college experiences and traits as well as holding institutional type and major variables constant. Piehl's study also showed that when faculty display personal interest in students' inner lives, especially as related to helping students "navigate questions of meaning and purpose," students tend to report greater gains across spiritual development measures. This latter finding also reaffirms the important mediating role that students' perception of faculty support for personal expressions of spirituality and for fostering spiritual development has on students' openness to actively exploring issues of meaning and purpose in their lives (see, for example, Bowman and Small, 2013).

Of course, the feasibility of employing student-centered or developmental pedagogies varies based on institutional type, size, and resources. Across different types of colleges and universities, there are also notable variations in the degree to which faculty routinely employ such approaches to learning and teaching, depending on disciplinary affiliation (see, for example, Lindholm and Szelényi, 2006). However, we also know that faculty members who themselves are spiritually inclined are more likely (largely irrespective of disciplinary affiliation and personal demographic characteristics) to use student-centered teaching methods (Lindholm and Astin, 2008).

Again largely independent of institutional and disciplinary contexts, college and university faculty who themselves are spiritually oriented are also more likely to emphasize the importance of students' personal development (in addition to, not in lieu of, students' intellectual development). Such orientation is reflected by the personal priorities faculty place on goals for undergraduate education that include enhancing self-understanding, preparing for responsible citizenship, developing moral character, helping develop personal values, facilitating the search for meaning and purpose, and providing for emotional development. Not unexpectedly, faculty who are highly spiritual (whether or not they exercise those inclinations within the context of a particular religious faith) are also more inclined to endorse the value of explicitly supporting undergraduate students' spiritual development. Among 2012 Faculty Beliefs and Values Survey respondents, for example, 36 percent of faculty who self-identify as highly spiritual see promoting students' spiritual development as a "very important" goal for undergraduate education, and an additional 29 percent feel that such a focus is "essential."

Faculty interactions with students, both inside and outside the classroom, also affect undergraduate students' propensity to embrace an ethic of caring, or what Rhoads (2000) described as "a sense of self firmly rooted in concern for the well-being of others" (p. 37). Specifically, students who experience more mentoring interactions with faculty, especially (but not exclusively) when those interactions relate to discussion of ethical and spiritual issues, tend to place higher value on the "caring self" (Fleming, Purnell, and Wang, 2013). Rockenbach and Mayhew's research (2013) on undergraduate students' ecumenical development also reaffirms the value of faculty members' efforts (along with broader institutional efforts) to "challenge and support" (Sanford, 1968) students' spiritually related explorations and struggles. As academic role models for students and interpreters of institutional missions, faculty also play a potentially influential role in helping students make connections between academic knowledge and skills, social issues, and civic life (see, for example, Stanton, 1994).

Throughout the course of the Spirituality in Higher Education project, students and colleagues alike have expressed to our research team their desire to learn how to more purposefully facilitate students' spiritual development through campus initiatives. For example:

"As a professor, how might I create a course that explores spirituality within the context of my particular subject matter?"

"As a student leader, how can I work with my peers to bring awareness and attention to the different ways in which people experience spirituality in order to promote cross-cultural understanding?"

"As an administrator, what would be an effective approach for engaging different segments of the campus community in developing a strategic plan for addressing issues of meaning and purpose within student and faculty life?"

In response, over the course of several years during the latter stages of the project, we initiated four related efforts to collect information about "promising practices." Our initial effort in spring 2005 centered around collecting syllabi from courses in which faculty incorporated assignments and other activities to facilitate undergraduate students' spiritual inquiry and awareness.[1] In 2006, our research team hosted at UCLA the National Institute on Spirituality in Higher Education, which brought together teams from ten diverse campuses to discuss possibilities for integrating spirituality into the curriculum and cocurriculum.

Later, after a call put forth by our research team in 2007, faculty and administrators from forty campuses across the country sent us information on their campus's curricular and cocurricular practices designed to support undergraduate students' spiritual development. Finally, in summer 2010, we expanded the pool of information by surveying vice presidents for student affairs, vice presidents for academic affairs, and campus ministry directors or chaplains at 1,580 four-year campuses nationwide. The online questionnaire covered a variety of topics, from specific practices and programs that promote student spiritual development to programs tailored in support of faculty spiritual development. The resulting guidebook (Lindholm, Millora, Schwartz, and Spinosa, 2011)—developed as a resource for administrators, faculty, academic personnel, student affairs professionals, and student leaders within higher education who are interested in attending to issues of spirituality, meaning, and purpose as part of the undergraduate experience—includes descriptions of some of the practices, programs, and syllabi that campus personnel shared with us.

FACULTY PERSPECTIVES ON SPIRITUALITY AND UNDERGRADUATE EDUCATION

Our Spirituality in Higher Education research team's early analyses showed that fully three-quarters of college students were "searching for meaning and purpose in life," yet more than half also said that their professors "never" provide opportunities to discuss these topics. Similarly, nearly two-thirds of students said that their professors "never" encourage discussion of spiritual and religious matters. Moreover, although 39 percent said that their religious and spiritual beliefs have been strengthened by "new ideas encountered in class," 53 percent reported that their classroom experiences had no impact. Only 55 percent were satisfied with how their college experience had provided "opportunities for religious/spiritual reflection."

When it comes to questions of the "appropriateness" of a place for spirituality in undergraduate education, faculty opinion is considerably divided. Respondents to the 2012 Faculty Beliefs and Values Survey, for example, tend to agree in large proportion (75%) that "this campus should be as concerned about students' personal development as it is with their intellectual development." However, underscoring the discomfort many faculty feel with the use of the term "spiritual" within higher education contexts, they predominately *dis*agree (56%) with the notion that "colleges should be concerned with facilitating students' spiritual development." Among faculty at public universities, that figure rises to 77 percent disagreement. As we highlighted in *Cultivating the Spirit*, concerns include fear of being criticized by colleagues because discussions about spirituality may be perceived as antithetical to academic norms, the perceived need to maintain separation of church and state, feeling a lack of expertise, and worrying that such discussions might be perceived as a form of indoctrination or proselytizing (Astin, Astin, and Lindholm, 2011b). As one professor we interviewed offered:

> There are many of my colleagues who would say, "Look, we are at a university and what I do is math; what I do is history; and, really, that's my competence. Moving into this other area is not my competence." I don't feel [that my reluctance] comes from a place of, "I'm not doing that," you know, like resentment. It comes from a place that, "This is not my area of expertise."

In considering how faculty could be better prepared to purposefully engage with students to support their spiritual development, another faculty member told us:

> I think some of the resistance in faculty that would have to be overcome is when spirituality gets connected with politicized religion. I think you would have to have some programming on what spirituality really is. What does [it] mean? And how is it connected to religion, and how is it not connected to religion? How can you understand it in the most productive way possible, rather than the most problematic way?

In an earlier interview study, Astin and Astin (1999) also found that the discomfort and uncertainty that some faculty experience in connection with "spirituality" largely dissipates upon suggesting that they substitute the phrase "search for meaning and purpose."

Palmer (1983, 1999) has written eloquently about the emotional and spiritual dimensions of life and the unique potential that educators have to help students develop their capacity for connectedness, responsiveness, and accountability. Similarly, Laurence and Kazanjian (2000) maintain that colleges and universities have tremendous potential to shape society positively through examining issues of purpose and meaning within the context of the campus environment, acknowledging the multiple aspects of self that operate simultaneously within individuals, and celebrating the diverse experience that people bring to their encounters with one another. Student affairs professionals have an especially rich legacy of concern for holistic education and personal development and, certainly, the significance of their contributions to the "softer" aspects of undergraduate student development should not be underestimated or overlooked. However, for spirituality to have a truly "authentic" place in campus life, its fundamental components must also be reflected in the core values, beliefs, and commitments of academic affairs personnel. Faculty members are the heart of the academic community. It is therefore critical to understand their views on spirituality, its expressions in their personal and professional lives, and the challenges they encounter in the quest for meaningfully integrated lives and a sense of wholeness are critical to understand.

As reflected throughout this book, those who participated in the 2012 Faculty Beliefs and Values Survey took much treasured time to share their perspectives on the meaning that spirituality has in their own lives; the intersections they may see between the spiritual dimension of their lives and their work as professors, along with associated tensions they may experience; and their broader views on the roles they and their institutions "should" play in supporting students' spiritual growth and development. With thanks for the candor—and, often, the passion—with which those views were offered, and for the receptivity of most respondents to the idea of potentially continuing the conversation, I close this chapter with a spirit of gratitude.

NOTE

1. Syllabi are available at http://spirituality.ucla.edu/publicatinos/ newsletters/2/syllabi.php.

EPILOGUE

Taken collectively, "the faculty's intellectual capital" has been described as "the institution's foremost asset" (Gappa, Austin, and Trice, 2007, p. 4). Too often overlooked, however, is the potentially powerful asset of the faculty's spiritual capital. As highlighted throughout this book, the spiritual and religious connections in faculty members' lives are variable. So too are their conceptualizations of whether (and how) one's spiritual life interfaces with professorial work. Indeed, the answers to those questions tend to depend heavily on who one is; the disciplinary contexts in which one's scholarly endeavors are housed; and the type of college or university in which one works, including issues of institutional culture and climate. The associated complexities make it difficult to offer definitive, universally applicable recommendations for how "best" to create and sustain academic communities that draw on spirituality's multifaceted qualities of quest, ecumenical worldview, ethic of caring, charitable involvement, and equanimity. However, in the interest of facilitating dialogue centered around how key institutional purposes, values, and practices inform and support interests in addressing spiritual considerations within specific campus communities, I offer a few concluding thoughts in this Epilogue.

In its most potentially transformative role, a spiritual orientation to life stresses what Lerner (1998) described as "the unity of all human beings and the unity of all being . . . without negating the importance and value of individual difference and individual freedom" (p. 1). Community development that is oriented around

this goal includes recognizing personal values, respecting individual human rights, reducing inequality, enhancing personal
security, promoting social justice, facilitating empowerment, and
enriching people's essential humanity (Chile and Simpson, 2004).
Reflecting in the 1950s on "the university and the spiritual life,"
Smith (1951) highlighted the value of higher education's
community-based attributes and described the college campus as
"the spirit's most natural home, its splendid habitat" (p. 402).
More recently, Spano (2008) framed his discussion on nurturing
institutional cultures of caring by highlighting the "blessings" of
the campus environment, as reflected in the taxonomy of human
virtues that Peterson and Seligman (2004) identified as accepted
by virtually all cultures of the world: wisdom, courage, humanity,
justice, temperance, and transcendence. Spano contends that by
understanding what makes us strong, and through working toward
enhancing the qualities that give universities their strength of
character, we can grow stronger.

In reconnecting higher education with human wholeness,
reinvigorating the integrative capacity of college and university
campuses, and making valued space for the spirit within the
academy, we are challenged to consider how our ways of being
ultimately extend to our ways of doing and relating. Within
campus communities, this process necessarily begins with self-
reflection and group dialogue. Writing about the "disconnected"
life of educators, Palmer (1999) explained how our cultural habits
within the academy—namely our competitiveness and our tendencies to think oppositionally, question others' perspectives
aggressively, and respond dismissively or with quick fixes for whatever might seem to be wrong—tend to result in environments
where it feels threatening to listen openly or to speak genuinely
(see also Twale and DeLuca, 2008). Within academic work environments, one essential consideration is finding ways to create
time and space for more open exchanges among colleagues.

Engaging in new conversations, such as how we make meaning
of our work, how we experience our work environments, and what
connections (if any) we may see between our spiritual/religious
lives and our work, makes all of us vulnerable. Especially valuable
in these circumstances are effective leadership from department
heads, coupled with the engagement of well-respected senior

faculty, who, by all accounts, are in the "safest" position career-wise to share the joys, trials, and tribulations of their own academic careers and to offer perspective on how they—whether spiritually oriented or otherwise—have made meaning of their academic careers and life experiences (Lindholm and Szelényi, 2003; Miller and Scott, 2000). In terms of opening the conversation, the direct similarity of experiences is likely to matter far less than the openness to share one's own journey as well as an expressed interest in learning what others' experiences might be. Indeed, in revealing our individual experiences, we often come to see more clearly not only the ways in which we are unique but also how our perceptions and experience are like those of some others and how they are like those of all others.

Dialogue and reflection centered around what Chickering (2006) refers to as "institutional formation" are foundational for developing academic units and broader work environments that excel in maintaining a place for individuality while also promoting community (see also Cooperrider and Whitney, 1999; Manning, 2000). Wilcox's volume (2013) on "revisioning mission" within Catholic higher education provides a wealth of additional insight into options and approaches for engaging colleagues in discussion and action around issues of spirituality, meaning, and purpose. As illustrated by Felten, Bauman, Kheriaty, and Taylor (2013), faculty mentoring communities can also play a powerful role in supporting faculty personal and professional growth interests and, by extension, laying the foundation for transformative institutional change. Included within each chapter are questions for reflection and growth that can help facilitate purposeful dialogue. Palmer and Zajonc's call to renew higher education through collegial conversations (2010) includes promising examples of how colleges and universities can help faculty, staff, and students realize their deepest potential.

Ultimately, it takes an engaged and committed community of faculty, staff, administrators, and students to nurture the development of campus cultures and climates that contribute to cultivating a sense of meaning and wholeness within and among institutional members and, through that process, honor the spiritual and religious connections in many of our lives. As acknowledged at the outset, the findings contained in this book are necessarily incomplete with respect to answering a multitude of pertinent research-oriented and practitioner-focused questions. My hope is that you will be stimulated to build on the largely descriptive profile incorporated here to examine in greater depth and detail the complexities of faculty members' spiritual and religious lives, particularly as those lives intersect with their roles as college professors. Ultimately, through the continued process of empirical, theoretical, and practical discovery, we can provide additional insights to help promote the development of spiritually enriching academic workplaces, teaching and learning environments, and campus communities.

APPENDIX
Study Methodology

The institutional sample for the 2012 Faculty Beliefs and Values Survey was designed to ensure diversity with respect to type (colleges and universities), control (public, private nonsectarian, Roman Catholic, Protestant, Evangelical), and selectivity level (high, medium, and low, based on the average SAT/ACT scores of entering students). Institutional participation in HERI's 2004–2005 Triennial National Faculty Survey and in the 2004–2007 longitudinal College Students' Beliefs and Values Survey along with geographical location (that is, Northeast, Northwest, Southeast, Southwest, and Midwest) were also taken into account to ensure a balanced representation within the final sample.

Once the institutional sample was created, faculty contact information (email address) was retrieved from college or university websites (via departmental pages and/or publicly accessible directory information). If email contact information was restricted from public access by the college or university, a "replacement" institution of the same type, control, selectivity level, and geographical location was selected for inclusion in the sample. On the basis of information provided on campus and departmental websites, effort was made to include within the population to be surveyed all full-time faculty who teach undergraduates at each campus that was part of the institutional sample. Primary interest for this study was in analyzing the beliefs, values, behaviors, and issues of meaning and purpose in the lives of traditionally appointed (that is, full-time tenured or tenure-track) professors, or "core" faculty members. Consequently, those listed on institutional websites who (1) had the title of assistant professor, associate professor, or professor and (2) were not designated as part-time faculty were included in each institutional sample. At large institutions where such determinations could not be made readily, random samples of faculty by department were selected for inclusion.

Faculty in the starting sample were sent an advance notification correspondence via email that described the purpose of the survey in general terms and encouraged their participation. The correspondence also asked the recipient to indicate via email if he or she would prefer to be removed from the survey administration list. In response, 3 percent asked to be removed.

The 2012 Faculty Beliefs and Values Survey administration was conducted in summer and fall 2012 using SurveyMonkey. First-wave surveys were sent out in five groups based on the institution's fall term start date for academic year 2012–2013. Potential survey respondents (that is, those who had not asked to be removed from the survey list) received via email an invitation to participate that included an electronic link to the survey questionnaire as well as an "opt out" link. (Faculty who had been invited previously to complete other SurveyMonkey administered questionnaires that were not associated with this study and who had indicated at that time via the same email address used to contact them for this study that they preferred not to receive any more surveys were automatically removed from the sample.) Approximately two weeks after the initial invitation was sent, a reminder correspondence was sent urging participation from those who had not responded and thanking those who had already completed the survey. Approximately two weeks later, a final reminder correspondence was sent. Of the 33,184 faculty in the final sample pool, 9,291 elected to participate, reflecting a 28 percent response rate. The survey questionnaire was designed such that if, for whatever reason, faculty preferred not to respond to any particular items in the survey, they could skip those items and continue. Most who elected to skip particular questions opted not to respond to one or more of the open-ended items that enabled them to elaborate on responses provided elsewhere on the survey or to offer other perspective. Overall, between 46 percent and 58 percent also responded to the open-ended questions. In response to the final survey item that asked permission for the principal investigator to retain the respondents' contact information for potential follow-up purposes, 74 percent indicated their consent.

The final sample comprised 8,447 respondents whose survey responses confirmed that they were employed as full-time, traditionally appointed, nonretired faculty members who teach undergraduates. Overall, the final 2012 Faculty Beliefs and Values sample proportions were quite similar to the starting sample proportions that had been based on the nationally normative faculty data we collected in 2004 and 2005. Consequently, for purposes of the analyses presented here, 2012 Faulty Beliefs and Values Survey data were not weighted.

DEFINING HIGH AND LOW SCORES ON SPIRITUAL AND RELIGIOUS MEASURES

Given that raw scores on the five spiritual and four religious factor scales have no absolute meaning, it is useful for research purposes to be able to classify individuals according to their scores (for example, "How many faculty obtained high scores on Equanimity?"). Because an individual's score on any of the spiritual and religious measures that our Spirituality in Higher Education research team created reflects the degree to which he or she possesses the quality being measured, defining high or low scores is to a certain extent an arbitrary decision. Nevertheless, an effort was made to introduce a certain amount of rationality into such definitions by posing the following question: In order to defend the proposition that someone possesses a "high" (or "low") degree of the particular trait in question, what *pattern* of responses to the entire set of questions would that person have to show? The quality of Equanimity can be used to illustrate the procedure that was followed in answering such a question for each measure.

Equanimity is defined by five items, all of which happen to have three possible responses (scored 1, 2, or 3). The highest possible score (the highest "degree" of Equanimity) is thus 5×3, or 15; the lowest possible score is 5×1, or 5. For three of the items, individuals were asked, "Please indicate the extent to which each of the following describes you," with the following response options: "to a great extent" (score 3), "to some extent" (score 2), and "not at all" (score 1):

> Seeing each day, good or bad, as a gift
> Being thankful for all that has happened to me
> Feeling good about the direction in which my life is headed.

To be classified as a high scorer on Equanimity, our research team decided (through the process of analyzing 2004 and 2007 College Students' Beliefs and Values Survey data) that the individual should respond "to a great extent" to at least two of these items and at least "to some extent" to the third item. This would generate 8 points on the Equanimity scale (3 + 3 + 2).

The other two items in the Equanimity scale were preceded by the following instructions: "During the last year, how often have you . . .," with the response options "frequently" (score 3), "occasionally" (score 2), and "not at all" (score 1):

> Being able to find meaning in times of hardship
> Felt at peace/centered

A person possessing a high degree of equanimity, we felt, would not respond "occasionally" to either of these items. Consequently, we decided that in order to be classified as a high scorer on Equanimity, the individual should answer "frequently" to both items, which would generate 6 points on the Equanimity scale. Thus the minimum score required to be classified as a high scorer on Equanimity would be 8 + 6, or 14. (Note that if an individual happened to respond "occasionally" to either of the last two items, then that individual would have to respond "to a great extent" on *all three* of the first three items in order to be classified as a high scorer.)

Looking at the other extreme, we decided that the respondent with a low degree of equanimity should answer "not at all" to at least one of the first three items and no more than "to some extent" on the other two, yielding a maximum of 5 points (1 + 2 + 2). If an individual happened to respond "to a great extent" on any of these three items, then he or she would have to answer "not at all" to *both* of the other two in order not to exceed 5 points.

On the final two items, we decided that an individual with a low degree of equanimity should answer no higher than "occasionally" on both, generating 4 additional points (2 + 2). Answering "frequently" to one of these last two items would require a "not at all" response to the other in order not to exceed the total of 4 points. (A similar trade-off in individual responses would be possible, of course, between the first three and the last two items.) Thus the maximum score to qualify as low on Equanimity is 5 + 4, or 9 points.

A similar reasoning process was followed in choosing high and low cutting points on each of the other measures. Tables A.1 and A.2 show the survey items making up each of the measures of spirituality and religiousness. This table also provides statistical details for each measure, including reliability estimates (Cronbach's alpha) both for the faculty members who responded to the 2012 Faculty Beliefs and Values Survey and for the students who responded to the 2004 and 2007 College Students' Beliefs and Values Surveys. Table A.3 shows the intercorrelations for these measures.

TABLE A.1 ITEM CONTENT OF FIVE SPIRITUAL MEASURES

	Score Ranges	
	High	Low
Spiritual Quest (Faculty alpha = .85; student alphas in 2004 and 2007 were .83 and .82)	9–19	26–34
Searching for meaning and purpose in life[a]		
Having discussions about the meaning of life with my friends[a]		
Finding answers to the mysteries of life[b]		
Attaining inner harmony[b]		
Attaining wisdom[b]		
Seeking beauty in my life[b]		
Developing a meaningful philosophy of life[b]		
Becoming a more loving person[b]		
Close friends are searching for meaning and purpose[c]		
Equanimity (Faculty alpha = .73; student alphas in 2004 and 2007 were .76 and .72)	5–9	14–15
Been able to find meaning in times of hardship[d]		
Felt at peace/centered[d]		
Feeling good about the direction in which my life is headed[a]		
Being thankful for all that has happened to me[a]		
Self-description: Seeing each day, good or bad, as a gift[a]		
Ethic of Caring (Faculty alpha = .82; student alphas in 2004 and 2007 were .79 and .22)	8–14	22–31
Trying to change things that are unfair in the world[a]		
Helping others who are in difficulty[b]		
Reducing pain and suffering in the world[b]		
Helping to promote racial understanding[b]		
Becoming involved in programs to clean up the environment[b]		
Becoming a community leader[b]		
Influencing social values[b]		
Influencing the political structure[b]		

TABLE A.1 (continued)

	Score Ranges	
	High	*Low*
Charitable Involvement (Faculty alpha = .62; student alphas in 2004 and 2007 were .67 and .71)	5–6	10–16
Participated in community food or clothing drive[d]		
Performed volunteer work[d]		
Donated money to charity[d]		
Helped friends with personal problems[d]		
Ecumenical Worldview (Faculty alpha = .72; student alphas in 2004 and 2007 were .72 and .70)	12–29	38–45
Having an interest in different religious traditions[a]		
Believing in the goodness of all people[a]		
Feeling a strong connection to all humanity[a]		
Understanding of others[e]		
Accepting others as they are[a]		
Improving my understanding of other countries and cultures[b]		
Improving the human condition[b]		
All life is interconnected[b]		
Love is at the root of all the great religious[b]		
Nonreligious people can lead lives that are just as moral as those of religious believers[b]		
We are all spiritual beings[b]		
Most people can grow spiritually without being religious[b]		

[a]3-point scale: (1) "Not at all" to (3) "To a great extent"
[b]4-point scale: (1) "Not important" to (4) "Essential"
[c]4-point scale: (1) "None" to (4) "All"
[d]3-point scale: (1) "Not at all" to (3) "Frequently"
[e]5-point scale: (1) "Lowest 10%" to (5) "Highest 10%"

Table A.2 Item Content of Four Religious Measures

	Score Ranges	
	High	Low
Religious Commitment (Faculty alpha = .97; student alphas in 2004 and 2007 were .96 and .97)	12–20	41–47
Seeking to follow religious teachings in everyday life[a]		
Religiousness[b]		
I find religion to be personally helpful[c]		
I gain spiritual strength by trusting in a Higher Power[c]		
Feeling a sense of connection with God/Higher Power that transcends my personal self[d]		
Felt loved by God[e]		
My spiritual/religious beliefs:		
Are one of the most important things in my life[c]		
Provide me with strength, support, and guidance[c]		
Give meaning/purpose to my life[c]		
Lie behind my whole approach to life[c]		
Have helped me develop my identity[c]		
Help define the goals I set for myself[c]		
Religious Engagement (Faculty alpha = .89; student alphas in 2004 and 2007 were .87 and .88)	7–11	5–36
Attended a religious service[e]		
Attended a class, workshop, or retreat on matters related to religion/spirituality[e]		
Reading sacred texts[f]		
Religious singing/chanting[f]		
Other reading on religion/spirituality[f]		
Prayer[f]		
Go to church/temple/other house of worship[f]		

TABLE A.2 *(continued)*

	Score Ranges	
	High	*Low*
Religious Struggle (Faculty alpha =.74; student alphas in 2004 and 2007 were .75 and .77)	7–10	16–21
Feeling unsettled about spiritual and religious matters[d]		
Feeling disillusioned with my religious upbringing[d]		
Struggled to understand evil, suffering, and death[e]		
Felt angry with God[e]		
Questioned [my] religious/spiritual beliefs[e]		
Felt distant from God[e]		
Disagreed with [my] family about religious matters[e]		
Religious Skepticism (Faculty alpha = .84; student alphas in 2004 and 2007 were .83 and .86)	9–13	23–33
Believing in life after death[d] (reverse coded)		
Conflict; I consider myself to be on the side of science[d]		
The universe arose by chance[c]		
In the future, science will be able to explain everything[c]		
I have never felt a sense of sacredness[c]		
Whether or not there is a supreme being doesn't matter to me[c]		
What happens in my life is determined by forces larger than myself[c] (reverse coded)		
It doesn't matter what I believe as long as I lead a moral life[c]		
While science can provide important information about the physical world, only religion can truly explain existence[c] (reverse coded)		

[a]4-point scale: (1) "Not important" to (4) "Essential"
[b]5-point scale: (1) "Lowest 10%" to (5) "Highest 10%"
[c]4-point scale: (1) "Disagree strongly" to (4) "Agree strongly"
[d]3-point scale: (1) "Not at all" to (3) "To a great extent"
[e]3-point scale: (1) "Not at all" to (3) "Frequently"
[f]6-point scale: (1) "Not at all" to (6) "Daily"

TABLE A.3 CORRELATIONS AMONG SPIRITUAL AND RELIGIOUS MEASURES

	SQ	EQ	CI	EC	EW	RC	RS	RE	RSK
SQ		.30	.20	.38	.42	.38	.23	.34	−.31
EQ			.28	.18	.30	.40	−.07	.33	−.30
CI				.30	.23	.31	−.12	.33	−.25
EC					.43	.14	.13	.10	−.05
EW						.23	.16	.15	−.10
RC							.13	.78	−.75
RS								.17	−.12
RE									−.75
RSK									

Key: SQ (Spiritual Quest); EQ (Equanimity); CI (Charitable Involvement); EC (Ethic of Caring); EW (Ecumenical Worldview); RC (Religious Commitment); RS (Religious Struggle); RE (Religious Engagement); RSK (Religious Skepticism)

References

Aguirre, A. J. An interpretive analysis of Chicano faculty in academe. *Social Science Journal, 24*(1) (1987): 71–81.

Aldridge, D. Spirituality, healing and medicine. *Cancer Prevention International, 3* (1998): 287–95.

Alport, G. W. *The individual and his religion.* New York: Macmillan (1950).

Allport, G. W., and J. M. Ross. Personal religious orientation and prejudice. *Journal of Personality and Social Psychology, 5*(4) (1967): 432–43.

Amabile, T., and S. J. Kramer. How leaders kill meaning at work. *McKinsey Quarterly, 1*(2) (2012): 124–31.

Ammons, S. K., and P. B. Edgell. Religious influences on work-family trade-offs. *Journal of Family Issues, 28* (2007): 794–826.

Antonio, A. L. Faculty of color reconsidered: Reassessing contributions to scholarship. *Journal of Higher Education, 73* (2002): 582–602.

Antonio, A. L., H. S. Astin, and C. M. Cress. Community service in higher education: A look at the nation's faculty. *Review of Higher Education, 23*(4) (2000): 373–98.

Ashford, B. E., and Pratt, M. G. Institutionalized spirituality. In R. A. Giacalone and C. L. Jurkiewicz (Eds.), *Handbook of workplace spirituality and organizational performance.* Armonk, NY: M. E. Sharpe (2003): 93–107.

Ashmos, D. P., and D. Duchon. Spirituality at work: A conceptualization and measure. *Journal of Management Inquiry, 9*(2) (2000): 134–45.

Astedt-Kurki, P. Religiosity as a dimension of well-being: A challenge for professional nursing. *Clinical Nursing Research, 4* (1995): 405–28.

Astin, A. W. *What matters in college? Four critical years revisited.* San Francisco: Jossey-Bass (1993).

Astin, A. W. Why spirituality deserves a central place in liberal education. *Liberal Education, 90*(2) (2004): 34–41.

Astin, A. W., and H. S. Astin, with the assistance of A. L. Antonio, J. S. Astin, and C. M. Cress. *Meaning and spirituality in the lives of college faculty: A study of values, authenticity, and stress.* Higher Education Research Institute, UCLA (1999).

Astin, A.W., H. S. Astin, and J. A. Lindholm. Assessing students' spiritual and religious qualities. *Journal of College Student Development, 52*(1) (2011a): 39–61.

Astin, A. W., H. S. Astin, and J. A. Lindholm. *Cultivating the spirit.* San Francisco: Jossey-Bass (2011b).

Astin, A. W., and J. P. Keen. Equanimity and spirituality. *Religion and Education, 33*(2) (2006): 1–8.

Astin, H. S., and D. E. Davis. Research productivity across the life and career cycles: Facilitators and barriers for women. In M. F. Fox (Ed.), *Scholarly writing and publishing: Issues, problems, and solutions.* New York: Westview Press (1985): 147–60.

Astin, H. S., and K. Twede. Institutional and personal correlates of shared values in academe. Unpublished manuscript, Higher Education Research Institute, UCLA (1989).

August, L., and J. Waltman. Culture, climate, and contribution: Career satisfaction among female faculty. *Research in Higher Education, 45* (2004): 177–92.

Austin, A. E. Faculty cultures, faculty values. In W. G. Tierney (Ed.), *Assessing academic climates and cultures.* New Directions for Institutional Research, no. 68. San Francisco: Jossey-Bass (Winter 1990): 61–74.

Austin, A. E., M. D. Sorcinelli, and M. McDaniels. Understanding new faculty: Background, aspirations, challenges, and growth. In R. P. Perry and J. C. Smart (Eds.), *The scholarship of teaching and learning in higher education: An evidence-based perspective.* Dordrecht, The Netherlands: Springer (2007): 39–89.

Baker, D. C. Studies of the inner life: The impact of spirituality on quality of life. *Quality of Life Research, 12* (Supp.1) (2003): 51–57.

Barnes, L.L.B., M. O. Agago, and W. T. Coombs. Effects of job-related stress on faculty intention to leave acadaemia. *Research in Higher Education, 39*(4) (1998): 457–69.

Batson, C. D. Religion as prosocial agent or double agent? *Journal for the Scientific Study of Religion, 15*(1) (1976): 29–45.

Batson, C. D., P. Schoenrade, and L. W. Ventis. *Religion and the individual.* New York: Cambridge University Press (1993).

Baumeister, R. F., and K. D. Vohs. The pursuit of meaningfulness in life. In C. R. Snyder and S. Lopez (Eds.), *The handbook of positive psychology.* New York: Oxford Univerity Press (2002): 608–18.

Beal, T. *Religion in America: A very short introduction.* New York: Oxford University Press (2008).

Beck, C. Education for spirituality. *Interchange, 17*(2) (1986): 148–56.

Beck, R., and R. K. Jessup. The multidimensional nature of quest motivation. *Journal of Psychology and Theology, 32*(4) (2004): 283–94.

Bennett, J. B. *Academic life: Hospitality, ethics, and spirituality.* Boston: Anker (2003).

Berrett, D. Today's faculty: Stressed, focused on teaching, and undeterred by long odds. *Chronicle of Higher Education* (October 24, 2012). http://chronicle.com/article/Todays-Faculty-Stressed-and/135276.

Berry, T. R., and N. Mizelle. *From oppression to grace: Women of color and their dilemmas within the academy.* Sterling, VA: Stylus (2006).

Biglan, A. The characteristics of subject matter in different scientific areas. *Journal of Applied Psychology, 57* (1973): 195–203.

Boice, R. *The new faculty member: Supporting and fostering professional development.* San Francisco: Jossey-Bass (1992).

Bowman, N. A., and J. L. Small. The experiences and spiritual growth of religiously privileged and religiously marginalized students. In A. N. Rockenbach and M. J. Mayhew (Eds.), *Spirituality in college students' lives: Translating research into practice.* New York: Routledge (2013): 19–34.

Bozeman, B., and Gaughan, M. Job satisfaction among university faculty: Individual, work and institutional determinants. *Journal of Higher Education, 82*(2) (2011): 154–86.

Braskamp, L. A. *Fostering student development through faculty development: A national survey of chief academic officers at church-related colleges.* Chicago: Loyola University Chicago (2003).

Braskamp, L. A., L. C. Trautvetter, and K. Ward. *Putting students first: How colleges develop students purposefully.* Boston: Anker (2006).

Burack, E. Spirituality in the workplace. *Journal of Organizational Change Management, 12*(4) (1999): 280–91.

Burkhardt, M. A. Characteristics of spirituality in the lives of women in a rural Appalachian community. *Journal of Transcultural Nursing, 4* (1993): 12–18.

Burns, C. T., L. M. Jackson, W. R. Tarpley, and G. J. Smith. Religion as quest: The self-directed pursuit of meaning. *Personality and Social Psychology Bulletin, 22*(10) (1996): 1068–76.

Cannister, M. W. Enhancing spirituality among college freshmen through faculty mentoring. *Research on Christian Higher Education, 5* (1998): 83–103.

Chickering, A. W. Planned change and professional development. In A. W. Chickering, J. C. Dalton, and L. Stamm (Eds.), *Encouraging authenticity and spirituality in higher education.* San Francisco: Jossey-Bass (2006): 189–219.

Chickering, A. W., J. C. Dalton, and L. Stamm. (Eds.). *Encouraging authenticity and spirituality in higher education.* San Francisco: Jossey-Bass (2006).

Chile, L. M., and G. Simpson. Spirituality and community development: Exploring the links between the individual and the collective. *Community Development Journal, 39*(4) (2004): 318–31.

Chiu, L., J. D. Emblen, L. Van Hofwegen, R. Sawatzky, and H. Meyerhoff. An integrative review of the concept of spirituality in the health sciences. *Western Journal of Nursing Research, 24*(4) (2004): 405–28.

Clark, B. R. *The academic life: Small worlds, different worlds.* Princeton, NJ: Carnegie Foundation for the Advancement of Teaching (1987).

Clark, R. T. The law and spirituality: How the law supports and limits the expression of spirituality on the college campus. In M. A. Jablonski (Ed.), *The implications of student spirituality for student affairs practice.* New Directions for Student Services, no. 95. San Francisco: Jossey-Bass (Fall 2001): 37–46.

Clark, S. M. The academic profession and career: Perspectives and problems. *Teaching Sociology, 14* (1986): 24–34.

Cohen, A. M. *The shaping of American higher education: Emergence and growth of the contemporary system.* San Francisco: Jossey-Bass (1998).

Conger, J. A. Introduction: Our search for spiritual community. In J. Conger and Associates (Eds.), *Spirit at work: Discovering the spirituality in leadership.* San Francisco: Jossey-Bass (1994): 1–18.

Cook, S. W., P. D. Borman, M. A. Moore, and M. A. Kunkel. College students' perceptions of spiritual people and religious people. *Journal of Psychology and Theology, 28*(2) (2000): 125–37.

Cooperrider, D., and D. Whitney. *Appreciative inquiry.* San Francisco: Berrett-Koehler (1999).

Dalton, J. C. Career and calling: Finding a place for the spirit in work and the community. In M. A. Jablonski (Ed.), *The implications of student spirituality for student affairs practice.* New Directions for Student Services, no. 95. San Francisco: Jossey-Bass (Fall 2001): 17–26.

Dalton, J. C. Integrating spirit and community in higher education. In A. W. Chickering, J. C. Dalton, and L. Stamm (Eds.), *Encouraging authenticity and spirituality in higher education.* San Francisco: Jossey-Bass (2006): 165–85.

Davie, G. Believing without belonging: Is this the future of religion in Britain? *Social Compass, 37* (1990): 455–69.

Dawson, P. J. A reply to Goddard's "spirituality as integrative energy." *Journal of Advanced Nursing, 25*(2) (1997): 282–89.

Dehler, G. E., and M. A. Welsh. Discovering the keys: Spirit in teaching and the journey of learning. *Journal of Management Education, 21*(4) (1997): 496–508.

Dehler, G. E., and M. A. Welsh. The experience of work: Spirituality and the new workplace. In R. A. Giacalone and C. L. Jurkiewicz (Eds.), *Handbook of workplace spirituality and organizational performance.* Armonk, NY: M. E. Sharpe (2003): 108–22.

de Janasz, S. C., and S. E. Sullivan. Multiple mentoring in academe: Developing the professorial network. *Journal of Vocational Behavior, 64* (2004): 263–83.

Denton, D., and W. Ashton. (Eds.). *Spirituality, action, and pedagogy: Teaching from the heart.* New York: Peter Lang (2004).

De Souza, M. Contemporary influences on the spirituality of young people: Implications for education. *International Journal of Childhood Spirituality, 8*(3) (2003): 269–79.

Dik, B. J., and R. D. Duffy. *Make your job a calling: How the psychology of vocation can change your life at work.* West Conshohocken, PA: Templeton Press (2012).

Dik, B. J., R. D. Duffy, and A. P. Tix. Religion, spirituality, and a sense of calling in the workplace. In P. C. Hill and B. J. Dik (Eds.), *Psychology of religion and workplace spirituality: A volume in advances in workplace spirituality: Theory, research, and application.* (L. W. Fry, Series Ed.). Charlotte, NC: Information Age (2012): 113–33.

Dill, D. D. The management of academic culture: Notes on the management of meaning and social integration. *Higher Education, 11*(3) (1982): 303–20.

Dillard, C. B. *On spiritual strivings: Transforming an African American woman's academic life.* Albany: State University of New York Press (2006).

Dillard, C. B., D. Abdur-Rashid, and C. A. Tyson. My soul is a witness: Affirming pedagogies of the spirit. *International Journal of Qualitative Studies in Education, 13*(5) (2000): 447–62.

Dobbie, B. J. Women's mid-life experience: An evolving consciousness of self and children. *Journal of Advanced Nursing, 3* (1991): 6–8.

Duchon, D., and D. A. Plowman. Nurturing the spirit at work: Impact on work unit performance. *Leadership Quarterly, 16* (2005): 807–33.

Duerr, M., A. Zajonc, and D. Dana. Survey of transformative and spiritual dimensions of higher education. *Journal of Transformative Education, 1*(3) (2003): 177–211.

Dyson, J., M. Cobb, and D. Forman. The meaning of spirituality: A literature review. *Journal of Advanced Nursing, 26*(6) (1997): 1183–88.

Eddy, P. L., and J. L. Gaston-Gayles. New faculty on the block: Issues of stress and support. *Journal of Human Behavior in the Social Environment, 17*(1–2) (2008): 89–106.

Edwards, M. U., Jr. *Religion on our campuses: A professor's guide to communities, conflicts, and promising conversations.* New York: Palgrave Macmillan (2006).

Eisler, R., and A. Montuori. The human side of spirituality. In R. A. Giacalone and C. L. Jurkiewicz (Eds.), *Handbook of workplace spirituality and organizational performance.* Armonk, NY: M. E. Sharpe (2003): 46–56.

Elkins, D. N., L. J. Hedstrom, L. L. Hughes, J. A. Leaf, and C. Saunders. Toward a humanistic-phenomenological spirituality: Definitions, description, and measurement. *Journal of Humanistic Psychology, 28*(4) (1988): 5–18.

Ellison, C. W., and J. Smith. Toward an integrative measure of health and well-being. *Journal of Psychology and Theology, 19*(1) (1991): 35–48.

Emmons, R. A. *The psychology of ultimate concerns: Motivation and spirituality in personality.* New York: Guilford Press (1999).

Fagenson, E. A. The mentor advantage: Perceived career/job experiences of proteges v. nonproteges. *Journal of Organizational Behavior, 10* (1989): 309–20.

Feldman, D. C. A socialization process that helps new recruits succeed. In J. R. Hackman, E. E. Lawler, and L. W. Porter (Eds.), *Perspectives on behavior in organizations* (2nd ed.). New York: McGraw-Hill (1983).

Felton, P., H. L. Bauman, A. Kheriaty, and E. Taylor. *Transformative conversations: A guide to mentoring communities among colleagues in higher education.* San Francisco: Jossey-Bass (2013).

Fernandes, L. *Transforming feminist practice: Non-violence, social justice, and the possibilities of a spiritualized feminism.* San Francisco: Aunt Lute Books (2003).

Fetzer Institute/National Institute on Aging Working Group. *Multidimensional measurement of religiousness/spirituality for use in health research.* Kalamazoo, MI: John E. Fetzer Institute (2003).

Finkelstein, M. J. *The American academic profession: A synthesis of social scientific inquiry since World War II.* Columbus: Ohio State University (1984).

Fleming, J. J., J. Purnell, and Y. Wang. Student-faculty interaction and the development of an ethic of care. In A. N. Rockenbach and M. J. Mayhew (Eds.), *Spirituality in college students' lives: Translating research into practice.* New York: Routledge (2013): 153–69.

Frankl, V. E. *Man's search for meaning: An introduction to logotherapy.* Boston: Beacon Press (1963).

Fryback, P. B. Health for people with a terminal diagnosis. *Nursing Science Quarterly, 6* (1993): 147–59.

Fryback, P. B., and B. Reinert. Spirituality and people with potentially fatal diagnoses. *Nursing Forum, 34*(1) (1999): 13–22.

Fuller, R. C. *Spiritual but not religious: Understanding unchurched America.* New York: Oxford Press (2001).

Gallup, G. H., Jr. *Why are women more religious?* (December 17, 2002). http//www.gallup.com/poll/7432/why-women-more-religious .aspx.

Gappa, J. M., and A. E. Austin. Rethinking academic traditions for twenty-first-century faculty. *AAUP Journal of Academic Freedom, 1* (2010): 1–20.

Gappa, J. M., A. E. Austin, and A. G. Trice. *Rethinking faculty work: Higher education's strategic imperative.* San Francisco: Jossey-Bass (2007).

Genia, V. The Spiritual Experience Index: A measure of spiritual maturity. *Journal of Religion and Health, 30*(4) (1991): 337–47.

Geroy, G. D. Preparing students for spirituality in the workplace. In S. L. Hoppe and B. W. Speck (Eds.), *Spirituality in higher education.* New Directions for Teaching and Learning, no. 104. San Francisco: Jossey-Bass (Winter 2005): 67–74.

Gibbons, P. Spirituality at work: Definitions, measures, assumptions, and validity claims. In J. Bieberman and M. D. Whitty (Eds.), *Work and spirit: A reader of new spiritual paradigms for organizations.* Scranton, PA: University of Scranton Press (2000): 111–31.

Gibson, J. L., J. M. Ivancevich, and J. H. Donnelly. *Organizations: Behavior, structure, process* (8th ed.). Burr Ridge, IL: Irwin (1994).

Glazer, S. (Ed.). *The heart of learning: Spirituality in education.* New York: Tarcher/Putnam (1999).

Goddard, N. C. A response to Dawson's critical analysis of "spirituality" as integrative energy. *Journal of Advanced Nursing, 31*(4) (2000): 968–79.

Greenleaf, R. K. *Servant leadership: A journey into the nature of legitimate power and greatness.* Mahwah, NJ: Paulist Press (1977).

Gross, N. *Why are professors liberal and why do conservatives care?* Cambridge, MA: Harvard University Press (2013).

Gross, N., and S. Simmons. *How religious are America's college and university professors?* (2007). http://religion.ssrc.org/reform/Gross -Simmons.pdf.

Hall, B. A. Patterns of spirituality in persons with advanced HIV disease. *Research in Nursing and Health, 21,* (1998): 143–53.

Hall, T. W., and K. J. Edwards. The Spiritual Assessment Inventory: A theistic model and measure for assessing spiritual development. *Journal for the Scientific Study of Religion, 41*(2) (2002): 341–57.

Hamer, D. *The God gene: How faith is hardwired into our genes.* New York: Anchor Books (2004).

Hayes, S. C. Making sense of spirituality. *Behaviorism, 12*(2) (1984): 99–110.

Helminiak, D. A. *Spiritual development: An interdisciplinary study.* Chicago: Loyola University Press (1987).

Hendel, D. D., and A. S. Horn. The relationship between academic life conditions and perceived sources of faculty stress over time. *Journal of Human Behavior in the Social Environment, 17*(1/2) (2008): 61–88.

Higgins, M. C., and K. E. Kram. Reconceptualizing mentoring at work: A developmental network perspective. *Academy of Management Review, 26* (2001): 264–88.

Hill, P. C., and B. J. Dik. Toward a science of workplace spirituality: Contributions from the psychology of religion and spirituality. In P. C. Hill and B. J. Dik (Eds.), *Psychology of religion and workplace spirituality: A volume in advances in workplace spirituality: Theory, research, and application.* (L. W. Fry, Series Ed.). Charlotte, NC: Information Age (2012): 1–22.

Hill, P. C., and R. W. Hood Jr. (Eds.). *Measures of religiosity.* Birmingham, AL: Religious Education Press (1999).

Hill, P. C., and K. I. Pargament. Advances in the conceptualization and measurement of religion and spirituality. *American Psychologist 58*(1) (2003): 64–74.

Hill, P. C., K. I. Pargament, R. W. Hood Jr., M. E. McCullough, J. P. Swyers, D. B. Lawson, and B. J. Zinnbauer. Conceptualizing religion and spirituality: Points of commonality, points of departure. *Journal for the Theory of Social Behavior, 30*(1) (2000): 51–77.

Hill, P. C., and E. Smith. Measurement in the psychology of religiousness and spirituality: Existing measures and new frontiers. In K. Pargament (Ed.-in-Chief), J. Exline and J. Jones (Assoc. Eds.), *APA handbook of psychology, religion, and spirituality.* Washington, DC: American Psychological Association (in press).

Hindman, D. M. From splintered lives to whole persons: Facilitating spiritual development of college students. *Religious Education, 97*(2) (2002): 165–82.

Hodge, D. R. The intrinsic spirituality scale: A new six-item instrument for assessing the salience of spirituality as a motivational construct. *Journal of Social Sciences Research, 30*(1) (2003): 41–61.

Holland, J. *Making vocational choices: A theory of careers.* Upper Saddle River, NJ: Prentice Hall (1973).

Holland, J. *Making vocational choices: A theory of vocational personalities and work environments* (3rd ed.). Odessa, FL: Psychological Assessment Resources (1997).

Hoppe, S. L. Spirituality and leadership. In S. L. Hoppe and B. W. Speck (Eds.), *Spirituality in higher education.* New Directions for Teaching and Learning, no. 104. San Francisco: Jossey-Bass (Winter 2005): 83–92.

Hurtado, S., L. Ponjuan, and G. Smith. *Women and faculty of color on campus: Campus diversity and civic engagement initiatives* (2003). http://umich.edu/~divdemo/Final_Engaged_Paper_kinkos.pdf.

Idler, E. Organizational religiousness. In Fetzer Institute/National Institute on Aging Working Group, *Multidimensional measurement of religiousness/spirituality for use in health research: A report to the Fetzer Institute/National Institute on Aging Working Group.* Kalamazoo, MI: John E. Fetzer Institute (1999): 75–80.

Johnson, W. B., and C. R. Ridley. *The elements of mentoring.* New York: Palgrave Macmillan (2004).

Karoly, P. A goal-systems self-regulatory perspective on personality, psychopathology, and change. *Review of General Psychology, 3* (1999): 264–91.

Kaye, J., and K. M. Robinson. Spirituality among caregivers. *Image: The Journal of Nursing Scholarship, 26* (1994): 218–21.

Kazanjian, V. H. Moments of meaning. *Connection: New England's Journal of Higher Education and Economic Development, 13*(3) (1998): 37–39.

Keen, C., and K. Hall. Engaging with difference matters: Longitudinal student outcomes of co-curricular service-learning programs. *Journal of Higher Education, 80*(1) (2009): 59–79.

King, A. S. Spirituality: Transformation and metamorphosis. *Religion, 26*(4) (1996): 343–51.

Klaas, D. Testing two elements of spirituality in depressed and nondepressed elders. *International Journal of Psychiatric Nursing Research, 4* (1998): 542–62.

Klaassen, D. W., and M. J. McDonald. Quest and identity development: Reexamining pathways for existential search. *International Journal for the Psychology of Religion, 12*(3) (2002): 189–200.

Klinger, E. *Meaning and void: Inner experience and the incentives in people's lives.* Oxford, England: University of Minnesota Press (1977).

Kosmin, B. A., and A. Keysar. *American Religious Identification Survey (ARIS) Summary Report.* Hartford, CT: Trinity College (2008).

Krahnke, K., and L. Hoffman. The rise of religion and spirituality in the workplace: Employees' rights and employers' accommodations. *Journal of Behavioral and Applied Management, 3*(3) (2002): 277–87.

Kristoff, A. L. Person-organization fit: An integrative review of its conceptualizations, measurement, and implications. *Personnel Psychology, 49*(1) (1996): 1–49.

Kuh, G. D., and E. J. Whitt. *The invisible tapestry: Culture in American colleges and universities.* ASHE-ERIC Higher Education Report No. 1. Washington, DC: Association for the Study of Higher Education (1988).

Lattuca, L. R., L. J. Voigt, and K. Q. Faith. Does interdisciplinarity promote learning? Theoretical support and researchable questions. *Review of Higher Education, 28*(1) (2004): 23–48.

Laurence, P., and V. Kazanjian. *Education as transformation: Religious pluralism, spirituality, and a new vision for higher education in America.* New York: Peter Lang (2000).

Lee, C., and R. Zemke. The search for spirit in the workplace. *Training, 30*(6) (June 1993): 21–28.

Leider, R. J., and D. A. Shapiro. *Whistle while you work: Heeding your life's calling.* San Francisco: Barrett-Koehler (2001).

Lerner, M. Spirituality in America. *Tikkun, 13*(5) (1998): 1.

Levin, J. Private religious practices. In Fetzer Institute/National Institute on Aging Working Group, *Multidimensional measurement of religiousness/spirituality for use in health research: A report to the Fetzer Institute/National Institute on Aging Working Group.* Kalamazoo, MI: John E. Fetzer Institute (1999): 39–42.

Lewis, C. A., and S. M. Cruise. Religion and happiness: Consensus, contradictions, comments and concerns. *Mental Health, Religion & Culture, 9* (2006): 213–25.

Lim, C., C. A. MacGregor, and R. Putnam. Secular and liminal: Discovering heterogeneity among religious nones. *Journal for the Scientific Study of Religion, 49*(4) (2010): 596–618.

Lindholm, J. A. *Establishing a "sense of space" within academic work environments.* Doctoral dissertation, UCLA Graduate School of Education & Information Studies (2001).

Lindholm, J. A., A. W. Astin, L. J. Sax, and W. S. Korn. *The American college teacher: National norms for the 2001–2002 HERI Faculty Survey.* Higher Education Research Institute, UCLA (2002).

Lindholm, J. A., and H. S. Astin. Spirituality and pedagogy: Faculty's spirituality and use of student-centered approaches to undergraduate teaching. *Review of Higher Education, 31*(2) (2008): 185–207.

Lindholm, J. A., H. S. Astin, and A. W. Astin. *Spirituality and the professoriate: A national study of faculty beliefs, attitudes, and behaviors.* Higher Education Research Institute, UCLA (2005).

Lindholm, J. A., M. L. Millora, L. M. Schwartz, and H. S. Spinosa. A guidebook of promising practices: *Facilitating college students' spiritual development.* Oakland: Regents of the University of California (2011).

Lindholm, J. A., and K. Szelényi. Becoming one of "us": Promoting a sense of institutional fit among faculty. *Department Chair* (Summer 2003): 7–9.

Lindholm, J. A., and K. Szelényi. *Disciplinary differences in faculty use of student-centered pedagogy.* Unpublished manuscript, Higher Education Research Institute, UCLA (2006).

Lindholm, J. A., and K. Szelényi. Faculty time stress: Correlates within and across academic disciplines. *Human Behavior in the Social Environment, 17*(1–2) (2008): 19–40.

Lindholm, J. A., K. Szelényi, S. Hurtado, and W. S. Korn. *The American college teacher: National norms for the 2004–2005 HERI Faculty Survey.* Higher Education Research Institute, UCLA (2005).

Lips-Wiersma, M. S., and L. Morris. *The map of meaning: A guide to sustaining our humanity at work.* Sheffield, England: Greenleaf Publishing (2011).

Locke, E. A. The nature and consequences of job satisfaction. In M. D. Dunnette (Ed.), *Handbook of industrial psychology.* Chicago: Rand-McNally (1976): 1297–1349.

Love, P. G., and D. Talbot. Defining spiritual development: A missing consideration for student affairs. *NASPA Journal, 37*(1) (1999): 361–75.

MacDonald, D. A. Spirituality: Description, measurement, and relation to the five factor model of personality. *Journal of Personality, 68*(1) (2000): 153–97.

Mahoney, A. Religion in families, 1999 to 2009: A relational spiritual framework. *Journal of Marriage and Family, 72*(4) (2010): 805–27.

Manning, K. *Rituals, ceremonies, and cultural meaning in higher education.* Westport, CT: Bergin & Garvey (2000).

Marsden, G. M. *The shaping of the American university: From Protestant establishment to established nonbelief.* New York: Oxford University Press (1994).

May, D. R., R. L. Gilson, and L. M. Harter. The psychological conditions of meaningfulness, safety and availability and the engagement of the human spirit at work. *Journal of Occupational and Organizational Psychology, 77* (2004): 11–37.

McLaughlin, C. Spirituality at work. *Bridging Tree, 1* (March 17, 1998): 11.

Menges, R. J., and Associates. *Faculty in new jobs: A guide to settling in, becoming established, and building institutional support.* San Francisco: Jossey-Bass (1999).

Mickley, J. P., K. Socken, and A. Belcher. Spiritual well-being, religiousness, and hope among women with breast cancer. *Image: The Journal of Nursing Scholarship, 24* (1992): 267–72.

Miller, V. W., and D. K. Scott. *Making space for spirit in the department.* (2000). http://www.umass.edu/pastchancellors/scott/papers/spirit.html.

Miller, W. R., and C. E. Thoresen. Spirituality, religion, and health: An emerging research field. *American Psychologist, 58*(1) (2003): 24–35.

Moberg, D. O. Assessing and measuring spirituality: Confronting dilemmas of universal and particular evaluative criteria. *Journal of Adult Development, 9*(1) (2002): 47–60.

Moody, J. *Demystifying the profession: Helping junior faculty succeed.* New Haven, CT: University of New Haven Press (2001).

Murphy, C. The academy, spirituality, and the search for truth. In S. L. Hoppe and B. W. Speck (Eds.), *Spirituality in higher education.* New Directions for Teaching and Learning, no. 104 (Winter 2005): 23–29.

Myers, D. G. *The American paradox: Spiritual hunger in an age of plenty.* New Haven: Yale University Press (2000).

Narayanasamy, A. A review of spirituality as applied to nursing. *International Journal of Nursing Studies, 36*(2) (1999): 117–25.

Nash, R. J., and M. C. Murray. *Helping college students find purpose: The campus guide to meaning-making.* San Francisco: Jossey-Bass (2010).

Newport, F. *God is alive and well: The future of religion in America.* New York: Gallup Press (2012).

Noddings, N. *Caring: A feminine approach to ethics and morals education.* Berkeley: University of California Press (1984).

Noddings, N. Educating moral people. In M. M. Brabeck (Ed.), *Who cares? Theory, research, and educational implications of the ethic of care.* New York: Praeger (1989): 216–32. (Earlier version appeared as N. Noddings, Do we really want to produce good people? *Journal of Moral Education, 16* [1987]: 177–88.).

Noddings, N. *The challenge to care in schools: An alternative approach to education.* New York: Teachers College Press (1992).

Noddings, N. *Starting at home: Caring and social policy.* Berkeley: University of California Press (2002).

O'Meara, K. A. *Scholarship unbound: Assessing service as scholarship for promotion and tenure.* New York: Routledge Falmer (2002).

O'Meara, K. A., A. L. Terosky, and A. Neumann. Faculty careers and work: A professional growth perspective. *ASHE Higher Education Report, 34*(3). San Francisco: Jossey-Bass (2008).

O'Reilly, C. A., J. Chatman, and D. F. Caldwell. People and organizational culture: A profile comparison approach to assessing person-organization fit. *Academy of Management Journal, 34* (1991): 487–516.

Ottaway, R. N. Defining spirituality at work. *International Journal of Value-Based Management, 16* (2003): 23–25.

Palmer, P. J. *To know as we are known: Education as a spiritual journey.* San Francisco: Jossey-Bass (1983).

Palmer, P. J. *The courage to teach: A guide for reflection and renewal.* San Francisco: Jossey-Bass (1999).

Palmer, P. J., and A. Zajonc. *The heart of higher education: A call to renewal.* San Francisco: Jossey-Bass (2010).

Paloutzian, R. F., and D. A. Lowe. Spiritual transformation and engagement in workplace culture. In P. C. Hill and B. J. Dik (Eds.), *Psychology of religion and workplace spirituality: A volume in advances in workplace spirituality: Theory, research, and application.* (L. W. Fry, Series Ed.). Charlotte, NC: Information Age (2012): 179–99.

Pargament, K. I. *The psychology of religion and coping: Theory, research, practice.* New York: Guilford Press (1997).

Pargament, K. I. The psychology of religion and spirituality? Yes and no. *International Journal for the Psychology of Religion, 9*(1) (1999): 3–16.

Park, C. L. Overview of theoretical perspectives. In C. L. Park, S. Lechner, M. H. Antoni, and A. Stanton (Eds.), *Positive life change in the context of medical illness: Can the experience of serious illness lead to transformation?* Washington, DC: American Psychological Association (2009): 11–30.

Park, C. L. Making sense of the meaning literature: An integrative review of meaning making and its effects on adjustment to stressful life events. *Psychological Bulletin, 136* (2010): 257–301.

Park, C. L. Religious and spiritual aspects of meaning in the context of work life. In P. C. Hill and B. J. Dik (Eds.), *Psychology of religion and workplace spirituality: A volume in advances in workplace spirituality: Theory, research, and application.* (L.W. Fry, Series Ed.). Charlotte, NC: Information Age (2012): 25–42.

Pelikan, J. *The idea of the university: A reexamination.* New Haven, CT: Yale University Press (1992).

Peterson, C., and M.E.P. Seligman. *Character strengths and virtues: A handbook and classification.* Washington, DC: American Psychological Association (2004).

Pew Forum on Religion & Public Life. *"Nones" on the rise.* Washington, DC: Pew Research Center's Forum on Religion & Public Life (October 9, 2012). http://www.pewforum.org/2012/10/09/nones-on-the-rise/.

Philipsen, M. I., T. B. Bostic, and M. A. Mason. *Helping faculty find work-life balance: The path toward family-friendly institutions.* San Francisco: Jossey-Bass (2010).

Piehl, T. A. *Enhancing classrooms and conversations: How interactions with faculty predict change in students' spirituality in college.* Doctoral dissertation, UCLA Graduate School of Education & Information Studies (2013).

Ponjuan, L., V. M. Conley, and C. Trower. Career stage differences in pre-tenure track faculty perceptions of professional and personal relationships with colleagues. *Journal of Higher Education, 82*(3) (2011): 319–46.

Posner, B. Z. Person-organization values congruence: No support for individual differences as a moderating influence. *Human Relations, 45* (1992): 351–61.

Potts, R. G. Spirituality and the experience of cancer in an African-American community: Implications for psychosocial oncology. *Journal of Psychological Oncology, 14* (1996): 1–19.

Putnam, R. D. *Bowling alone: The collapse and revival of American community.* New York: Simon & Schuster (2000).

Putnam, R. D., and D. E. Campbell. *American grace: How religion divides and unites us.* New York: Simon & Schuster (2012).

Reed, P. G. Preferences for spiritually related nursing interventions among terminally ill and nonterminally ill hospitalized adults and well adults. *Applied Nursing Research, 4* (1991): 122–28.

Reker, G. T., and P. T. P. Wong. Aging as an individual process: Toward a theory of personal meaning. In J. E. Birren and V. L. Bengston (Eds.), *Emerging theories of aging.* New York: Springer (1988): 214–46.

Reuben, J. A. *The making of the modern university: Intellectual transformation and the marginalization of morality.* Chicago: University of Chicago Press (1996).

Rhoads, R. A. Democratic citizenship and service learning: Advancing the caring self. In M.B.B. Magolda (Ed.), *Building faculty learning communities.* New Directions for Teaching and Learning, no. 82. San Francisco: Jossey-Bass (Summer 2000): 37–44.

Rice, R. E. The academic profession in transition: Toward a new social fiction. *Teaching Sociology, 14* (1986): 12–23.

Rice, R. E., and A. E. Austin. High faculty morale: What exemplary colleges do right. *Change, 20*(2) (March/April 1988): 51–58.

Rice, R. E., M. D. Sorcinelli, and A. E. Austin. *Heeding new voices: Academic careers for a new generation.* New Pathways Working Paper series, No. 7. Washington, DC: American Association for Higher Education (2000).

Riley, B. B., R. Perna, D. G. Tate, M. Forcheimer, C. Anderson, and G. Luera. Types of spiritual well-being among persons with chronic illness: Their relation to various forms of quality of life. *Archives of Physical Medicine and Rehabilitation, 79*(3) (1998): 258–64.

Robbins, S. P. *Organizational behavior: Concepts, controversies, applications* (8th ed.). Upper Saddle River, NJ: Prentice Hall (1998).

Rockenbach, A. N., and M. J. Mayhew. How institutional contexts and college experiences shape ecumenical worldview development. In A. N. Rockenbach and M. J. Mayhew (Eds.), *Spirituality in college students' lives: Translating research into practice.* New York: Routledge (2013): 88–104.

Rokeach, M. *The nature of human values.* New York: Free Press (1973).

Roof, W. C. *A generation of seekers: The spiritual journeys of the baby boom generation.* San Francisco: HarperCollins (1993).

Rose, S. Is the term "spirituality" a word that everyone uses, but nobody knows what anyone means by it? *Journal of Contemporary Religion, 16*(2) (2001): 193–207.

Rosser, V. J. Faculty members' intentions to leave: A national study on their worklife and satisfaction. *Research in Higher Education, 45* (2004): 285–309.

Sandage, S. J., C. M. Dahl, and M. G. Harden. The psychology of religion, spirituality, and diversity. In P. C. Hill and B. J. Dik (Eds.), *Psychology of religion and workplace spirituality: A volume in advances in workplace spirituality: Theory, research, and application.* (L. W. Fry, Series Ed.). Charlotte, NC: Information Age (2012): 43–62.

Sanford, N. *Where colleges fail: A study of student as person.* San Francisco: Jossey-Bass (1968).

Satow, R. L. Value-rational authority and professional organizations: Weber's missing type. *Administrative Science Quarterly, 20* (1975): 526–31.

Sax, L. J., and A. W. Astin. The benefits of service: Evidence of undergraduates. *Educational Record, 78*(3–4) (1997): 25–32.

Sax, L. J., S. Hurtado, J. A. Lindholm, A. W. Astin, W. S. Korn, and K. M. Mahoney. *The American freshman: National norms for fall 2004.* Higher Education Research Institute, UCLA (2005).

Schein, E. H. *Organizational culture and leadership* (3rd ed.). San Francisco: Jossey-Bass (2004).

Schlegel, R. J., J. A. Hicks, L. A. King, and J. Arndt. Feeling like you know who you are: Perceived true knowledge and the meaning of life. *Personality and Social Psychology Bulletin, 37*(6) (2011): 745–56.

Seidlitz, L., A. D. Abernethy, P. R. Duberstein, J. S. Evinger, T. H. Chang, and B. L. Lewis. Development of the Spiritual Transcendence Index. *Journal for the Scientific Study of Religion, 41*(3) (2002): 439–53.

Seifert, T. A., and P. D. Umbach. The effects of faculty demographic characteristics and disciplinary context on dimension of job satisfaction. *Research in Higher Education, 49* (2008): 357–81.

Shahjahan, R. A. Centering spirituality in the academy: Toward a transformative way of teaching and learning. *Journal of Transformative Education, 2*(4) (2004a): 294–312.

Shahjahan, R. A. Reclaiming and reconnecting to our spirituality in the academy. *International Journal of Children's Spirituality, 9*(1) (2004b): 81–95.

Shahjahan, R. A. Spirituality in the academy: Reclaiming from the margins and evoking a transformative way of knowing the world. *International Journal of Qualitative Education (QSE), 18*(6) (2005): 685–711.

Shahjahan, R. A. Toward a spiritual practice: The role of spirituality among faculty of color teaching for social justice. *Review of Higher Education, 33*(4) (2010): 473–512.

Sherman, D. W. Nurses' willingness to care for AIDS patients and spirituality, social support, and death anxiety. *Image: The Journal of Nursing Scholarship, 28* (1996): 205–13.

Silberman, I. Religion as a meaning system: Implications for the new millennium. *Journal of Social Issues, 61* (2005): 641–63.

Smart, J., K. A. Feldman, and C. A. Ethington. *Academic disciplines: Holland's theory and the study of college students and faculty.* Nashville, TN: Vanderbilt University Press (2000).

Smith, C. *The secular revolution: Power, interests, and conflict in the secularization of American public life.* Berkeley: University of California Press (2003).

Smith, D. M. *Women at work: Leadership for the next century.* Upper Saddle River, NJ: Prentice Hall (2000).

Smith, T. V. The university and the spiritual life. *Journal of Higher Education, 22*(8) (1951): 400–10.

Sorcinelli, M. D., and A. E. Austin. (Eds.). *Developing new and junior faculty.* New Directions for Teaching and Learning, no. 50. San Francisco: Jossey-Bass (Summer 1992).

Spano, D. B. Nurturing institutional cultures of caring. *About Campus,* *12*(6) (2008): 17–21.

Stanton, T. K. The experience of faculty participants in an instructional development seminar on service-learning. *Michigan Journal of Community Service Learning,* *1*(1) (1994): 7–20.

Stark, R. Physiology and faith: Addressing the "universal" gender differences in religious commitment. *Journal for the Scientific Study of Religion,* *41*(3) (2002): 495–507.

Steger, M. F. Work as meaning. In P. A. Linley, S. Harrington, and N. Page (Eds.), *Oxford handbook of positive psychology and work.* Oxford, England: Oxford University Press (2010): 131–42.

Steger, M. F. Spiritual leadership. In P. C. Hill and B. J. Dik (Eds.), *Psychology of religion and workplace spirituality: A volume in advances in workplace spirituality: Theory, research, and application.* (L. W. Fry, Series Ed.). Charlotte, NC: Information Age (2012): 223–38.

Steger, M. F., B. J. Dik, and R. D. Duffy. Measuring meaningful work: The Work and Meaning Inventory (WAMI). *Journal of Career Assessment,* *20*(3) (2012): 322–37.

Steger, M. F., P. Frazier, S. Oishi, and M. Kaler. The Meaning in Life Questionnaire: Assessing the presence and search for meaning in life. *Journal of Counseling Psychology,* *53*(1) (2006): 80–93.

Steger, M. F., B. M. Hicks, T. B. Kashdan, R. F. Krueger, and T. J. Bouchard Jr. Genetic and environmental influences on the positive traits of the values in action classification, and biometric covariance with normal personality. *Journal of Research in Personality,* *41*(3) (2007): 524–39.

Stockton, S., and Associates. *The private conversations about spirituality at a public university.* Research forum presented at the Going Public with Spirituality in Work and Higher Education conference, Amherst, MA (June 6, 2000).

Stoll, R. I. The essence of spirituality. In V. B. Carson (Ed.), *Spiritual dimensions of nursing practice.* Philadelphia: W. B. Saunders (1989): 4–23.

Strohl, J. E. Religion vs. spirituality. *Dialog: A Journal of Theology,* *40*(4) (2001): 274–76.

Tanyi, R. A. Towards clarification of the meaning of spirituality. *Journal of Advanced Nursing,* *11*(4) (2002): 500–09.

Testerman, J. K. *Spirituality vs. religion: Implications for healthcare.* Paper presented at the 20th annual Faith and Learning Seminar, Loma Linda, CA (June 15–27, 1997).

Tierney, W. G., and E. M. Bensimon. *Promotion and tenure: Community and socialization in academe.* Albany: State University of New York Press (1996).

Tisdell, E. J. *Spirituality in adult and higher education. ERIC digest. No. ED459370.* Columbus, OH: ERIC Clearinghouse on Adult Career and Vocational Education (2001).

Tisdell, E. J. *Exploring spirituality and culture in adult and higher education.* San Francisco: Jossey-Bass (2003).

Tobin, G. A., and A. K. Weinberg. *Profiles of the university.* Vol. 2, *Religious beliefs and behavior of college faculty.* Roseville, CA: Institute for Jewish and Community Research (2007).

Todd, K. L. A semantic analysis of the word spirituality. (2004) http://web.nwe.ufl.edu/~jdouglas/spiritual.pdf. (This site is no longer available.)

Trautvetter, L. C. Developing students' search for meaning and purpose. In G. I. Kramer and Associates (Eds.), *Fostering student success in the campus community* (2007): 236–61.

Trower, C. A. A new generation of faculty: Similar core values in a different world. *peerReview, 12*(3) (2010). http://www.aacu.org/peerreview/pr-su10/pr_su10_NewGen.cfm.

Turner, C. S. Women of color in academe: Living with multiple marginality. *Journal of Higher Education, 73*(1) (2002): 74–93.

Twale, D. J., and B. M. DeLuca. *Faculty incivility: The rise of the academic bully culture and what to do about it.* San Francisco: Jossey-Bass (2008).

Umbach, P. The contribution of faculty of color to undergraduate education. *Research in Higher Education, 47*(3) (2006): 317–45.

Underwood, L. G., and J. A. Teresi. The Daily Spiritual Experience Scale: Development, theoretical description, reliability, exploratory factor analysis, and preliminary construct validity using health-related data. *Society of Behavioral Medicine, 24*(1) (2002): 22–33.

Van Maanen, J., and E. H. Schein. Toward a theory of organizational socialization. In B. M. Staw (Ed.), *Research in organizational behavior,* vol. 1. Greenwich, CT: JAI (1979): 209–94.

Waggoner, M. D. (Ed.). *Sacred and secular tensions in higher education: Connecting parallel universities.* New York: Routledge (2011).

Waite, P. J., S. R. Hawks, and J. A. Gast. The correlation between spiritual well-being and health behaviors. *American Journal of Health Promotion, 13* (1999): 159–62.

Weathersby, R. *Being spiritually present at work in the academy: Possibilities and dilemmas.* Research session presented at the Going Public with Spirituality in Work and Higher Education conference, Amherst, MA (June 5, 2000).

Whitt, E. Hit the ground running: Experiences of new faculty in a school of education. *Review of Higher Education, 14*(2) (1991): 177–97.

Wigglesworth, C. Spiritual intelligence. In J. Neal (Ed.), *Handbook of faith and spirituality in the workplace: Emerging theory and practice.* New York: Springer Science + Business Media (2013): 675–95.

Wilcox, J. R., with J. A. Lindholm, and S. D. Wilcox. *Revisioning mission: The future of Catholic higher education.* Wilcox (2013).

Williams, D. R. Commitment. In Fetzer Institute/National Institute on Aging Working Group, *Multidimensional measurement of religiousness/ spirituality for use in health research: A report to the Fetzer Institute/ National Institute on Aging Working Group.* Kalamazoo, MI: John E. Fetzer Institute (1999): 71–74.

Wright, S. Life, the universe, and you. *Nursing Standard, 14* (2000): 23.

Wrzesniewski, A. Callings. In K. Cameron and G. Spreitzer (Eds.), *The Oxford handbook of positive organizational scholarship.* New York: Oxford University Press (2013): 45–55.

Wrzesniewski, A., J. E. Dutton, and G. Debebe. Interpersonal sensemaking and the meaning of work. *Research in Organizational Behavior, 25* (2003): 93–135.

Wuthnow, R. *After heaven: Spirituality in America since the 1950s.* Berkeley: University of California Press (1998).

Zinnbauer, B. J., K. I. Pargament, B. Cole, M. S. Rye, E. M. Butter, T. G. Belavich, K. M. Hipp, A. B. Scott, and J. I. Kadar. Religion and spirituality: Unfuzzying the fuzzy. *Journal for the Scientific Study of Religion, 36*(4) (1997): 549–64.

Zinnbauer, B. J., K. I. Pargament, and A. B. Scott. The emerging meanings of religiousness and spirituality: Problems and prospects. *Journal of Personality, 67*(6) (1999): 889–919.

Zohar, D., and I. Marshall. *Spiritual capital: Wealth we can live by.* San Francisco: Berrett-Koehler (2004).

SUBJECT INDEX

A

Academic disciplines: belief in God and, 126–127; Charitable Involvement scale and, 115; Ecumenical Worldview items and, 98–100; equanimity and, 162–164; Ethic of Caring scale and, 88–89; religious commitment and, 134–136; religious disagreements among, 204*f*; religious skepticism and, 148–149; religious-science relationship and, 152–154; spiritual quests and, 77–80; spirituality *versus* religiousness and, 62–67; values of faculty in, 59–62

Academic work: benefits of holistic approach to, 12; as calling, xiv–xvii, 76; core elements of, 76; equanimity and, 164–166; essential aspects of, 165*f*; Ethic of Caring items and, 91–96; spiritual quests and, 74–83; tensions in, 82. *See also* Work

Accountability, 112

Administration, 110–111

Advice, from faculty, 184–197

African American faculty members: charitable involvement of, 113, 115; Ecumenical Worldview and, 100; equanimity of, 162; religious commitment of, 132, 133; religious skepticism of, 148; reported religious self-identity in, 28, 29*t*, 32, 37*t*; reported

spirituality of, 26*t*, 27, 32, 40, 41*t*; spiritual quests of, 74

Age: and rejection of spirituality and religion, 51–52*t*; and self-reported religiousness, 33*t*, 37*t*; and self-reported spirituality, 26*t*, 27, 33*t*, 41–42*t*

Altruism scale (Elkins and colleagues), 20

Altruism, spirituality *versus* religion and, 44–45

Applied fields, faculty in, 63

Artistic personalities, 79

Asian American/Asian faculty: religious self-identification of, 36, 37*t*; spiritual quests of, 74

Atheism, viii

Autonomy, 164

Awareness scale (Hall and Edwards), 19

B

Baby boomers, 206

Behavioral studies, 11

Belonging, sense of, 107

Business faculty: Ethic of Caring scale and, 89; religious commitment of, 134*f*; spiritual quests of, 77

Business-oriented approaches, 6

C

Calling: crafting of, in faculty, xvi–xvii; definition of, xv, 76; ecumenical worldview and, 104–105; maintaining perspective

U.S. Constitution, xiii
U.S. population, spirituality of, 1

V

Value-rational organizations, 60–61
Values, of faculty: description of, 59–67; equanimity and, 167–170; importance of, 8–9; of spiritual but not religious faculty, 40; spirituality *versus* religion and, 44–45, 49
Values, societal: conceptualization of, 10–11; importance of, in behavioral studies, 11; of liberal education, 6; spirituality as a reflection of, 5
Vocation. *See* Calling, scholarly work as

W

Women faculty: charitable involvement of, 113; equanimity of, 162; rejection of spirituality and religion by, 50, 51*t*; religious commitment of, 134, 135*t*; spiritual quests of, 74; spiritual self-identification of, 32, 40, 41*t*; work-life balance of, 205–206
Work: interactions with colleagues at, 107–108; job satisfaction in, 106, 107; meaningful nature of, 74–75; schedule of, for religiously engaged faculty, 142–143. *See also* Academic work
Workaholism, 174
Work-life integration, 172–177, 194–195, 205–206

NAME INDEX

If you enjoyed this book, you may also like these:

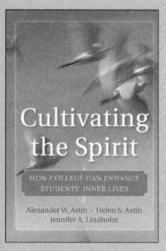

Cultivating the Spirit
by Alexander W. Astin, Helen S. Astin,
Jennifer A. Lindholm
ISBN: 9780470769331

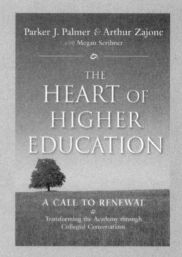

The Heart of Higher Education
by Parker J. Palmer and
Arthur Zajonc, with Megan Scribner
ISBN: 9780470487907

Transformative Conversations
by Peter Felton, H-Dirksen L. Bauman,
Aaron Kheriaty, Edward Taylor
ISBN: 9781118288276

Contemplative Practices in Higher Education
by Daniel P. Barbezat, Mirabai Bush
ISBN: 9781118435274